Genre Fiction of New India

This book investigates fiction in English, written within, and published in India since 2000 in the genre of mythology-inspired fiction. In doing so it introduces the term 'Bharati Fantasy'. This volume is anchored in notions of the 'weird' and thus some time is spent understanding this term linguistically, historically ('wyrd') as well as philosophically and most significantly socio-culturally because 'reception' is a key theme to this book's thesis. The book studies the interface of science, Hinduism and *itihasa* (a term often translated as 'history') within mythology-inspired fiction in English from India and these are specifically examined through the lens of two overarching interests: reader reception and the genre of weird fiction. The book considers Indian and non-Indian receptions to the body of mythology-inspired fiction, highlighting how English fiction from India has moved away from being identified as the traditional Indian postcolonial text. Furthermore, the book reveals broader findings in relation to identity and Indianness and India's post-millennial society's interest in portraying and projecting ideas of India through its ancient cultures, epic narratives and cultural (Hindu) figures.

E. Dawson Varughese is an independent global cultural studies scholar and the author of *Beyond the Postcolonial: World Englishes Literature* (2012) and *Reading New India* (2013). She has published in *Contemporary South Asia*, *South Asian Popular Culture* and *English Today*.

Routledge Studies in Contemporary Literature

For a full list of titles in this series, please visit www.routledge.com.

5 **Food and Culture in Contemporary American Fiction**
 Lorna Piatti-Farnell

6 **Intertextual and Interdisciplinary Approaches to Cormac McCarthy**
 Borders and Crossing
 Edited by Nicholas Monk with a Foreword by Rick Wallach

7 **Global Issues in Contemporary Hispanic Women's Writing**
 Shaping Gender, the Environment, and Politics
 Edited by María Cibreiro and Francisca López

8 **Trauma and Romance in Contemporary British Literature**
 Edited by Jean-Michel Ganteau and Susana Onega

9 **Spatial Politics in Contemporary London Literature**
 Writing Architecture and the Body
 Laura Colombino

10 **Diseases and Disorders in Contemporary Fiction**
 The Syndrome Syndrome
 Edited by T.J. Lustig and James Peacock

11 **Identity and Form in Contemporary Literature**
 Edited by Ana María Sánchez-Arce

12 **The Vampire in Contemporary Popular Literature**
 Lorna Piatti-Farnell

13 **Religion in Cormac McCarthy's Fiction**
 Apocryphal Borderlands
 Manuel Broncano

14 **The Ethics and Aesthetics of Vulnerability in Contemporary British Fiction**
 Jean-Michel Ganteau

15 **Genre Fiction of New India**
 Post-Millennial Receptions of 'Weird' Narratives
 E. Dawson Varughese

Genre Fiction of New India

Post-Millennial Receptions of 'Weird' Narratives

E. Dawson Varughese

LONDON AND NEW YORK

First published 2017 by Routledge

2 Park Square, Milton Park, Abingdon, Oxfordshire OX14 4RN

52 Vanderbilt Avenue, New York, NY 10017

Routledge is an imprint of the Taylor & Francis Group, an informa business

First issued in paperback 2019

Copyright © 2017 Taylor & Francis

The right of E. Dawson Varughese to be identified as author of this work has been asserted by her in accordance with sections 77 and 78 of the Copyright, Designs and Patents Act 1988.

All rights reserved. No part of this book may be reprinted or reproduced or utilised in any form or by any electronic, mechanical, or other means, now known or hereafter invented, including photocopying and recording, or in any information storage or retrieval system, without permission in writing from the publishers.

Notice:
Product or corporate names may be trademarks or registered trademarks, and are used only for identification and explanation without intent to infringe.

Library of Congress Cataloging-in-Publication Data

Names: Dawson Varughese, Emma author.
Title: Genre fiction in new India: post-millennial receptions of 'weird' narratives / by E. Dawson Varughese.
Description: New York; London: Routledge, 2016. | Series: Routledge studies in contemporary literature; 15 | Includes bibliographical references and index. Identifiers: LCCN 2016013297
Subjects: LCSH: Indic fiction (English)—21st century—History and criticism. | Mythology, Indic, in literature.
Classification: LCC PR9492.6.M95 V38 2016 | DDC 823/.9209954—dc23
LC record available at https://lccn.loc.gov/2016013297

ISBN: 978-1-138-02320-8 (hbk)
ISBN: 978-0-367-86856-7 (pbk)

Typeset in Sabon
by codeMantra

For M. V. V.
... for we are stardust only ...

Contents

	Foreword	ix
	Preface	xi
	Acknowledgements	xiii
	A Note on Transliteration and use of Terms	xv
1	Introducing the Post-Millennial Scene	1
2	The 'Wyrd': Numinosity and Estrangement	21
3	Bharati Fantasy: Eternal *Bhāva*	54
4	Bharati Fantasy: Modern-Day Sensibilities	96
5	Conclusion	149
	Index	167

Foreword

A. K. Ramanujan famously claimed that no Hindu reads the *Mahabharata* or the *Ramayana* for the first time. It is also true, I think, that these great epics (and the religious stories of which they are a part) will never have a last reader. A remarkable aspect of post-millennial Indian fiction in English is the record-breaking popularity of these ancient stories, repackaged for a modern Indian audience. About fifteen years ago, an Indian novel was a bestseller if it sold over ten thousand copies; these days it is more like a hundred thousand copies.

This is a remarkable phenomenon for at least two reasons. First, an Indian reader in English has access to a variety of fiction from different parts of the world, especially American and British fiction. So these ancient stories must have a compelling advantage that other tales do not. The second reason is that these books are being written by a new breed of authors typically not from the Indian literary establishment. Many are relatively young, first-time, middle-class authors with technocratic backgrounds. So these authors must know something about their readers that others do not.

Not everyone is enamoured with this turn of events. It isn't unusual for these myth-inspired works to be dismissed as commercial works of poor quality; works capitalizing on a low-brow readership whose grasp of English is limited, but who view the ability to read in English as a sign of status. Such dismissals are unjust, inaccurate and, in a sense, tragic.

It is unjust because such quality judgements are typically pronounced by people who don't like to read these sorts of stories. We don't ask aficionados of lawn croquet to judge rugby; why should it be any different with literary genres? The dismissals are inaccurate because these works, as this volume shows, are produced with a great deal of thought and effort. For example, Pervin Saket's *Urmila* took its author some five years to write and by any measure is an elegant and subtle work. Finally, such dismissals are tragic because it can lead one to miss the major impact these works are having on the Indian zeitgeist.

E. Dawson Varughese offers a much more nuanced view. She's not interested in deciding whether these works are of high literary quality or not. What does interest her is to understand what unites these fantasy works, what motivates their writers to write them, and whether there are universal aspects to these stories which can be appreciated by non-Indian readers as well. She shows how the concept of the Weird (and its more recent incarnations) is a useful way to characterize the unitary essence. This is an intriguing idea, and in my view, it offers a powerful approach for the analysis of these myth-inspired stories. But the Weird is mediated in the Indian context by Indian concepts like *itihaas, dharma, moksha* and so on. It is useful to have a term that characterizes both the universal and particular aspects of such stories, and E. Dawson Varughese's term 'Bharati Fantasy' does the job admirably. It points to the fantastic nature of these stories but also indicates that reality, as place and situation, is mediated by ideas rooted in an Indian substrate.

All this is fine, but what do the Indian writers have to say about the how and why of their works? The interviews here are a first, I think, in a theoretical work of this sort. They wonderfully complement the theoretical discussions. It becomes clear that the authors are aware that they're in the process of creating a corpus that is neither easily classified nor simply about selling as many copies as possible.

It is true many Bharati fantasy novels happen to be commercially successful. However, commercial success is neither a necessary nor a sufficient criterion for inclusion in this category. In any event, a work's commercial value shouldn't be a strike against it. It is all too tempting to turn a classification of labour into a classification of labourers. Thus a "writer *of* commercial novels" becomes a "commercial writer". In actual fact, commercial fiction has a set of rules, a certain stylistics if you will, that marks it as a distinct species of fiction rather than an inferior form of fiction. It is a bit like realising beetles are a distinct species rather than failed birds.

This book will be of interest to literary scholars in India and those outside it. I see it as the beginning of a research program that takes modern Indian fantasy seriously. For young researchers, it points to a number of open research questions. For seasoned scholars, while asking them to rethink their models of the fantastic, it also suggests new domains of application. As mentioned, the great inspiration behind E. Dawson Varughese's most recent work is a collection of ancient stories that neither have a first reader nor a last one. I have every confidence that this book too will serve to inspire many other works to come.

Anil Menon
Author of *Half of What I Say*

Preface

Currently, India is the Second largest English-language book market and it is posited to be the largest within the next twenty years. Not only are mainstream catalogues of Indian publishing growing at pace, so too is the market of genre fiction. This book investigates fiction in English, written within and published from India since 2000 in the genre of mythology-inspired fiction and in doing so, it introduces the term 'Bharati Fantasy'.

The volume is anchored in notions of the 'weird' and thus some time is spent understanding this term linguistically and historically ('wyrd') as well as philosophically and most significantly socio-culturally because 'reception' is a key theme to this book's thesis. The book studies the interface of science, Hinduism and *itihasa* within mythology-inspired fiction in English from India and these are specifically examined through the lens of two overarching interests: reader reception and the genre of weird fiction. To this end, the book considers configurations of Indian and non-Indian receptions to the body of mythology-inspired fiction, highlighting how English fiction from India is less recognisable by the tropes of the Indian postcolonial novel. In addition to the conclusions about reader reception, the book reveals broader findings in relation to identity and Indianness and India's post-millennial society's interest in portraying and projecting ideas of India through its ancient cultures, epic narratives and cultural (Hindu) figures.

Overall, I suggest that it is the advent of New India, its economic prosperity, its growing (reading) middle classes and a new sense of innovation in literary production which has led to – and continues to sustain – a proliferation of popular mythology-inspired fiction.

Acknowledgements

I would like to thank BASAS-British Academy for the fellowship in Pune to support the writing of this book and during my time there, at Deccan College Dr Kshirsagar, Dr Deodhar, Dr Dixit, and Dr Kulkarni-Joshi and at Savitribai Phule Pune University, Dr Jawaare and the students of the English Department.

Some of my writing from *Reading New India* has been developed here – namely the genre term 'Bharati Fantasy' and some analyses of novels such as *Bali and the Ocean of Milk* and *Chanakya's Chant*. Earlier work on Bharati Fantasy appeared in *Contemporary South Asia* as: '"Celebrate at home": post-millennial Indian fiction in English and the reception of "Bharati Fantasy" in global and domestic markets' in December 2014, vol. 22, issue 4. My earliest work on the 'weird' of New India was presented as a paper at 'What Happens Now' Lincoln, 2014 and I am grateful for that early feedback.

In writing this book my own ideas of truth, history and belief have been challenged, enlightened and then challenged once again. It was during the last stages of writing this book that I came to learn of the passing of someone who made it his life's work to interrogate the very same and so I remember Michael here; how sad it will always be that you left us all so soon.

I would like to thank the 'A.M. library' which helped me access resources that otherwise, as an independent scholar I would have missed out on, I'd like to thank Robert Eaglestone for his continued support and Nat Golden who may or may not like to hear about Bharati Fantasy and related projects *again*! To spsandqs: with love and thanks.

This book would not have been possible without the support of Number 5. Thank you. To my mum who absolutely without fail supports me and does whatever she can to help me reach my goals.

Finally, to the two who have travelled the *Triloka* of mythology-inspired fiction with me: SJV and MVV – it's now time to have a rest.

A Note on Transliteration and use of Terms

Unless appearing in citations, the transliteration policy in this book uses a minimal, standard level of diacritical marks in order to provide an equivalent translation into English although such instances are few (such as *bhāva*). Lexical items of 'Indian' origin widely recognised in English (or whose meanings are discussed in this volume) such as *dharma*, *itihasa*, *asura*, *deva* appear italicised but without their diacritics. Throughout, the *Mahabharata*, the *Ramayana* and the *Harivarsha* are italicised but without italicisation of the definite article, in the case of *The Bhagavad Gita* this term appears in italics including the definite article. Proper names (or attributed names) of deities are capitalised throughout but do not appear in italics: Lord Ram, Lord Krishna, Neelkanth as examples. The same system of capitalization is applied to the spelling of sacred Hindu texts such as the Vedas and the Puranas.

Hindu gods and deities are respectfully referred to as Lord, Sri, or Goddess where in doing so the text's meaning is not compromised i.e. referring to Ram as Lord Ram when in the text at hand he is referred to as 'Ram' as this can conflate meaning on various levels of interpretation. Another instance is when Lord Shiva is presented as the 'human Shiva', the man he was before his 'blue throat' was revealed and thus before he was recognised as divine.

On *itihasa*: I wish to stress that this volume does not assert that all Hindus believe that *itihasa* represents that which historically, truthfully happened; it is a personal choice to believe the extent to which an *itihasa* text represents true, historical events. Rather, this volume respectfully appreciates that belief in *itihasa* (and its manifestation in the epics) as representation of true, historical events is a notion that Hindus (and non-Hindus) understand and believe in variously and to differing degrees.

On *weird*, *wyrd*: the term 'weird' is used throughout this book to articulate issues of reception with regard to mythology-inspired fiction written in English, published from within India since 2000. 'weird' is employed here as a term relating to 'the Weird' as a body of supernatural and speculative fiction and *not* in its everyday semantic of 'abnormal' when wanting to describe something (or someone) in a derogatory manner.

On the *Ramayana*: Unless otherwise stated, I refer to the *Ramayana* of Valmiki, as this functions as a recognisable cultural touchstone given that

Valmiki's *Ramayana* has come to be considered authoritative, often referred to being the 'original' within popular, contemporary culture. This volume however, explores the multiplicity of the telling of the *Ramayana* or the *Rama katha* and this is recognised in the discussion of the novels and with the authors in the interviews.

On *Indian* and *Hindu*: Given this volume discusses the epic texts of the *Mahabharata* and the *Ramayana*, that it looks at Vedic and other sacred Hindu texts as inspiration for a body of fiction generally referred to as being 'mythology-inspired', ideas of Indianness run throughout this volume and the word 'Indian' appears on most pages. The term 'Indian' is obviously not used to only refer to Indians who are Hindu and furthermore, the book recognises that the Indian experience and understanding of *itihasa* texts is various and long-reaching across Indian society and cultures.

1 Introducing the Post-Millennial Scene

This chapter provides an overview of the post-millennial context of writing, publishing and reading Indian genre fiction in English within India. It details the economic and political changes that have led to increased consumerism in the leisure markets which have in turn grown and developed the book publishing industry. Issues of marketing and distribution through both domestic and global publishing houses are unpicked as well as the habits of book consumerism within India. The chapter then moves on to consider the labels of genre fiction as 'commercial fiction' and as 'popular fiction', investigating how the proliferation of this body of writing challenges notions of 'literary' Indian fiction and, moreover, how Indian fiction in English has not historically been of the 'commercial' type. During this discussion, the idea that India is a postcolonial literature-producing nation is challenged, suggesting that such notions are of an erstwhile India and that a lack of insight on the part of the Western academy as to India's domestic fiction production is responsible for this blinkered position.

The chapter demonstrates that the hugely successful genre of 'mythology-inspired' fiction, as it is referred to within India, is one such example of the Western academy disregarding certain domestic fiction production. The discussion closes by considering how the mythology-inspired genre fiction of the last ten years poses important questions of reception given the very specific frames of reference and aesthetics it invokes. Despite the cultural specificity of this body of writing, this chapter concludes by suggesting that a degree of universal experience exists through the narrative plots of this writing and thus the chapter reviews some of the debate around narrative and story as part of the human condition.

1.1 Reading and Publishing in Post-Millennial India

Changes to Indian society have taken place on many levels since liberalisation of the economy was initiated in the 1990s. Physical changes to urban centres, the installation of metro systems and the construction of malls and housing blocks are some of the more noticeable changes to Indian society but equally so, changes to media reporting, mobile phone and Internet provision have also impacted society and its knowledge-generating industries, most markedly since the mid-2000s (see *The Caravan: A Journal of Politics and Culture*, 'The Media Issue', December 2015). Television and satellite, often central to the urban, middle-class home, have not only changed family life but have also impacted and shaped notions of youth culture within India. Echoes of New India have been seen in Bollywood production, whether through the masala films of Salman Khan or the film adaptations of popular novels by Chetan Bhagat, namely the film *Kai Po Che!* (2013) based on Bhagat's novel *The 3 Mistakes of My Life* and *2 States* (2014), based on the novel of the same name. The rise of shopping malls and consumption of 'leisure' consumables have similarly changed how a family might spend time together and also how young people interact during their free time.

The outcomes of the decisions to open up the Indian economy were felt most intensely in the late 1990s into the 2000s. The early post-liberalisation period revealed a more economically minded India, an India which concentrated on its domestic market, on consumption more than investment, on the service industry and on high-tech manufacturing. The liberalisation was driven through by Manmohan Singh as finance Minister, radically changing the Indian economy through the deregulation of markets, lowering of taxes and allowance of greater foreign investment. The effects of these then fundamental reforms were not fully experienced until the early 2000s and, significantly, 2007, when India experienced its highest post-liberalisation growth rate. Manmohan Singh, who served a decade as prime minister from 2004, following five years as finance minister, was known as the architect of 'Manmohanomics'. In 2014, this economic tagline morphed into 'Modinomics' as Narendra Modi stood for prime minister in the 2014 elections with the promise of bringing the economic (and governance) successes seen in Gujarat (where he had been chief minster) to a national scale. Winning a landslide victory in the 2014 prime ministerial election, Narendra Modi became the 15th prime minister of India and in so doing, brought about yet more change. In many ways, Mr Modi is regarded as a prime minister for a 21st-century India, not least because of his savvy media presence and website,[1] through which you can 'interact with PM' [*sic*], write to him and share thoughts and ideas. The inevitability of such a contemporary prime minister follows the significant changes Indian society has known in the past twenty years, particularly regarding the evolution of the Indian middle-class identity. As the middle class has grown in size, a revised definition of this demographic has been necessary, of which Radhakrishnan (2011) writes:

> This 'new' middle class is most often described as compromising those who are employed in high-end service sector jobs. What appears to be 'new' about this class, however, is not its composition. Most of those who make up what has been dubbed as India's 'new' middle class had parents who were part of the 'old' one. (42)

The middle class that Radhakrishnan speaks of here is also composite of a generation of Indian Institute of Technology (IIT) and Indian Institute of Management (IIM) graduates who have contributed to New India's economic and social growth. Interestingly, many of the authors of post-millennial genre fiction in English are IIT or IIM graduates and such authors include: Amish Tripathi, author of the hugely successful 'Shiva Trilogy', whose work is discussed here in Chapter 3; Chetan Bhagat, a graduate from IIM Ahmedabad whose 'Inspi-Lit' (see Dhar, 2013) has sold widely and has been adapted into several successful Bollywood films (mentioned earlier); and Christopher C. Doyle, author of *The Mahabharata Secret* (2013) and *The Mahabharata Quest* (2014), also discussed here (in Chapter 4), is a graduate from IIM Calcutta. These young professionals, alongside a growing middle class of entrepreneurs and other professional workers, are, for a large part, both the readers and the authors of post-millennial Indian fiction in English.

Literary activity post millennium within India has been shaped by the successful Jaipur Literature Festival (JLF), which takes place annually in Jaipur, Rajasthan. It was started in 2006 by Namita Gokhale and William Dalrymple with the vision to showcase both South Asian authors as well as writers from around the world – of the South Asian diaspora and otherwise. The festival has impacted the formation of the South Asian canon of fiction, particularly English-language works, although literary works in various Indian languages appear at the festival too. Commercial fiction alongside literary fiction authors have appeared at Jaipur, notably Amish Tripathi and Ashwin Sanghi for our discussions here. Ashwin Sanghi also appeared at the sister JLF at the Southbank in London in May 2015 as part of the annual 'Alchemy' festival, a point of interest for the question of reception that Chapters 2, 3 and 4 concentrate on. In 2015, the JLF appeared in Boulder, Colorado, in the United States. The JLF is the biggest literary festival in India in terms of speakers and audience numbers, however, many literary festivals now take place across the country and most of these have been inaugurated during the post-millennial years – IANS (2015) puts the number of literary festivals in India at around 90. Examples of these 'new' festivals include: Pune International Literary Festival which started in 2013, Hyderabad Literary Festival which began in 2010, Kochi International Book Festival from 2000 and Bangalore Literature Festival which started in 2012.

In a bid to engage the publishing sector, the JLF launched the 'Jaipur BookMark' (JBM) in 2014, and according to its website:

> JBM is held parallel to JLF and provides a platform for publishers, literary agents, authors, translation agencies and writers to meet, talk business deals, listen to speakers from across the world and perhaps even sign the occasional contract.[2]

The publishing scene in India has also been affected by the economic changes and development, most notably post millennium. Narayanan (2012) writes of the new de/reterritorialization of publishing houses and cites Penguin as one such example. She writes:

> No longer identified as just a UK-based company, the publisher is regarded as a 'worldwide' corporation since its locations are spread across the US, Canada, the UK, Ireland, Australia, New Zealand, India, South Africa and China. This polycentric configuration has made it possible for books, like other commercial products, to be produced, designed, translated, and marketed across the world. (107)

Other such publishing companies with an office in India include HarperCollins India and Hachette India, but as Narayana warns, 'if the global visuality of Indian writers is a significant consequence of de/reterritorialized corporations, its most adverse effect is the hegemony of these corporations as the prime global producers of Indian writing' (2012: 107). In late 2013, Penguin merged with Random House and now trades as Penguin Random House India. In a complementary move of sorts, the independent presses of India have also flourished under this post-millennial sky. Notable examples are seen in Westland Ltd, one of the biggest independent and domestically orientated publishers, Zubaan and Rupa (although Zubaan's trade list is distributed by Penguin Random House), as well as in a renaissance of sorts for Jaico Books of Mumbai, established in 1946, and a newly established company called Leadstart Publishing, also based in Mumbai. In short, independent presses are proving successful in their own right in post-millennial India. Noteworthy for the interests of this book, the novels discussed in Chapters 3 and 4 are chiefly published by Westland Ltd, Zubaan, Jaico and Leadstart Publishing. This correlation of independent or domestically orientated publishing houses and mythology-inspired genre fiction is not an arbitrary one, as the following chapters will demonstrate. The cultural specificity and frames of reference of these novels demand a particular publishing and marketing understanding, even if the 'global visuality of Indian writers' that Narayanan writes of is somewhat relegated in that very process. In a recently published collection of short stories titled *Great Stories From Modern India* by the New Delhi-based publisher Om Books International, the editor writes:

> Science, modernity coupled with a consumer culture, the fathomless limits ushered in by the Internet revolution, have opened up fresh vistas with the result that contemporary literature around the globe seems to be deeply impacting the very character of today's literary output.
> (Kohli, 2015: 13)

India is no exception in experiencing these 'fresh vistas' that Kohli speaks about here. The post-millennial publishing scene of Indian fiction in English has proved explosive, with significant areas of growth in 'commercial fiction', notably in chick lit, crime writing and young, urban India-centred narratives. Publishing trends (and thus reading trends) have shifted significantly with an increase in commercial or 'popular' Indian fiction being published domestically in the last fifteen years. From within this publishing boom, a curious phenomenon continues to unfold between Indian authors (based in India), Indian publishers and global publishing houses with regional or India-based offices. As an example, HarperCollins India is a branch of HarperCollins Publishers LLC, one of the largest English-language publishing houses globally, with its headquarters in New York City. Outside of the United States, HarperCollins has publishing groups in Canada, the United Kingdom, Australia, New Zealand and India. It is evident that India, although boasting a strong English-language publishing market, is the only country out of these six which is not regarded as a 'Western' nation. Domestic Indian fiction, published under the HarperCollins name, has often been published with this proviso: 'For Sale in the Indian Subcontinent Only', usually printed on the back cover of the novel. The same (or similar phrasings) can also be found with Penguin India (now Penguin Random House) and Hachette India – both publishers whose headquarters are located outside of India. Examples of novels carrying such a 'restricted sales' clause include several of Anuja Chauhan's chick-lit/rom-com novels (HarperCollins India), Hachette India's *Sita's Curse* (2014) and Eraly's *Night of the Dark Tress* (2006), published by Penguin, which carries the following statement on its back cover: 'For Sale in the Indian Subcontinent and Singapore only.'[3] Interestingly, such geographical sales restrictions do not apply with Indian publishers such as Westland Ltd, Jaico and Leadstart Publishing and no such sales conditions are found on the book covers. As stated earlier, it is these very publishing companies – Westland Ltd, Jaico and Leadstart Publishing – which have produced most of the mythology-inspired fiction post millennium. It is particularly striking that the independent domestic Indian presses are publishing mythology-inspired fiction, which, as it is examined in this book, produces cultural-specific and very 'Indian' stories. Despite the novels' domestic foci, the publishing houses of Westland Ltd, Jaico and Leadstart Publishing impose no restrictions on how this fiction may travel and thus, with no sales restrictions, the fiction has a chance to find new global audiences over the books published by the (global) corporations of HarperCollins, Penguin Random House and the like. This kind of unevenness within literary worlds suggests Casanova (2007) but as the following quote details, the unevenness usually favours the bigger, global companies:

> Autonomy is nonetheless a fundamental aspect of world literary space. The most independent territories of the literary world are able to state their own law, to lay down the specific standards and principles applied by their internal hierarchies, and to evaluate works and pronounce judgments without regard for political and national divisions.
> (Casanova, 2007: 86)

She continues to outline that '… the structural internationalism of the most literary countries strengthens and guarantees their independence. Autonomy in the world of letters is always relative' (86). And yet this position seems at odds with the wider global situation that Cooppan (2004: 10) describes: 'The constitutive flows of goods, persons, capital, ideas, information, and technologies have shrunk our contemporary world, rendering geographic borders less distinct and placing cultures in deeper contact with one another'. And it is indeed through these global flows that the smaller, domestic Indian presses are able to make their books available to an audience outside of India; an irony of sorts when we consider how some of the novels published by the global companies through the Indian offices are restricted in their circulation, as they are 'For Sale in the Indian Subcontinent Only'. On the one hand, it is challenging to realise that even with the economic rise of India and the world's 'constitutive flows', India's domestic fiction market remains somewhat unknown to the Western academy and, moreover, to a large section of a Western audience. Indeed, a Western audience may not have heard of Amish Tripathi, Anuja Chauhan or Ashwin Sanghi, despite these authors' impressive sales figures within India. On the other hand, living in India and being 'English reading', it is hard not to have come across them, if not read them. Burke (2014: online) writes how a 'new wave of homegrown [sic] writers are climbing the country's bestseller lists, challenging the dominance of international heavyweights such as Dan Brown, John Grisham and Tom Clancy …' As India's 'popular' canon of fiction in English continues to grow at pace, it seems that the Western academy's limited interest in its production and proliferation is both manifest and outmoded. We are left wondering what the relationship between the Western academy and popular domestic Indian fiction in English really is and why there seems to be a chasm of (mis)knowledge around this particular body of writing. As this chapter has already highlighted, the domestic Indian market and matters of 'restricted sales' certainly impede global knowledge exchange about this body of fiction, but there are also other, pressing debates such as the place (and the role) of 'commercial fiction' in literary culture and the various issues around differing frames of reference on which this volume focuses in significant detail. The mythology-inspired fiction presented and discussed in this volume is generally available outside of India and we can measure this by using the e-commerce giant Amazon to benchmark the availability of the titles discussed later in this book. The books of Ashwin Sanghi published by Westland Ltd are available as paperbacks through amazon.co.uk (accessed October 2015), as are the books of Amish Tripathi, also published by Westland Ltd – the Shiva Trilogy and his recent 2015 novel, the first book in his Ram Chandra series. Anand Neelakantan's novels, published by Leadstart, are equally available on amazon.co.uk as well as Christopher C. Doyle's first book *The Mahabharata Secret* (2013) by Om Books International. Even Nayak's book by a small independent press called Amaryllis, published in early 2014, is available on amazon.co.uk.

Published by Fingerprint, an Indian publisher started in 2012, *Exiled Prince* (2014) is only available for download to an electronic device and is therefore not currently available as a paperback on amazon.co.uk. Within India, the aforementioned books are easily obtained through the online e-commerce companies of Flipkart and Infibeam.com as well as amazon.co.in (July 2015). The increase in e-commerce has been so rapid that both software developers and courier companies in India have experienced great demand for logistics in this field (see Panda, 2013), and there has been some recent discussion about India Post linking up with e-commerce firms to provide delivery services for their customers (see Nair, 2015).

Reading and publishing in New India are unrecognisable in many ways from the practices of twenty years ago. The impact of technology in terms of publishing, marketing, buying and receiving fiction has transformed the way people spend their leisure time and their money; moreover, *what* people are reading has also changed, and with authors writing new narratives that often echo the spirit of New India, the readership is both growing and evolving. The genre fiction of New India discussed in this opening section reveals a new aspect of the appetite for fiction domestically and, alongside the success of chick lit, crime narratives and other urban-centred storylines, mythology-inspired fiction has proven to be a successful avenue for both author and publisher.

The next section of this chapter looks at the production of genre fiction in more detail, unpicking some of the terms associated with it, namely 'commercial fiction', and what we might mean by 'popular' fiction. It also looks at this new body of mythology-inspired writing against a history of more 'literary' offerings in English and challenges the idea of Indian postcolonial fiction, suggesting that historically, Indian fiction in English has not been of the 'commercial' type. During this discussion, the idea that India is a postcolonial literature-producing nation is challenged, suggesting that such notions are of an erstwhile India and that a lack of insight on the part of the Western academy as to India's production of domestic fiction is responsible for this blinkered position.

1.2 Genre Fiction of New India

The identity of Indian writing in English has changed significantly and also relatively quickly over the course of the last fifteen years (see Dawson Varughese, 2013), and this is due to the considerable rise of 'commercial' Indian fiction over Indian 'literary' fiction. The latter term, often 'regarded as coeval with "Indian English literature" *per se*' according to Gupta (2012: 47), has dominated the postcolonial Indian literary scene in English. In *The Picador Book of Modern Indian Literature* (2001), Amit Chaudhuri details the features of what is referred to as contemporary Indian fiction. Chaudhuri suggests the creation of these defining characteristics has been influenced greatly by the critical and commercial reception of Rushdie's works, most notably by the reception of *Midnight's Children*. For Chaudhuri, the new Indian novel is written in English and has 'edged out from everyday consciousness those indigenous languages and their modern traditions that seemed so important a few decades ago, and were so crucial to the evolution of modern Indian identity or identities' (2001: xxiii). Chaudhuri also describes the new Indian novel as having to mirror Indian life and culture as being 'plural, garrulous, rambling, lacking a fixed centre' (xxv) and (following Rushdie's style) 'robustly extroverted, rejecting nuance, delicacy and inwardness for multiplicity and polyphony' (xxv). This connection between form/voice and the idea of Indianness is clearly too simplistic and unsophisticated to hold true (see Chaudhuri, 2001 and Chakrabarty, 2000, in particular) but in spite of this, the idea has formed and impacted the global literary marketplace, pandering as it does to notions of the oriental 'other' and more specifically the 'other' that is India (see also Rockwell, 2003). Focussing on domestic Indian fiction that is written from within and distributed from India, which is the case for the fiction analysed in Chapters 3 and 4 of this book, Rayan (2002) calls for critics to 'study how Indianness is a pervasive presence in Indian English writing and is its chief distinguishing characteristic' (112). As has been widely documented, India has long been made accessible for the wider English-speaking world, and as Huggan writes, this has been wrought through 'a culturally mediated view' (2001: 80), making India more palatable and, indeed, exoticised for Western readerships. Like Huggan, Brouillette (2011) interrogates how the marketing of postcolonial novels indulges in the exoticisation, commodification and fetishism of the Other and in this sense Rushdie's works belong to a much wider body of writing which is marketed and consumed in these ways.

If Rushdie is to be considered a game changer in the recent history and identity of Indian writing in English, then so we might also consider Arundhati Roy and her novel *The God of Small Things* (1997) and its impact through both domestic and international receptions. Claire Squires (2009: 140) writes: 'In Roy's home country of India, *The God of Small Things* was not only successful in itself but also a stimulus to opening up the market ...', but this success was not without issues of 'reception'. Hugely popular in the West, and winner of the Man Booker Prize in the autumn of 1997, some reviews of the time captured the 'magic' of Roy's novel, or the 'magic' that had enchanted Western readers at least. On the one hand, *The God of Small Things* proffered India as exotic yet accessible through Roy's Anglophile family of characters, set against the backdrop of a deeply lush and tropical Kerala, a not unlikely holiday destination for a particular echelon of Western society in the late 1990s. Part of its enchantment was this positioning of elements familiar to a Western readership, set against the unfamiliar and the foreign. On the other hand, the reception of *The God of Small Things* within India was somewhat mixed, and for some readers the publication of the novel was controversial. Squires writes: 'The particular case of offence was Roy's portrayal of a sexual relationship between an Untouchable man and a Syrian Christian woman' (2009: 141). It was this mixed East-West reception that catapulted the book into notoriety and into a literary marketing relationship beyond the control of the author herself. Despite its somewhat tainted reputation within India, *The God of Small Things* amassed critical acclaim because, as Gupta (2012: 47) reminds us: 'Success in literary fiction is measured by texts which have circulated well in a wider Anglo-American market, and have enjoyed concordant critical attention and cultural currency'.

Although controversy does play a role in the literary scene, more commonplace in a novel's promotional activity is the use of branding and literary activity such as readings and festival appearances. Genre is often central to the branding and marketing of literary works and it is also key to the business of literary prizes, given that prizes use the genre groupings to categorise and grant awards. Squires (2009) exemplifies the impact of literary prizes when she writes that they are 'integrally involved with the process of canonisation, both by choosing works to reward and promote, but also by defining the ways in which they are chosen' (101). In the context of post-millennial India, many literary prizes have entered the market, such as the Vodafone Crossword Book Award (formerly the Hutch Crossword Book Award from 2004 to 2007) and The Hindu Best Fiction Award, as well as one of the most influential literary prizes which is currently affiliated to the JLF, the DSC Prize for South Asian Literature, inaugurated in 2011. The 2013 winner of the $50,000 DSC prize was Jeet Thayil for his novel *Narcopolis*, followed in 2014 by Cyrus Mistry's *Chronicle of a Corpse Bearer*, Jhumpa Lahiri's *The Lowland* in 2015 and Anuradha Roy in 2016 for *Sleeping On Jupiter*. Although the prize accepts works in translation, the winners to date have all been authors of Indian fiction in English. Post millennium, as with the increase in literary festival and prize activity (as detailed in Section 1.1), there has also been a sharp rise in the production of genre fiction. This new body of writing is a marked departure from the 'literary fiction' of Rushdie and Roy. Critically labelled as 'paraliterature', such writing might be described as 'commercial', 'popular' or 'genre' fiction. In the case of India, Gupta (2012) describes both literary and commercial fiction production when he writes:

> The Indian commercial fiction in English which circulates predominantly within the country can be regarded as reasonably distinct from the 'literary fiction' in English which has a larger-than-Indian presence. Neither are, however, mutually impervious or exclusive areas.
>
> Despite numerous efforts to describe these terms according to content – as if texts have immanent qualities of commercialness and literariness – both are plausibly understood as market-led categories. (46)

For Gupta, this new 'commercial fiction' is 'consumed primarily within India', seen to display a kind of 'Indianness' that Indians appreciate and is not meant to be taken 'seriously' or regarded as 'literary'. He writes that 'literary fiction is the respectable public face of Indian literature in English abroad and at home, while commercial fiction is the gossipy café of Indian writing in English at home' (47). McCrum (2010: online) also describes the demographic of the commercial fiction readership, stating:

> This new middle-class audience – small entrepreneurs, managers, travel agents, salespeople, secretaries, clerks – has an appetite for literary entertainment that falls between the elite idiom of the cultivated literati, who might be familiar with the novels of Amitav Ghosh and Salman Rushdie, and the Indian English of the street and the supermarket. Theirs is the Indian English of the outsourcing generation.

Both Gupta and McCrum are careful to benchmark the readership of commercial fiction against the literary, the elite and the transnational. Such a comparison reveals that commercial fiction within India belongs firmly with a class of people who would not normally buy 'literary' novels, who are blue- and grey-collar workers, who are Indian (domestic) in their reading tastes and choices and who are Indian English reading/speaking. If such a demographic is one of the defining features of the 'commercial' fiction readership, then the sales performance of these books is another feature of how this body of new writing might be defined. Joshi (2015) tells us that: 'The previous "Hindu" print run of 500 copies has now been replaced by 30,000 to 1 million-plus first printings for writers such as Chetan Bhagat and Anuja Chauhan' (314). Indeed, print runs testify to the 'popularity' of genre fiction in India and these are often boosted by the hype, marketing, book trailers and launches that accompany the release of the books. Post millennium, it is the genre of mythology-inspired fiction that has proven explosive in sales and reception, some books appearing with backing from popular film stars, music composers and inventive marketing strategies. Amish Tripathi's 'Shiva Trilogy' is an example of such a marketing strategy and it is reported to have been one of the fastest-selling book series in the history of Indian publishing. Tripathi's *The Oath of The Vayuputras* (2013), the last of the Shiva Trilogy, enjoyed particular hype and publicity given the success of the preceding novels. On the phenomenal success of Tripathi's Shiva Trilogy, Sunaina Kumar writes:

> His [Amish's] publisher Westland offers up sale figures for the new book, 3,50,000[4] copies presold compared with 2,40,000 for the last Harry Potter novel in India. You don't have to join too many dots to see that Amish is being marketed as our answer to JK Rowling. (2013: online)

Moreover, Tripathi was featured in the Nielsen BookScan in the top five best-selling authors every week throughout 2012/2013. He has since launched a new series of novels, the 'Ram Chandra' series; where his Shiva Trilogy had celebrated the life of Lord Shiva, the Ram Chandra series is focussed on

Lord Ram. Given the sales figures and the following that Amish Tripathi has amassed as a 'popular' fiction author (his books have been translated into several other Indian languages), Amish Tripathi's Ram Chandra series is set to be a successful one. Indeed, a significant proportion of commercial fiction is published in series or as a trilogy: Amish Tripathi's 'Shiva Trilogy'; Anuja Chauhan's chick-lit and rom-com novels *Those Pricey Thakur Girls* (2013) followed by *The House That BJ Built* (2015); Anand Neelakantan's 'Epic of The Kaurava Clan' series; Christopher C. Doyle's 'The Mahabharata Quest' series; Shatrujeet Nath's 'Vikramaditya Trilogy'; and Jagmohan Bhanver's 'The Krishna Trilogy' as recent examples. Where an author of commercial fiction does not publish in a series or trilogy, it is the genre of her/his work which tightly binds the narratives together. As an example, the Ashwin Sanghi novels *The Rozabal Line* (2008), *Chanakya's Chant* (2010) and *The Krishna Key* (2012) do not follow each other as a series but the genre of 'thriller' links all three and in India at least, the three books are often seen for sale as a box set. Whether bound by a genre type or as part of a series, these post-millennial genre novels sustain readership through both their marketing and their commitment to continuing the story – whether that be through the key protagonists or through a specific genre. There is no doubt that such a technique is also a feature in the production and marketing of literary fiction, but I suggest that it is more commonplace within genre fiction to find serialisation or the employment of a specific genre throughout an author's portfolio of work. Having said this, it is evident that mythology-inspired fiction 'plays' with genre – something that is explored in Chapters 3 and 4 here – 'because the competition is so numerous and so fierce, there is a great deal of pressure to transform the formula, be it theme, plot twist, or narrative technique, in order to surprise and score a winner at the sales counter' (Swirski, 2007: 45). This creativity is clearly true of mythology-inspired fiction overall, taking the established genres of the 'thriller', 'historical' or 'fantasy' fiction and twisting, shaping and culturally moulding the genres to form what I call 'Bharati Fantasy' (Chapter 2 details its definition). Commercial or popular fiction has so far been defined by its non-literariness (according to Gupta, 2012), its sales performance and its large print runs as well as its leaning towards serialisation or employment of a specific genre type. Another defining feature of popular fiction is the interface of the genre fiction with the contemporary. Scott McCracken (1998) writes:

> Popular narratives play a vital role in mediating social change, informing their audience of new currents and allowing the reader to insert him or herself into new scenarios in a way that can be related to her or his own experience. Its engagement in the present, in now-time, means that the political nature of popular fiction is never in doubt. (185)

The popular fiction I explored in *Reading New India* (2013) engages with the 'now' through its various genres, themes, protagonists and story contexts. Whether it be through chick lit, rom-coms, what I have termed as Crick

Lit[5] – commercial fiction based on cricket – or through the mythology-inspired fiction I am exploring here in this book, the post-millennial scene of genre fiction in English from India interfaces with the contemporary moment. Of this approach Gupta (2015: 21) writes '[T]he nascent move to analyse Indian commercial fiction in English is now similarly defensive about and separated from literariness, and similarly celebratory about the 'Indianness' of commercial fiction texts.' As India has undergone significant economic and social change since 2000, the idea of India, notions of Indianness and India's own philosophy of modernity have emerged as urgent and contentious topics of debate. For such societies changing at pace, McCracken suggests that popular fiction 'can supply us with the narratives we need to resituate our*selves* in relation to the world' (1998: 17, original emphasis). Many of the storylines of post-millennial Indian fiction in English revise ideas of India and Indianness through narratives of both globalisation and older, more ancient eras of Indian civilisation. Again, McCracken suggests that popular fiction can offer a space for such 'remaking' to take place, stating that 'the reader of popular fiction is actively engaged in the remaking of him or herself and this act of remaking has a utopian potential' (17). As I have written elsewhere (Dawson Varughese, 2013, 2014, 2016), the combining of popular genres in Indian post-millennial fiction in English can be seen in Anuja Chauhan's rom-com/Crick-Lit novel *The Zoya Factor*, in Geeta Sundar's Crick-Lit and crime novel *The Premier Murder League* or in Ashwin Sanghi's novels, where thriller and mythology-inspired fiction combine. Following McCracken's argument that popular fiction allows for a 'remaking' of oneself, he also suggests that the combining of popular genres in a narrative 'can allow a more complex exploration of self-identity, while still giving the reader familiar boundaries within which to project his or her fantasies' (1998: 13). For our interests here, this particular quote highlights how the post-millennial mythology-inspired novels function within the current Indian popular fiction scene given that they are anchored in ideas of Indian identity, culture and belief ('Hinduism'). Chapters 3 and 4 of this book investigate eight authors and their mythology-inspired popular fiction and the analyses of their work in these two chapters highlight their connection to the 'commercial' and 'popular' fiction worlds that they inhabit (it is, however, the overarching interest of this volume that guides the analysis, namely the novels' connections with *itihasa*, myth and the (Indian) scientific imagination).

The terms 'commercial', 'popular' and 'genre' fiction are therefore understood and employed in this volume with the following meanings: 'commercial' is understood here as pertaining to large print runs, paperback books with large sales and complementary marketing campaigns; 'popular' fiction is understood here to mean fiction that is consumed by blue- and grey-collar workers, interfacing with the contemporary moment (to a greater or lesser degree) and 'commercial' in its sales figures. Additionally, for the Indian context, the 'popular' is also domestic and (often) employs Indian English. Just as we might import Western terms to understand and categorise ideas of 'modernity' in India, we are also at risk of importing Western ideas of genre fiction, imposing them on the fiction that is being produced domestically. In this sense, the term 'genre' here is used to talk about groupings of 'types' of fiction production such as the established categories of 'fantasy', 'sci-fi', 'thriller' or 'romance' (and their sub-genres). This present volume therefore creates a new genre term in response to the growing body of fiction referred to in India at least, as mythology-inspired fiction (Chapter 2, Section 2.2 details this). My work has previously coined a genre term in order to categorise a body of new writing thematically linked to cricket (see Dawson Varughese, 2016 for more detail). In creating a new genre term for a body of fiction, the process is significantly (not completely) de-centralised from Western academic discourse and classification. Such an intervention is necessary, I believe, since these days, the post-millennial, domestic, Indian popular novel in English is only tangentially connected to Western readers and the Western academy.

It feels like a long time since the (generally reported) first Indian novel in English, *Rajmohan's Wife*, was published, not simply because it appeared in 1864 but because the idea of the Indian novel in English has developed and changed considerably since the mid-1880s. As the late 20th century gave us Rushdie and 'Indian writing in English began to glitter with glossy paperback covers in airport bookstores all around the world' (Black, 2015: online), the novel developed not only in form, style and genre but also in how it was read, distributed and critiqued. Arriving in the post-millennial years, although 'literary' Indian novels in English continue to be produced, they emanate from all corners of the globe, from various and hybrid author identities and have thus unquestioningly expanded the idea of the Indian novel that the early 20th century proffered. The growing body of contemporary commercial fiction within India asserts anew the identity of the Indian novel in English. It does this by re-anchoring the novel in India and by its appeal to the mass, domestic market. Moreover, the genre fiction which is the focus of this present volume – generally referred to as mythology-inspired fiction – further anchors the Indian novel to, and in, India, its culture(s), people(s) and histories. This is particularly noteworthy 'given the predominance of developmental realist concerns in Asian writing, and consequently the relative absence of a strong tradition of speculative fiction among Asian writers' (Goh, 2013: 46). Goh goes on to explain how 'most of the imaginative Asian futures have been articulated by non-Asian writers' (46). But for Menon, the speculative can enhance the experience of encountering the Indian epics, when he writes: 'The Ramayana with its fantasy tropes should arouse the *adbhut rasa* – the savor of wonder – but it cannot, because in India the pleasure of a first contact with the epics is not possible. [...] We need the novum for wonder, and that is precisely what tradition cannot offer. But speculative fiction can' (2012: x). We shall return to this idea of the speculative, extending, enhancing and revalidating traditional epics in Chapters 3 and 4.

As I have discussed elsewhere (Dawson Varughese, 2012, 2013), contemporary, commercial Indian fiction in English challenges the idea of India as a postcolonial literature-producing nation, and although we do not have the scope to rehearse such debate in full here, it is important to state how problematic it would be to suggest that India's domestic fiction in English is recognisable by the tropes of (earlier) Indian postcolonial novels. By way of concluding thoughts to this section, we might turn to the second *Granta: Magazine of New Writing* devoted to India, where Guest Editor Ian Jack writes in his 'Introduction': 'The Indian writer need no longer look over his shoulder at his imagined audience abroad; many if not most of his readers are much closer – are Indian like him and need no telling about samosas' (2015: 12).

As this chapter has detailed, the Indian domestic literary scene in terms of writing activity, publishing prospects and, importantly, domestic readership, has meant most latterly that India is no longer substantially beholden to the Western academy for publishing opportunity, endorsement or canon formation. India grows, publishes, celebrates and awards its authors independent of Western intervention and although much combined literary activity continues to take place between India and Western academies, it is no longer emphatically necessary for India to curate such relationships for its literary survival, given that plenty is happening 'at home'.

1.3 Reception, Universalism and Difference

This chapter has thus far outlined the context of publishing and reading Indian fiction in English in India since 2000 and has provided an overview of how genre fiction in English from India has emerged over the last fifteen years and how this body of writing challenges erstwhile notions of Indian fiction in English. As Section 1.2 details, Roy's novel *The God of Small Things* was hugely successful in terms of its Western reception as it portrayed India as exotic yet accessible. Roy crafted an Anglophile family of characters and set the story against a backdrop of a deeply lush and tropical Kerala. A principal reason for the success of this novel in the West was the balance Roy struck between the positioning of elements that are familiar to a Western readership amidst the elements of the unfamiliar and the foreign (i.e. the Indian, the Keralite). And thus we are reminded of the essence of the reading (and the reception) process. Indeed, literacy skills, the recognition of graphemes and their phoneme counterparts and the understanding of syntax, grammar and semantics are all essential for reading to take place. Yet equally so, our abilities to cognitively process and culturally process and interpret what we read are as important, as essential. How can a text mean without its social, cultural content – at its very base, its human content or its relation to humanity? Montgomery et al. (2000) say of the process of reading:

> [...] reading involves two complementary processes or dimensions: not only making sense of various aspects of the language, sounds or images of the text itself, but also continuously constructing possible models of the text's surrounding social and historical context, on the basis of our own views about the world and understanding of other possible or likely views about the world. (7–8)

This chapter has already highlighted the cultural specificity of the mythology-inspired novels explored in Chapters 3 and 4. These English-language novels – they are not works in translation – require what Montgomery et al. (2000) outline as the process of reading. Although accessing the text linguistically is reasonably straightforward – names of places, people and specific cultural terms aside – these mythology-inspired novels demand from a non-Indian reader the construction of textual worlds, drawing on the reader's knowledge of India, its history, religion and cultures. Where aspects of this knowledge base are absent, an enhanced 'to-and-fro spiral' (Rosenblatt, 1976) is constructed between text and reader to help make the text 'mean'. In her book *Literature As Exploration* (1976), Louise Rosenblatt explores the concept of a reader-text relationship in detail. Rosenblatt's position with regard to the prevailing ideas of the time was that reading was more than an interaction of marks on the page where the reader extracted the meaning. Rosenblatt argued that the process was actually one of a to-and-fro spiral, meaning that both text and reader are equally challenged by what each one brings to the reading at the time of that reading. Through her work, she claimed that we as readers all have a role to play in making the text mean and the author has little control over the meaning of the literary work as soon as it is published and open to readers. For Rosenblatt at least, the words on the page were indeed the author's in the sense that she had produced them, and somewhere in there the author's meaning or intention may be found, but it was only the reader who could make the text mean. Rosenblatt's assertion that it is the reader who makes the text 'mean' is a principle that we shall return to in Chapters 2, 3 and 4 as we discuss the reception of Indian literary texts in non-Indian cultural contexts. Iser, like Rosenblatt, advocates that literary communication can be seen as a two-way relationship; in reading a message of a text, it is the reader who is actually composing the message, thus, in line with Rosenblatt's earlier work, Iser asserts:

> If meaning is imagistic in character, then inevitably there must be a different relationship between text and reader from that which the critic seeks to create from his referential approach. Such a meaning must clearly be the product of an interaction between the textual signs and the reader's acts of comprehension. And, equally clearly, the reader cannot detach himself from such an interaction; on the contrary, the activity stimulated in him will link him to the text and induce him to create the conditions necessary for the effectiveness of that text. (1994: 9)

Where Iser was concerned with the aesthetic aspects of reading, Jauss (1970) was more interested in placing the text historically. Jauss was not concerned with investigating the history of the text in terms of author or literary trend, rather he was interested in seeing how the text was 'received' by the readers, reading that text in their own moment of history. Freund (1987) speaks of Jauss' work as one that aimed

> ... to develop a new mode of literary history based not on a simple positivistic acceptance of received tradition but rather on an investigation of the literary reception of canonical works, and on the ways in which the experience of the literary work by its readers mediates the relationship of past and present. (135)

Although the manner in which the mythology-inspired novels discussed in this book are received by their readers is not a direct concern here, Jauss' approach to understanding how these texts are currently received and interpreted, given that the novels' interests are anchored in the (re)telling of India's epic narratives, history and folklore, remains a tangential affair. As we read in Section 1.2, McCracken advocates that the popular's engagement in the present, in 'now-time', means that the political nature of popular fiction is never in doubt (1998: 185). Chapters 3 and 4 explore the reading of these texts in 'now-time' despite their deep anchoring in ancient or older Indias. This is made particularly manifest by the fact that Chapter 3 focuses on mythology-inspired fiction whose narratives are of an ancient epoch, whereas Chapter 4 focuses on mythology-inspired fiction whose narratives are of a 'now-time', a post-millennial epoch or a near future – and in some of the novels examined in Chapter 4 there is some 'narrative time travel' to older Indias in order to evoke epic narrative, such as in the *Mahabharata*.

Returning then to ideas of reading and reception, the type of reception both Iser (1994) and Jauss (1970) advocated was not without its difficulties, and Ingarden (1973) attempted to highlight these. Iser's perception of interpretation is difficult to completely advocate: if we are free to interpret as we wish, then any one text could have a hundred interpretations if one hundred people read it, but there must be something there in the text which governs a sense of general, universal interpretation. If not, then the text becomes insignificant and one reader could not talk to another reader about the 'same' text as it would appear not to be exactly that, 'the same text'. The discussion and analyses of the mythology-inspired fiction texts which follow in Chapters 3 and 4 challenge ideas of interpretation and universalism, but this debate is made all the more interesting by the fact that the fiction is written in English from the outset. Indeed, these texts are in some cases translated into other Indian languages *from* English (Amish Tripathi's 'Shiva Trilogy' being an example), but the fact that these texts were originally produced in English suggests a certain universalism in their 'potential' distribution to readers of English and particularly so as the publishers of some mythology-inspired fiction do not impose region- or country-only sales. Indeed, such distribution secures a far more global audience than the books being produced and read in Marathi or Hindi as examples. Yet the narrative content of much of this canon of new writing is not easily accessible despite it being expressed in a language that in theory allows these books to travel to a global audience. As Matravers (2001) writes:

> [A] representation produced for the purposes of communication is, implicitly or explicitly, produced for a particular audience. The author

may assume that his audience has certain background beliefs necessary to make certain inferences which may well be necessary in order for the representation to be understood. (60)

This issue of audience and their 'background beliefs' is revisited throughout this book. Given that my interest here is with fiction that is anchored in Indian epic narrative and history (what I term as 'Bharati Fantasy' – to follow in Chapter 2), it is necessary to consider narrative as a universal experience in order to explore how epic narrative foregrounds tropes that appear to travel across cultures. Turner (1996) highlights the link between human existence and parable. In citing many acclaimed literary works, he argues that we read life through story; story laden with emotions that are inherently part of human existence. He reminds us of the universal in narrative:

> Parable is the root of the human mind – of thinking, knowing, acting, creating, and plausibly even of speaking. But the common view, firmly in place for two and a half millennia, sees the everyday mind as unliterary and the literary mind as optional. (v)

Miall (1998) argues that our human ability to respond to literature, including emotional response, is an ability endowed by erudition and he refutes the idea that literature is a response process which has grown out of recent cultural developments. From this evolutionary-based point of view, Miall probes questions on what makes literature literature, reminding us that it appears in all cultures, produced across millennia. He asks whether literature fulfils some long-standing function which has evolved in the human species and argues that response to literature uses emotional and cognitive schemata, making for an argument of the universality of narrative. Meanwhile, Wierzbicka (1992) warns of the dangers of ethnocentrism and cultural relativism when she writes: '[C]ultural relativism, too, presents dangers to any pursuit of truth, and to scholarly inquiry into language, thought, and culture' (26). And so Chapter 2 argues that it is the appearance of certain themes and characteristics of both India's mythology-inspired fiction and the Western academy's 'weird fiction' as a genre that unearths a certain universalism across these two canons of writing, and Chapters 3 and 4 explore this idea through textual analysis. The themes and characteristics found across India's mythology-inspired fiction and the 'Weird' include: awe at strangeness, the numinous, cultural notions of science and technology and the subverting of the 'real'. The reception of these themes, however, is a more complex matter and this is explored in length throughout Chapters 3 and 4.

Given that this book interrogates popular Indian mythology-inspired fiction through interests of reading reception, cultural notions of science, history and belief (Hinduism), a sociology of literature is at the heart of this volume. Specifically, this book is interested in how 'weird fiction' is defined through its own cultural anchorage and, in turn, how new fictions from India are yet to be studied within Western academia, as the challenge of how to read them (if not through postcolonial theory) is a very real one. Equally so, the nature of these fictions as 'commercial' or 'popular' has meant that the Western academy has been less ready to study such texts given that the tradition, especially within postcolonial studies in England at least, has been to study 'literary' works of which the popular is not considered part. Accordingly, a cultural studies approach to the novels examined here, rather than a literary studies approach, is advocated. I believe this approach offers a way to study this body of recent fiction by focussing on the complex intersections between the public (this is, after all, 'popular' fiction) and private subjectivity around matters of science, faith, belief and ideas of 'Indianness'. The narratives of this body of mythology-inspired fiction are in a sense publicly circulating narratives which are very specific to India, both in terms of cultural literary heritage, belief and spirituality as well as being indicative of a contemporary post-millennial India, and I therefore advocate that they demand an approach and interpretation grounded in the Indian experience. To this end, Chapters 3 and 4 feature narrative interviews. The insistence on the 'narrative' rather than the short question form of interview method is to develop the discussions more deeply than the short form would usually allow. Although the interviews were completed as written documents over some months, they were preceded by face-to-face meetings in India (with four of the six authors), through which ideas were generated for the narrative interview questions and ensuing discussion. This approach to the formulation of the interviews anchors itself in the 'interview guide approach' rather than in 'standardized open-ended interviews' (see Cohen et al., 2005: 271), in that the topics and issues covered are agreed in advance. This agreement was reached during the meetings and then, as the interviewer, I determined the sequence and wording of the questions post meeting and, as it were, 'pre-interview'. My approach to the interviews deviates from the 'standardized open-ended interviews' in that the same questions were not asked of all the interviewees, rather the narrative interviews were tailored to the authors' particular interests in the topic and the novels' themes and foci. Such an approach is unsuitable for data coding given that the questions asked are different for each interviewee. However, the narrative interviews served a different purpose; specifically they created a dialogue with the analyses of the fiction written by the authors who were also interviewed. The narrative interviews were conducted at the same time as the analyses of the fiction were being carried out, thus the narrative interviews and analyses informed each other concurrently.

Notes

1. www.narendramodi.in.
2. https://jaipurliteraturefestival.org/jbm.
3. I have written elsewhere (Dawson Varughese, *forthcoming*) on the related subject of book cover design and its part in the (restricted) sales of Indian genre fiction.
4. 3,50,000, as written by the author, Kumar, is the number 350,000 according to the conventions of the Indian numbering system.

5. See Dawson Varughese (2016), 'Genre fiction of New India: post-millennial configurations of Crick Lit, Chick Lit and crime writing' for a detailed definition of Crick Lit.

References

Black, S. (2015) 'Post-Humanitarianism and the Indian Novel in English', in Anjaria, U. (ed.) *A History of the Indian Novel in English*, New York: Cambridge University Press.
Brouillette, S. (2011) *Postcolonial Writers in the Global Literary Marketplace*, Basingstoke: Palgrave Macmillan.
Burke, J. (2014) 'Indian publishers wake up to new generation of homegrown thrillers', *The Guardian* 12 October 2015. http://www.theguardian.com/world/2014/oct/12/india-new-generation-thrillers [accessed October 2014].
Casanova, P. (2007) *The World Republic of Letters* (translated by M. B. Debevoise), Cambridge: Harvard University Press.
Chakrabarty, D. (2000) *Provincializing Europe*, Princeton: Princeton University Press.
Chaudhuri, A. (2001) *The Picador Book of Modern Indian Literature*, London: Picador.
Cohen, L., Manion, L. and Morrison, K. (eds.) (2005) *Research Methods in Education*, London: RoutledgeFalmer.
Cooppan, V. (2004) 'Ghosts in the disciplinary machine: the uncanny life of world literature', *Comparative Literature Studies*, vol. 41, no. 1, pp. 10–36.
Dawson Varughese, E. (2012) *Beyond the Postcolonial: World Englishes Literature*, Basingstoke: Palgrave.
Dawson Varughese, E. (2013) *Reading New India: Post-Millennial Indian Fiction in English*, London: Bloomsbury.
Dawson Varughese, E. (2014) 'Celebrate at home': post-millennial Indian fiction in English and the reception of 'Bharati Fantasy', in global and domestic markets, *Contemporary South Asia*, vol. 22, issue 4.
Dawson Varughese, E. (2016) 'Genre Fiction of New India: Post-millennial configurations of Crick Lit, Chick Lit and crime writing', in Tickell, A. (ed.) *South Asian Fiction in English: Contemporary Transformations*, Basingstoke: Palgrave.
Dawson Varughese, E. (Forthcoming) 'Consuming post-millennial Indian Chick Lit: visual representations of Chauhan's females', in Houlden, K. and Atia, N. (eds.) *Popular Postcolonialisms: Popular Cultural Forms and the Postcolonial Paradigm*, London: Routledge.
Dhar, S. (2013) 'Inspiring India: The fiction of Chetan Bhagat and the discourse of motivation', in Sen, K. and Roy, R. (eds.) *Writing India Anew: Indian English Fiction 2000–2010*, Amsterdam: Amsterdam University Press.
Freund, E. (1987) *The Return of The Reader: Reader Response Criticism*, London: Methuen & Co.
Goh, R. B. H. (2013) 'Engaging Future Asia: techno-orientalisms, ethnography, speculative fiction', *Creative Industries Journal*, vol. 6, no. 1, pp. 43–56.
Gupta, S. (2012) "Indian 'Commercial' Fiction in English, the Publishing Industry, and Youth Culture." *Economic and Political Weekly*, vol. 46, no. 5, pp. 46–53.
Gupta, S. (2015) *Consumable Texts in Contemporary India: Uncultured Books and Bibliographical Sociology*, Basingstoke: Palgrave Macmillan.
Huggan, G. (2001) *The Postcolonial Exotic: Marketing the Margins*, London, New York: Routledge.

IANS (2015) 'Lit fests stimulated reading revolution in India: Literati' http://timesofindia.indiatimes.com/life-style/books/features/Lit-fests-stimulated-reading-revolution-in-India-Literati/articleshow/50340844.cms?from=mdr [accessed December 2015].

Ingarden, R. (1973) *The Literary Work of Art*, Evanston, IL: Northwestern University Press.

Iser, W. (1994) *The Act Of Reading: A Theory Of Aesthetic Response*, Baltimore: Johns Hopkins University Press. [original published 1978].

Jack, I. (2015) 'India Another Way of Seeing', *Granta: The Magazine of New Writing*, Issue 130, Winter, London: Granta Publications.

Jauss, H.R. (1970) 'Literary history as a challenge to literary theory', *New Literary History* 2 (1) Autumn: 7–37.

Joshi, P. (2015) 'Chetan Bhagat: remaking the novel in India', in Anjaria, U. (ed.) *A History of the Indian Novel in English*, New York: Cambridge University Press.

Kohli, S. (ed.) (2015) *Great Stories From Modern India*, Noida: Om Books International.

Kumar, S. (2013) 'The Pied Piper of Meluha', *Tehelka*, February, issue 10, vol. 10. Web. Accessed 5 April 2013.

Matravers, D. (2001) *Art and Emotion*, Oxford: Oxford University Press.

McCracken, S. (1998) *Pulp: Reading Popular Fiction*, Manchester: Manchester University Press.

McCrum, R. (2010) "Chetan Bhagat: The Paperback King of India." *The Observer*, January 24 2013.

Menon, A. (2012) 'Introduction', in Menon, A. and Singh, V. (eds.) *Breaking the Bow: Speculative Fiction Inspired by the Ramayana*, New Delhi: Zubaan.

Miall, D. S. (1998) 'An evolutionary approach to literary reading: theory and predictions' www.ualberta.ca/~dmiall/reading/evolut.htm [accessed 5 October 2005].

Montgomery, M., Durant, A., Fabb, N., Furniss, T., Mills, S. (2000) *Ways of Reading*, 2nd edition, London: Routledge.

Nair, R. P. (2015) 'Why India Post could become e-commerce's most potent delivery partner' http://yourstory.com/2015/06/india-post-ecommerce/ [accessed October 2015].

Narayanan, P. (2012) *What Are You Reading?: The World Market and Indian Literary Production*, London: Routledge.

Panda, P. (2013) 'Review of Indian courier services for ecommerce companies, IndiaPost Tops' www.thetechpanda.com/2013/03/18/ [accessed October 2015].

Radhakrishnan, S. (2011) *Appropriately Indian: Gender and Culture in a New Transnational Class*, Durham, NC: Duke University Press.

Rayan, K. (2002) 'Towards an Indian critical tradition for Indian Writing in English', in Arjunwadkar, K. S. (ed.) *The Lamp and the Jar: Essays by Krishna Rayan*, New Delhi: Sahitya Akademi.

Rockwell, D. (2003) 'The shape of a place: translation and cultural marking in South Asian fictions' *Modern Philology*, vol. 100, no. 4, May, pp. 596–618.

Rosenblatt, L. (1976) *Literature As Exploration*, New York: Modern Language Association. [original published 1938].

Squires, C. 2009. *Marketing Literature: The Making of Contemporary Writing in Britain*. Basingstoke: Palgrave.

Swirski, P. (2007) *From Lowbrow to Nobrow*, Canada: McGill-Queen's University Press.

Turner, M. (1996) *The Literary Mind*, Oxford: Oxford University Press.

Wierzbicka, A. (1992) *Semantics, Culture, and Cognition: Universal Human Concepts in Culture-Specific Configurations*, New York: Oxford University Press.

2 The 'Wyrd'

Numinosity and Estrangement

The first section of this chapter (Section 2.1) looks at how the term 'weird fiction' has been used in the Western academy to date and begins by exploring its origins. We trace the linguistic etymology of the term 'weird' as 'wyrd' and thus consult its Old Norse and Anglo-Saxon usage. This discussion presents ideas of the numinous, fate and the endurance of life's trials and connects the Old Norse myths of the Norns (the three Fates) with epic narrative texts from Hinduism. In doing so, the focus is on how the wyrd depicts a 'presence' and in turn, how such a presence is a defining characteristic of weird fiction and by extension, how it also appears in 'Bharati Fantasy' – a term I introduce in detail in the second part of this chapter. Following this exploration of the wyrd, the chapter goes on to define weird fiction and in doing so, draws on the critical writing of Miéville, Vandermeer and S. T. Joshi in particular. The history of the Weird as a body of fiction is discussed here, from Lovecraft's 'weird tales' to contemporary ideas of the 'New' or 'Recent' Weird. Section 2.1 closes by considering how these ideas of weird fiction are manifest in Bharati Fantasy before exploring this in greater detail in Section 2.2.

Section 2.2 discusses Bharati Fantasy as a genre term in addition to presenting a definition of this growing body of new writing. Here, discussion about sacred texts in terms of myth and *itihasa* in Hinduism are presented and I explore how these texts have acted as inspiration for Bharati Fantasy novels. Discussion of the Indian scientific imagination closes Chapter 2 with its focus on Indian scientific and cosmological achievements, theories of creationism and Hinduism's connections with modern science.

2.1 The (New) Weird

The production of weird fiction is mostly attributed to Lovecraft and the weird tales of the early 1900s. Joshi (2004), a leading scholar on Lovecraft, writes that Lovecraft was imbued with a sense of the '… relative insignificance of all human life when measured on the scale of cosmic infinity …' (78). The early part of the 1900s was a time when ideas of God, science and human existence were at the forefront of the popular imagination, and with the onset of World War I, these ideas moved to take up a very real position in people's lives. Lovecraft himself identified the 'modern masters' of weird fiction in Arthur Machen, Algernon Blackwood, Lord Dunsany and M. R. James (Joshi, 2004: 7), all of whom published weird stories in the early 1900s. Joshi refers to this period of weird fiction as the 'Golden Age' and to Lovecraft as 'the linchpin of the twentieth-century weird tale, not only for its absorption of the best weird work of the past but for his nurturing of a fair proportion of the best work that followed him' (8). The motifs of the cosmic and of natural law are at the heart of weird fiction, as China Miéville (2009) writes: 'The focus is on awe, and its undermining of the quotidian. This obsession with numinosity under the everyday is at the heart of "Weird Fiction"' (510), and Kincaid (2014) writes: 'H.P. Lovecraft, whose stories, time and again, suggested that forces incomprehensible to man steered a fundamentally alien universe, and that any contact between man and this cosmic horror could result in only madness' (45). In short, the numinous, the cosmos and the distorting of the laws of nature all feature as part of the weird tale. It is these elements of weird fiction that are of particular interest to this volume as the term Bharati Fantasy, defined later in this chapter, foregrounds the numinous and instances of 'awe', especially in relation to superhuman beings and, by extension, the flouting of natural law. Moreover, the cosmic features as a background narrative to Bharati Fantasy more generally given that the cosmic is anchored in the numinous and more broadly features as part of Hindu belief (creationism, Brahman as examples). In anchoring itself in the cosmic and the numinous, weird fiction (of the Western academy) I suggest links back to a linguistic etymology and concept of wyrd.

2.1.1 *Wyrd*

The contemporary noun and adjective 'weird' is rooted linguistically in Anglo-Saxon culture and is cognate with the Old English word wyrd, further connected (albeit more broadly) to the common Germanic verb 'verda' (werden), 'to become'. The term wyrd is an Old Norse word, 'Urdr', which, in turn, expresses the past tense of 'verda', translating as 'became' or 'happened'. The notion of Urdr – known more commonly as 'Urd' – is a powerful one as it is personified in the Norns of Norse mythology: three female beings who spin time – the past, present and the future (not unlike the Greek 'Fates' or 'Moirae', although there are clearly some significant differences between the two cultures). Wyrd has been translated as 'fate' and in common literary culture is often remembered through Shakespeare's *Macbeth* and the 'three weird sisters' prophesising Macbeth's eventual demise. Weil (1989) writes of wyrd here as

> the implacable arbiter of men's struggles resounds throughout the Anglo-Saxon canon like a perpetual minor chord, the synonymous nature of fate and shaping in Old English should not be surprising: the singers of the canon were always aware that the events of their lives had been 'shaped' by a force (or forces) beyond their control. (94, original emphasis)

Importantly, though, in Norse mythology, the Norns were only able to *influence* the unfolding of a person's destiny, they did not completely prescribe one's fate and, therefore, one would live in a dialogue of sorts with the Norns. Life was never set by them, neither was it completely free from their hand, as Weil explains: '[E]ven the three Norns who spun and snipped the threads of fate for each man were shadowy figures, spinning, not quite shaping, apparently acting without a purpose of their own' (1989: 95). Despite the Norns' control over causality and thus their hand over all human existence, McNish (2004) explains:

> European paganism to either a greater or a lesser extent sensed the reality of causality as the moving force behind all natural phenomena. Their gods were immortal and possessed superhuman powers, but they did not create the Universe and were themselves only one aspect of it. (3)

This causal force known as wyrd signals that these early Germanic peoples were pursuing proto-scientific ideas of causality, although this was quickly curtailed with the arrival of Christianity wherein the wyrd was explained away as Divine intervention or Providence (see in particular Lochrie, 1986). Of interest here to our understanding of weird fiction is how the Anglo-Saxon philosophy of wyrd connects in particular to a body of fiction I refer to as Bharati Fantasy; a canon of popular mythology-inspired fiction from post-millennial India which this chapter details extensively later.

Tracing the word weird back to its wyrd roots is particularly helpful in providing insights into Bharati Fantasy fiction as well as generating ideas around the interface of science and belief. Although, overall, this book connects with McNish's description of the current semantic of the word weird; 'a distorted and degenerate form [of weird] with all the fearful and ungodly connotations that are associated with "weird" to this day' (2004: 5). This idea of the Weird is applied to both Chapter 3 ('Bharati Fantasy: Eternal *Bhāva*') and Chapter 4 ('Bharati Fantasy: Modern-Day Sensibilities') where, amongst other interests, the texts are analysed for their connection with McNish's words.

A deeper connection between the Old Norse wyrd (Urd) and the texts of Hinduism that inspire Bharati Fantasy novels can be found in the two cultures' epic (poetic) texts. As this chapter will go on to detail, for the Hindu texts it is the Vedas – epic, lyrical narratives such as the *Mahabharata*, the *Ramayana* and the Puranas, and in the case of Old Norse, it is the *Poetic Edda*. The collection of mythological and heroic poetry that is the *Poetic Edda* explores the lives of the gods, battles of good over evil, the wisdom of the gods and the creation of the world. It is in the 'Seeress's Prophecy' ('Voluspa') that the beginning of the world is presented, a poem recited by a seeress who can remember a period before the beginning of the world. It is in the *Poetic Edda* and in the 'Seeress's Prophecy' in particular that we learn of the three Fates (the Norns) and their ability to shape man's fortune. Part of the poem tells of the Fates residing by a sacred tree called 'Yggdrasill' which stands over Urd's well. It reads:

> From there come girls, knowing a great deal,
> three from the lake standing under the tree;
> Urd one is called, Verdandi another –
> they carved on a wooden slip – Skuld the third;
> they laid down laws, they chose lives
> for the sons of men, the fates of men.
>
> (Larrington, 2014: 6, *trans.*)

Urd who features here is the Fate most closely associated with wyrd and she is also mentioned at other points in the *Poetic Edda*, for example, in 'Groa's Chant' it reads:

> This second one I will chant for you: if you must go on this errand,
> whether you like it or not;
> may Urd's charms keep you safe on all sides
> when you are on your way!
>
> (Larrington, 2014: 257, *trans.*)

Another occasion is in 'The Sayings of Fiolsvinn' where Svipdag, who has gained supernatural protection from his dead mother, is in dialogue with the giant Fiolsvinn. Svipdag reveals part of his identity by saying:

> 'Svipdag I'm called, Sun-bright is my father;
> I've wandered wind-cold ways from there;
> no man can overcome Urd's decree -
> even if it's been shamefully laid down'.
>
> (Larrington, 2014: 267, *trans.*)

Where Urd appears in these parts of the *Poetic Edda* it is clear that she is a force that cannot be overcome. Despite being gentle in her nature as a female figure and through her relatively placid activity of spinning, Urd's hand on man's life remains a powerful, omnipresent force. Weil (1989) writes of the Norns' presence, saying: 'Given the primacy of tactile imagery throughout their poetry, their vision of destiny as a process of shaping is characteristic' (94). This looming, numinous presence that is symbolic of Urd is sensed in the fiction of Lovecraft, in the New or Recent Weird of Miéville, as well as in the growing body of Bharati Fantasy fiction from India. This presence for Weil *is* wyrd: 'The Anglo-Saxon universe seems curiously without cause, yet brimming with effects – all subsumed under the murky heading of *wyrd*, which remains a force, not a figure. Who, then, is the Shaper?' (95, original emphasis). I suggest, through my analyses of the Bharti Fantasy novels in Chapters 3 and 4, that both a looming presence of wyrd and that of a

'Shaper' feature in this fiction, sometimes the Shaper is more manifest, there is, however, usually a sense of a looming, numinous presence throughout. In such a way, the body of writing I define as Bharati Fantasy connects with ideas and definitions of weird fiction. I am not suggesting, however, that Bharati Fantasy is weird fiction per se, rather its reception in a Western context may be akin to that of (New) Weird fiction.

2.1.2 Weird Fiction

Returning then to an understanding of how the term weird fiction has been defined and also how it continues to be defined as New or Recent Weird fiction, we turn to Miéville's chapter titled 'Weird Fiction' in *The Routledge Companion to Science Fiction* (2009),[1] where Miéville begins by detailing the eminent authors of the original weird fiction canon (often referred to as The Weird) before moving on to current defining characteristics of weird fiction. In the 1930s, Lovecraft wrote an essay titled 'Notes on Writing Weird Fiction' in which he outlined his interests in and motivations for what he called 'the weird tale'. He writes:

> I choose weird stories because they suit my inclination best—one of my strongest and most persistent wishes being to achieve, momentarily, the illusion of some strange suspension or violation of the galling limitations of time, space, and natural law which for ever imprison us and frustrate our curiosity about the infinite cosmic spaces beyond the radius of our sight and analysis. (Lovecraft, 2009: online)

Miéville writes in detail of the characteristics of weird fiction, although he begins by saying that 'if considered at all, Weird Fiction is usually, roughly, conceived of as a rather breathless and generically slippery macabre fiction, a dark fantastic ("horror" plus "fantasy") often featuring nontraditional alien monsters (thus plus "science fiction")' (2009: 510). From the lengthier discussion of weird fiction that Miéville offers in the chapter, I have distilled the following characteristics of Weird Fiction that he presents:

- an awe at strangeness
- the numinous which is a threatening force
- less narrative plot and more emphasis on 'weird presence' within the narrative
- revolutionary teratology

In this same chapter, Miéville posits how 'The Weird' of Lovecraft and other weird authors writing in the early 20th century took place during 'a period of crisis in which its cruder nostrums of progressive bourgeois rationality are shattered' (2009: 513). Writers who quickly followed Lovecraft's lead, inspired by the creation of other worlds that Lovecraft produced in his short life (he died at the age of 46), included a writer called August Derleth. Kincaid (2014) says that 'Derleth, who invented the term "Cthulhu Mythos", tended to work closer to Lovecraft's own model ...' but Kincaid goes on to point out that '... where Lovecraft presented an amoral universe, Derleth's Christianity led him to recast the Mythos as an eternal struggle between the evil of the Elder Gods and the good of the Old Ones' (45). Indeed, ideas of good over evil were an echo of the reality of the time, of which Miéville cites the crisis of the First World War, 'where mass carnage perpetrated by the most modern states made claims of a "rational" modern system a tasteless joke' (2009: 513).

Much the same, New or Recent Weird authors, post millennium, are writing against a backdrop of 21st-century crisis and warfare: whether it be financial ('Global Financial Crisis 2008'), nuclear (the Fukushima Daiichi nuclear disaster of 2011), revolutionary (Occupy Wall Street, the Arab Spring as examples), world health (the Ebola outbreak of 2014) or natural disasters such as the South Asian tsunami (of 2004), Hurricane Katrina (2005) or the Haiti earthquake (2010). During this timeframe, warfare has continued to plague the planet, with the Iraq War (2003–2011), the war in Afghanistan, the rise of the Islamic State (2014), and 'terror' seems to reign in its many manifestations, from 9/11 at the start of the millennium, to the Mumbai Attacks in 2008, the terror attacks in Paris (2015) and the downing of civilian aircraft (flight MH17 in eastern Ukraine in 2014, the Russian Airbus over the Sinai Peninsula in 2015) and there also remains the mysterious case of MH370 which disappeared on its flight from Kuala Lumpur to Beijing. Csicsery-Ronay (2012) explores the correlation between 'event-streams' and artistic responses, writing:

> Event-streams that affect all of humanity or the natural world – epidemics, meltdowns, refugee waves, global warming, the Net, electronically accelerated and expanded booms and busts, transnational jihads and democratic mobilizations, labor migration, transnational sex and drug trafficking, media hyperrealization, electronic commodomy, and collective traumas all the way down – inevitably encourage new artistic responses, new forms adequate for the new conditions. (480)

For our interests here, analysis of some of the texts in Chapters 3 and 4 reveals the connection between our globalised world, crisis and terror (see in particular Doyle, 2013; Sanghi, 2012; Arni, 2013). An overriding motif of Lovecraft's work is the depiction of places and 'things' unknown, whether that be through the numinous, teratology or 'awe at strangeness'. Kneale (2006) writes that Lovecraft's stories 'are centrally concerned with the paradox of representing entities, things and places that are beyond representation' (106). Through his writing, Lovecraft illustrates humankind's inadequate understanding of the cosmos and, in turn, he tries to show how our existence has little significance when understood as being part of such a large and limitless whole. This bleak view of not only man's existence but also of the supposed horrors that exist in the vast universe beyond contribute to the sense of terror that one encounters in Lovecraft's works. The question of 'time' plagued Lovecraft and thus the connection with space was easily made through his ruminations on 'the vast gulfs of time and space revealed by sciences like astronomy and geology' (Kneale, 2006: 109). In his own critical writing, *Supernatural Horror in Literature*, first published in 1945, although written in the mid-1920s and revised in the mid-1930s, Lovecraft acknowledges how advances in scientific understanding will impact the development of what he refers to as 'supernatural horror' in the future. He writes, 'through the stimulation of wonder and fancy by such enlarged vistas and broken barriers as modern science has given us with its intra-atomic chemistry, advancing astrophysics, doctrines of relativity, and probings into biology and human thought' (Lovecraft 1973: 106). The developments in these fields of enquiry (alongside others) have certainly shaped speculative fiction, whether it be in the genre of horror, science fiction or fantasy, and in the case of the Weird, such developments have helped craft narratives and plot lines that continue to question and subvert the laws of nature. A cognate genre term for such writing is 'slipstream', described by Ashley as one which 'uses the tropes and ideas of science fiction, fantasy and horror but it is not bound by their rules and will make those elements only a minor feature of the story rather than its raison d'être. Likewise a plot and set-up may appear conventionally literary but fall outside the staid boundaries of mainstream' (2008: ii). Frelik (2009) also concedes that 'slipstream novels, novellas and short stories share their territory with other literary entities', and making a reference to Miéville's New Weird, Frelik goes on to say that

> like the inhabitants of Beshel and Ul Qoma, Slipstream's readers and critics peer into the spaces of their self-approved texts, 'unseeing' and 'unhearing' other readers and the claims made by proponents of other conventions about the same literary property. And yet, these different territorial markings do not necessarily invalidate and cancel out each other. (2009: online)

Returning though to how we might define the (New) Weird, in her 'Foreword' to *Year's Best Weird Fiction Volume Two*, Kelly (2015) writes that

> ... weird fiction is speculative and often (but not always) works to subvert the Laws of Nature. More than any other mode or stream or genre fiction, The Weird is a feeling. A kind of continuous distortion of ambient space. So, weird tales can be comprised of elements of science fiction, fantasy, and horror, but can also occupy those more sensate liminal areas. (vii)

Known as the 'New Weird' and also as the 'Recent Weird', the genre term has been shaped by writers like Miéville, K. J. Bishop, Paul di Filippo, Kelly Link, Nick Mamatas and others. By 2005, the term New Weird had gained some significant momentum and had developed an understanding of the defining characteristics of the New Weird through online discussion boards (in particular, www.weirdfictionreview.com) and, significantly, from the introduction to Jeff Vandermeer's anthology *The New Weird* (2008). Vandermeer's introduction offers a (somewhat lengthy) working definition of the term; I include some of the wording of his 'working definition' here:

> New Weird is a type of urban, secondary-world fiction that subverts the romanticized ideas about place found in traditional fantasy, largely by choosing realistic, complex real-world models as the jumping off point for creation of settings that combine elements of both science fiction and fantasy. [...] New Weird fictions are acutely aware of the modern world, even if in disguise, but not always overtly political. (2008, xvi)

In addition to the four characteristics of weird fiction that I have taken from Miéville's chapter ('Weird Fiction', 2009) mentioned earlier, I add two definitions here put forward by Vandermeer in order to create a framework by which the novels in Chapters 3 and 4 can be analysed. These are:

- subverting traditional fantasy, largely by choosing realistic, complex real-world models
- elements of both science fiction and fantasy

The defining characteristics of the Weird that Miéville and Vandermeer advocate manifest themselves in the fiction I call Bharati Fantasy. This body of post-millennial Indian fiction calls upon a central tenant of the Weird which Koja (2015) details in her introduction to *Year's Best Weird Fiction: Volume Two* titled 'At Home with the Weird':

> We all know that there's more to the world than what our senses combined can convey, though we use those hard-working senses (including the less-documented but no less real 'sixth' sense, proprioception) to daily investigate our outer and inner geographies, and decide from the information we take in whether a thing is actual or not, able to give pleasure or cause danger, something to welcome, to flee or to watch. (xi)

Bharati Fantasy cannot be categorised as science fiction or simply as fantasy according to their respective definitions within the Western academy (see more on this in Section 2.2).[2] Weird fiction on the other hand offers some workable definitions to describe the characteristics of Bharati Fantasy and more so when it concerns the reception of this body of fiction in non-Indian cultural milieus. Weird fiction has long been defined by its ability to create an atmosphere of dread from unknown forces or beings, but the genre has never been science fiction or fantasy per se, it has never been simply a 'ghost story' or of the 'horror story' genre. Given that the original iterations of weird fiction were inter-genre and thus a blend of horror, ghost story, fantasy and quasi-science fiction, it is of little surprise that the New Weird also treads such blended ground. The genre term of the New Weird offers a space where contemporary fiction responds to topics of science, numinosity, awe at strangeness, specific cultural histories and philosophies interplay and, moreover, the globalised and connected world we now inhabit allows for such a space to showcase a variety of national and cultural fiction productions. In acknowledgement of this international dynamic, the definition of the New Weird may be shaped by these global fiction productions. In turn, the prevailing topics of the Old (and New) Weird such as science, numinosity and awe at strangeness might be redefined through specific cultural histories, aesthetics and philosophies. This re-visioning of such key terms which have to date been chiefly anchored in Western notions (and imaginations) of science, numinosity and awe of strangeness, is key to the development of the genre term Bharati Fantasy. Just as the Weird in the early 1900s blended genres with a fear of the unknown, out of which fixed laws of nature were not only challenged but often broken, so too does the New Weird continue to challenge fixed ideas of natural law, science, belief and strangeness. In an echo of this activity, Bharati Fantasy offers its own interpretation of writing the weird, most notably through its depiction of the numinous and scientific imagination but also through the manner in which Bharati Fantasy texts are received across cultures.

2.2 Bharati Fantasy: *Itihasa*, Myth and the Indian Scientific Imagination

This chapter section begins by focussing on ideas of truth, myth and *dharma* through the Sanskrit term *itihasa*. The sacred texts of the Vedas, the epics of the *Mahabharata* and the *Ramayana* as well as the Puranas are presented as part of this discussion and I demonstrate how these texts are connected to both ideas of *itihasa* and to the fiction of Bharati Fantasy. The chapter then moves to consider how the genre term I have coined as Bharati Fantasy is defined. This involves looking at Western ideas of fantasy fiction as well as exploring historical fiction and the receptions of Bharati Fantasy novels by Indian and non-Indian readers. The chapter concludes by exploring the Indian scientific imagination, considering Indian scientific and cosmological achievements, theories of creationism and its connections with modern science, the non-linearity of human existence in the Hindu world and the influence of *advaita Vedanta* on the Indian Hindu imagination and its relationship to the world.

2.2.1 Sacred Texts: Itihasa and Myth

In Section 2.1, I outlined how Old Norse mythology holds the linguistic anchor to the term weird (wyrd). As wyrd embodies a sense of prophecy and is linked to the three Norns of Old Norse mythology, it is important to demonstrate the connection that this has with Hindu ideas of mythology and epic narrative before we look at the defining features of the genre term Bharati Fantasy and this genre's connection with the Indian scientific imagination. Let us begin by considering the context of dharmic tradition. Cromwell Crawford (2003) writes:

> The Sanskrit word for ethics is *Dharma* ('to hold'). It signifies that which embodies law, custom, and religion, and is analogous to the concept of 'Natural Law' in Christian ethics, though the idea of 'law' should not detract from its dynamic character. *Dharma* is activity, mobility, and is possessed of catalytic qualities. (11)

Malhotra (2013) writes how the idea of 'myth' is expressed and understood in such traditions when he says: '[D]harma traditions deal with their past through "itihasa", a Sanskrit term sometimes translated as "myth" or simply "narrative"' (63). Malhotra also explains that the term 'myth' in the West is often seen 'as the opposite of truth' (63). Malhotra rightly sketches out that the popular semantic of 'myth' is often expressed as being 'imaginary, fantastical, fictional, or even superstitious, primitive or false' (63). Yet, in dharmic traditions, myth *uses* 'narrative' to convey certain truths. The question of 'truth' resonates through much of Hindu life given that *dharma* is the principal code for morality. Moreover, for a nation that is Hindu, Muslim, Sikh, Christian, Jain and otherwise, the national motto, adopted at India's independence, is the Sanskrit *satyam eva jayate*, which translates as 'truth alone triumphs' or 'truth alone is victorious'. This motto is part of a mantra from the *Athara Veda*, thus the words are of both ancient and sacred provenances.

How, then, do narratives convey aspects of 'truth', in particular those 'truths' of dharma? Malhotra (2013) asserts that 'accounts of the past are not made through *either* myth or history exclusively. Rather, these categories are replaced by itihasa, which combines "purakalpa" (past narrative) with words of advice regarding all aspects of life' (65, original emphasis). The term *itihasa* is broadly translated as 'history', although Thapar (2014a: 55) writes that it 'has come to be used now to mean history, but earlier it was not history in any modern sense of the term'. In literal translation *iti-ha-asa* conveys the following: 'thus it happened'[3] or 'thus indeed it was' (Thapar, 2014a: 55). The epics of the *Mahabharata* and the *Ramayana* when accepted as an *itihasa* text narrate past events as those 'that happened', which by extension implies a true account of historical events. Thapar warns against such an idea saying that 'the epic can be treated as among the genres reflecting a past, but this does not permit it being read literally as history' (211). Rather, she suggests we may consider the conjoint term *itihasa-purana* as more specific in meaning 'that which was believed to have happened in the past' (56). What has come to be regarded as *itihasa* in terms of texts, though, is a canon which has evolved over many years in terms of how it has been written, documented and the events within the narratives interpreted. So for historians like Thapar, the epic form has been shaped by the historical contexts it has known, therefore it 'can be viewed as the articulation of a consciousness relating to the historical past, even if the events which it narrates may not all be historically authenticated' (2014a: 208). Close historical analysis of the *Ramayana*, for example, points towards a choice of narratives which had existed at various times, brought together in what is currently known as Valkimi's *Ramayana*.

Given, then, that the epics embody the zeitgeist of the time in which they were composed and (re)told, and are therefore not necessarily 'historic' facts of the kind that may be verified and substantiated, the epics are recognised for their ability to communicate moral and ethical 'truths'. Radhavallah Tripathi (2014) writes that the *Vācaspatyam* provides a standard definition of *itihasa*, saying, 'The *itihasa* comprises an account of past happenings and also preaches the way for the attainment of the *puruṣārthas* (four goals of human life)' (87). In this way, an *itihasa* text, Tripathi writes, 'presents a continuum of past, present and future. It is both descriptive and prescriptive' (87). She goes as far as to say that this view of *itihasa* is more concerned with 'what ought to be, rather than on what was or has been' (87). The guidance that the epic narratives of Hinduism convey can be grouped into the four goals or objectives of Hindu life which are *dharma* (righteousness), *artha* (the acquisition of wealth), *kama* (pleasure) and *moksha* (liberation from this mortal life). As Cromwell Crawford (2003) reminds us,

> ... the Hindu scriptures do not have systematic discussion of moral doctrines, fashioned in the manner of Aristotelian or Thomistic models. At the same time Hindu scriptures are rich repositories of certain theoretical statements that define the shape of reality and the nature of things, along with prescriptive and practical sayings, aimed at the cultivation of moral behaviour. (11)

It is *dharma* and *moksha*, the non-materialistic goals, which are the higher goals in life according to Hinduism but it is the epic narratives that communicate how, in pursuing both *artha* and *kama* (the materialistic goals), the higher goals of life may be attained. The protagonists of these stories are Hindu deities. In Sanskrit, the term *daivata shastra* is used to describe events and experiences related to the deities' lives and, in turn, *daivata shastra* can be regarded as a vehicle for the narrating of truth. The word 'mythology' appears as a translation of *daivata shastra* and, as such, has been assimilated into Indian English where speakers will use the term mythology over *daivata shastra*. However, the word mythology in Western contexts – in English at least – conjures up those ideas elucidated by Malhotra earlier, namely 'fantasy' and 'fiction', in short, narratives which do not tell of actual people or actual historical events. On myths and on epics, Thapar (2014b) suggests that whereas myths involve deities and humans, epics focus more on humans and so are assumed to contain some trace of an historical kernel. But this does not mean that all the events are historically accurate or that even the historically proved event is accurately described in the epic. (198)

The writing that I refer to as Bharati Fantasy anchors its narratives or at least takes considerable inspiration from various Hindu scriptures and epic texts through retellings, interpretation and inspired versions of the ideas and characters present in the 'original' material. The Hindu texts that Bharati Fantasy draws on are specifically the Vedas, the *arshamahakavya* – the *Mahabharata* and the *Ramayana* – the *Harivarsha* and the Puranas. To explain this a little further, here are some examples: Lord Shiva appears as Lord Rudra across the four Vedas and Amish Tripathi's 'Shiva Trilogy' is, as the name suggests, a re-visioning of the life of Lord Shiva; the life of Sri Krishna is elucidated in the Hindu text *Harivarsha* and Ashwin Sanghi's *The Krishna Key* (2012) draws on this Hindu text as he simultaneously narrates an ancient and contemporary tale; the life of Ram is most latterly being explored through Amish Tripathi's new collection – the Ram Chandra Series – drawing on various Hindu texts, although most evidently the *Ramayana*; the story of Sita in the *Ramayana* is re-visioned in Samhita Arni's *The Missing Queen* and the experience of Urmila in the *Ramayana* is also reimagined through Pervin Saket's novel *Urmila* (2016). The fact that the *Ramayana* is present in many of the Bharati Fantasy narratives might be explained through Sattar's (2011) observation that between 1997 and 2003 the *Ramayana* lost its inherent pluralism, something that is being rekindled and recelebrated today. She writes of this time period, saying:

> [T]hose were the years when the Hindu right was firmly entrenched in the national consciousness as well as in political power. This constellation of political parties, scholars, local politicians and people-on-the-street had appropriated Rama and his story, silencing its inherent pluralism and making it the basis of their antagonism to those they perceived as hostile to Hinduism and to the Indian nation. (x)

Sattar's book *Lost Loves: Exploring Rama's Anguish* appears alongside many other non-fiction and fictional works which explore the *Ramayana* from varying perspectives and viewpoints. Importantly, the texts from which these Bharati Fantasy authors named earlier (and others) take their inspiration are various but all are Hindu texts which hold different standings within Hinduism and broader 'Hindu' culture. To start with the most ancient of these texts, it is the Vedas which are regarded as the most sacred and divine of texts. These four ancient scriptures (the Vedas) are considered 'authorless'. The *Rig Veda*, *Yagur Veda*, *Sama Veda* and *Athara Veda* are scriptures that were 'heard' by the ancient seers (known also as *rishis*) and as these scriptures were 'heard', they remain divine, untouched by the human hand. They are referred to as *Sruti* (from the Sanskrit for 'heard') and are considered as 'truth' because of their divine provenance. The Vedas cover aspects of ritual, meditation, philosophy and knowledge of Brahman to detachment and emancipation from reality (Samhitas, Brahmanas, Aranyakas and the Upanishads). For our purposes here, it is the more esoteric aspects of the Vedas, rather than their provenance, that I am interested in and how they appear as part of Bharati Fantasy novels, connecting with ideas of the Weird.

For the esoteric, we turn to the Upanishads. Each of the four Vedas includes a latter section known as the Upanishad and it is this iteration of the Vedas which is considered the final and culminate. The Upanishad looks to offer a teaching made as simple as possible from subject matter which is deeply esoteric, centred around detachment and emancipation from earthly life with a focus on the relationship of this world with Brahman, the Supreme Being.[4] As Smith (2003) explains, the simple equation of the Upanishad is 'That [brahman] is You [the individual self]. The individual self (*atman*) is the universal self (*brahman*): this is the highest truth; everything else is ultimately unreal. This remains the dominant philosophy of Hinduism' (39). I return to discussion of Brahman later in this chapter in relation to science and the Indian imagination in order to explore the interface of science and Vedic thought. A second set of texts that Bharati Fantasy authors often draw on inspirationally, and at times directly, is the *arshamahakavya* and the *mahakavya*. The *mahakavya* refers to the epic narratives of the *Mahabharata*, the *Ramayana* and *Harivarsha*, whereas the *arshamahakavya* refers only to the *Mahabharata* and the *Ramayana*. Tripathi (2014) states how the *arshamahakavya* 'is imbued with the vision of a seer. Having visualized the past, present and future of a country and the continuum of time in flux, the seer presents the destiny of a nation and society and enables us to see it' (87–88). Given, then, that the epic, lyrical texts of the *Mahabharata* and the *Ramayana* are considered as *itihasa*, the stories of the warring Kauravas and Pandavas, the banishing of Lord Ram into forest exile and the kidnapping of Sita by Ravana might all be considered as 'truth' in the sense that they 'happened'. These lyrical narratives are authored most famously by Vyasa (the *Mahabharata*) and by Valmiki (the *Ramayana*) between 400 BC and AD 400. There have been multiple retellings of these epics, each one being its own interpretative retelling and narration of the events and shaped by the epoch in which it is found (a point we return to in Chapter 3, Section 3.7). This palimpsestic nature of the *arshakarvya* is echoed in the production of Bharati Fantasy novels as the narratives of Lord Shiva, Lord Ram, Ravana, Sita and Sri Krishna are told anew. Given that the (*arsha*) *mahakavya* (and the Puranas) are central to Hinduism in both belief and wider 'Indian' culture, it can be customary for Hindus to believe that the events and people portrayed in the aforementioned texts existed and to believe in the events described in these texts as 'truth'; the texts are understood to be *itihasa* ('thus it happened') in this regard.[5] Discussion on this continuum of belief – the degree to which *itihasa* texts narrate what really happened in the past – is taken up through the analysis of the Bharati Fantasy novels in Chapters 3 and 4 as well as through the author interviews at the end of these chapters respectively.

From these epic, lyrical texts, Bharati Fantasy authors have drawn on certain aspects of the narratives, such as locations mentioned in the epic texts, people named in the texts or objects such as coins or seals from the civilisations of that time (see Doyle's *The Mahabharata Secret* and Sanghi's *The Krishna Key* in Chapter 4, this volume, as examples). Bharati Fantasy authors have also focussed on the (divine) protagonists from these great texts, such as Lord Shiva, Lord Ram, Sita, Urmilla or Ravana from the *Ramayana* (see Amish's 'Shiva Trilogy', Chapter 3, this volume; Arni's *The Missing Queen*, Chapter 3, this volume; Saket's *Urmila*, Chapter 4, this volume) and Sri Krishna and his role in the *Mahabharata* and the portrayal of his life in the *Harivarsha* (see Sanghi's *The Krishna Key*, Chapter 4, this volume). Events such as the 'churning of the ocean' (*samudra manthan*) also appear in Bharati Fantasy storylines (see Nath's novel *The Guardians of the Halahala* discussed in Chapter 3 and Choudhury's *Bali and the Ocean of Milk* discussed in Chapter 4, this volume) as well as the birth of Sri Krishna (see Bhanver's *The Curse of Brahma*, Chapter 3, this volume). The Puranas are another text source that Bharati Fantasy writers draw on for their works. Of the Puranas, Malhotra writes '[T]he Puranas do use historical narratives and events, but in the form of parables to teach dharma, and not as indispensable and central strictures' (2013: 80). The *Bhagavata Purana* is one of the most popular Puranic Hindu texts as it describes the life of Sri Krishna. Although the Puranas are generally considered as *itihasa*, they do include regional aspects in their narrations and thus reflect variation in how the story is presented. This is in keeping with their function, which, in essence, is the communication of dharma.

2.2.2 Bharati Fantasy

Given the debate around 'truth' and 'history', it is important to foreground that both truth and history are understood as being composite of *itihasa* throughout my discussion of the term Bharati Fantasy. In my presentation of the term Bharati Fantasy, I consider another genre – historical fiction – given that both terms share a negotiated space of epic narrative as hegemonic history, identity and culture. In formulating the genre term Bharati Fantasy, the reception of this body of fiction is key. The matter of reception elucidated here concerns (comparatively) Indian receptions and Western receptions of mythology – inspired or mythology-inspired fiction. The anchor to this difference in reception lies in these words of Malhotra (2013): 'the dharmic relation between history and myth is [thus] not at all comparable to the Western relation between truth and fiction' (65), but as Chapter 1 has detailed, publishing trends in post-millennial India are bringing new, popular fiction to readers outside of India, thus to readers who are outside of dharmic traditions. I have developed Bharati Fantasy as a genre term in response to this situation. Although the retelling and reimaginings of Hindu epic narratives is not a new phenomenon, the entrance of Bharati Fantasy into the Indian writing in English scene is new in terms of how scholars have previously viewed the canon of Indian writing in English and in particular, its postcolonial identity. I have written elsewhere (Dawson Varughese, 2012, 2016, Forthcoming) on the relationship between the popular and the post-colonial and therefore will not be rehearsing such debates here; however, it is useful to consult Chaudhuri (2001), since he writes on the interface of the postcolonial novel and the Indian 'mythic imagination':

> While there are many differences between the traditional Indian epic and the post-colonial Indian English novel, one seems to be of particular importance; the mythic imagination from which those epics sprang was disturbingly amoral and estranging (I recall some of the British critics of Peter Brook's *Mahabharata* noting in wounded tones the Machiavellian, unfathomable nature of the Hindu god Krishna), and it is through this amorality that the epics reveal to us the mystery of human nature and the universe. The post-colonial novel on the other hand, is frequently rooted in the liberal middle-class conscience and founded in the liberal humanist verities: multiculturalism is good; colonialism and fundamentalism are bad, etc. (xxvi)

Bharati Fantasy, through its connection with epic Hindu narrative, explores the 'unfathomable', 'mythic imagination' and the 'mystery of human nature and the universe' that Chaudhuri writes of and yet it is fiction written in English targeting a popular, Indian, middle-class, upwardly mobile audience containing narrative plots which might be interpreted as clinging to 'liberal humanist verities'. As Malhotra (2013) reminds us: 'truth and not mere history is the concern of itihasa' (65), and in this sense Bharati Fantasy narrates both a shared history and a set of attitudes for living, albeit through a popular, 'commercial fiction' lens (see S. Gupta, 2012).

2.2.3 Marketing the Genre

Beyond the fact that Bharati Fantasy draws on ideas of *itihasa*, Bharati Fantasy is significant as a point of confluence of genres and receptions, for I suggest that one reader's fantasy novel might be another's historical fiction. The year 2010 saw the publication of Amish Tripathi's *The Immortals of Meluha* and Ashwin Sanghi's *Chanakya's Chant*, authors I consider to be the primary authors of Bharati Fantasy, and these books were 'for sale in India only' or more regionally orientated, 'available in the Indian Subcontinent only' (see Chapter 1 for more on restricted sales). The year 2014 started to see the sale of these authors' books on amazon.co.uk, both in paperback and as e-books; a shift in sales that I suggest opens up curious avenues of cultural reception. The delay in any dedicated global circulation of these authors' works together with this fiction's 'genre' identity have combined to powerful effect, as it is one which has resulted in a significantly self-sustaining and domestically inclined celebration of this writing trend within India (see, for example, Mumbai's Litomania Festival). The reach of this fiction domestically is in part due to being genre fiction and in turn 'popular' fiction, of which Glover and McCracken (2015) write,

> ... popular fiction is frequently thought of as those books that everyone reads, usually imagined as a league table of bestsellers whose aggregate figures dramatically illustrate an impressive ability to reach across wide social and cultural divisions with remarkable commercial success. (1)

Given how the works of Tripathi, Sanghi and other Bharati Fantasy writers have more recently become easily available through e-retailers such as Amazon, questions of reception arise, and none more readily than how such fictions might be genre classified. Sudarshan Purohit (2010: online) reminds us of the reality of the genre marketing of Indian fiction in English when he talks of the imported 'Western books ecosystem' and the 'genre names that are used to categorise the different types of writing, particularly evident in commercial fiction in English, in India today'. In coining the term Bharati Fantasy, I seek to readdress this inequality, making the case that genre terms imported from the West do not necessarily capture the essence of a fiction's narratives, its plots, readerships and circulation. Given that my term Bharati Fantasy is anchored in a familiar genre term of the West ('fantasy'), it recognises that certain readerships will respond to the fiction as a fantasy narrative whilst the term 'Bharati' places the fiction firmly in an Indian milieu (and by its name, within something of a Hindu milieu), thus shaping how the term fantasy is and should be interpreted.

As noted earlier, many of the Bharati Fantasy novels have titles that make reference to Indian mythology, the epics, religious texts, deities or political figures. Examples of the genre include: Tripathi's 'Shiva Trilogy' – *The Immortals of Meluha* (2010), *The Secret of the Nagas* (2011) and *The Oath of the Vayuputras* (2013) – and the first book of his 'Ram Chandra' series, *Scion of Ikshvaku* (2015); Nilanjan P. Choudhury's *Bali and the Ocean of Milk* (2011); R. G. Menon's 'Vedic' Trilogy *Thundergod* (2012); Anand Neelakantan's *Asura* (2012) and *Ajaya* (2013) followed by *The Rise of Kali* (2015) in the same series; Christopher C. Doyle's *The Mahabharata Secret* (2013); Bhanver's *The Curse of Brahma* (2015); Nath's *The Guardians of the Halahala* (2015); Samhita Arni's *The Missing Queen* (2013); Ashok Banker's 'Ramayana Series' and 'Krishna Coriolis' books; Dev Prasad's *The Curse of Surya* (2015); Pervin Saket's *Urmila* (2016); Mainak Dhar's *Vimana* (2012); Ashok Banker's *Gods of War* (2009); Rudra Krishna's *The Onus of*

Karma (2010); and Devdutt Pattanaik's *The Pregnant King* (2008). By book title alone, the marketing of these novels outside India (or outside the region of South Asia more broadly) can present a challenge. The cultural referents are not only found in the novels' titles, but also the book covers of these works which symbolise deep cultural and religious attachment, achieved through images of the Himalayas, the Ganga, Lord Shiva, Lord Ram and temples as examples. The endorsements found on the book covers are equally culturally bound – Shashi Tharoor, Anil Dharkar, Karan Johar, Rashmi Bansal – names that are little known or generally unknown to readerships outside of India, although there is some exception within the Indian diaspora, of course, which would be more likely to engage with and understand such cultural referents but, significantly, the Indian diaspora is not only vast, it is also Hindu, Sikh, Muslim, Jain, Christian and otherwise. Even within the various Hindu communities of the global Indian diaspora, receptions, beliefs and traditions vary to such an extent that a given 'reception' of this wave of fiction cannot be determined so easily. Through these observations, S. Gupta's suggestion that 'Indian commercial fiction in English, the argument goes, is geared expressively for an internal Indian audience and therefore does not need to be explanatory and demonstrative in the way that literary fiction, with a potentially international readership, feels it should be' (2012: 50) is fairly substantiated, not least because much detail of domestic (as opposed to diasporic) Indian life is captured within these texts.

In an interesting turn of events, the UK-based publisher and distributor Jo Fletcher Books decided to include the novels of Amish Tripathi in its catalogue from 2013. The publisher's website describes itself thus: 'Jo Fletcher Books is part of the Quercus family, a small but perfectly formed list publishing the very best in best science fiction, fantasy and horror'.[6] This statement from Jo Fletcher Books testifies to some degree that authors of Bharati Fantasy write within a recognisable Western construct of the fantasy genre; this is how the books of Amish Tripathi are marketed in the Western markets to which Jo Fletcher Books reaches out. Indeed, 2013 saw Quercus Books acquire the rights to produce a UK and US edition of Tripathi's *The Immortals of Meluha* (2010). Interestingly, it appears that Amish Tripathi's novels have not been changed for these 'new' markets; the book covers remain the same and the only addition is a blurb which describes him as 'India's first literary popstar'[7] in order to introduce him to new audiences. The emergence of Tripathi's *The Immortals of Meluha* (2010) and its marketing and distribution are in complete contrast to the manner in which the literary fiction of *The God of Small Things* (1997) was identified, endorsed and made known to its many (global) audiences. Bharati Fantasy, it must be acknowledged, is far from holding the *global* notoriety of Arundhati Roy's bestseller, but Amish Tripathi and Ashwin Sanghi in particular are comparable in their literary successes of a different (commercial) kind, within the domestic Indian market at least. *The Oath of the Vayuputras* (2013) by Tripathi, the last book of his Shiva Trilogy, reached sales of over one million copies in 2013. The success of Tripathi's novels echoes something of the success of

Roy's 1997 Man Booker Prize winner, only, conversely, the success has been generated and celebrated from within India and not from outside it.

Despite the current, enlarging distribution circuits of Bharati Fantasy, it must be emphasised that these novels remain discernibly (Hindu) Indian, in the sense that they draw on Hindu Indian epic narrative as well as on myths and folklore of various – although mostly Hindu – Indian cultures and traditions (as an example, 'Vikramaditya' in Nath's novel, see Chapter 3). It is such cultural anchoring that creates particular issues of reception. A reader with little or no knowledge of the history, religion and people of ancient Bharat will most likely read these new novels as significantly 'otherworldly'. Less so might a readership where Hindu mythology, history, religion and Sanskrit terms are more readily part of their cultural heritage. Definitions of fantasy (such as those of Clute and Grant, Mendlesohn and Roberts) detail how the characters, the plot and the narrative style are fantastical in the sense that the world depicted is not real. Clute and Grant (1999) say of fantasy, 'when set in an otherworld, that otherworld will be impossible, though stories set there will be possible in its terms' (338). Describing mythology-inspired fiction through such definitions and thus as simply fantasy has its own issues, given that for some readerships the Hindu epic narratives of the *Mahabharata* or the *Ramayana* are *itihasa* (see earlier discussion). Malhotra (2013) writes: 'Hindus participating in rituals at temples do, for the most part, follow a received and codified tradition, and a minority might believe in the narratives they celebrate as literally having happened' (65). For Yogashram (2015), 'as a result of listening to these stories, people developed a desire to shape their own lives according to the dharmas that they portrayed. The religion followed by countless Hindus today is based on what is portrayed by Valkami and Vyasa' (81).

Given the multitude of Hindu responses to the epic narratives of Valkami and Vyasa, it is not surprising that the reception of mythology-inspired fiction is a complex one; in cases where the author moves considerably away from the 'original' Hindu epic (or inspiration) or where contemporary sensibilities are stretched (Chapters 3 and 4 present such examples in detail), then certain Indian readerships may well consider the narrative as simply fantasy. A fine line exists in this debate, not simply in terms of cultural reception but also in terms of genre classification in how these narratives are actually crafted. Therefore, for some Indian readers (shall we say), the references to the Hindu epic narratives will mean references to spiritual beliefs, denoting that such epics are believed to be accounts of real events (*itihasa*), thus manifestly *not* fantasy. The bleeding of personal belief into popular culture is an ever-present and ever-challenging situation, in Nanda's (2003) opinion:

> [F]or at least three decades now, modernists and secular intellectuals have been on the defensive. Rather than engage with the continuing hold of religious traditions on popular imagination, they have been forced to fend off accusations of 'mental colonialism' and elitism coming from post-modernists and Hindu nationalists alike. (7)

And so the reception of Bharati Fantasy within an Indian context (that is, domestic and diasporic) becomes increasingly complicated, not only because of the challenge to the idea of *itihasa* but also, I would like to suggest, because this wave of mythology-inspired fiction might even be categorised as historical fiction, a point I return to shortly. The narratives that I refer to as Bharati Fantasy are generally set in early Bharat, consistent with (aspects of) the Hindu epics such as the *Ramayana* and the *Mahabharata* as well as the teachings of the Vedas and the Upanishads – as I have discussed at length earlier. There are also narratives where the historical setting of the book blends ancient times with contemporary thought or times, weaving modern-day political and cultural references into the narrative, albeit manifestly into another, much older era. Nilanjan P. Choudhury's *Bali and the Ocean of Milk* (2011) is an example of this technique and two of Ashwin Sanghi's novels also implement this technique, namely *The Krishna Key* (2012) and his earlier novel *Chanakya's Chant* (2010). *Chanakya's Chant* (2010) blends the ancient world of 340 BC with the modern day, alternating chapter by chapter. These two eras of over two millennia apart are linked through the lives of the two protagonists, through politics and the struggle for a united country. Both *The Krishna Key* (2012) and *Chanakya's Chant* (2010) are discussed in some detail in Chapter 4 in this volume. Although the Bharati Fantasy novels are mythology-inspired to greater or lesser degrees, the approaches to this genre can be quite different, as Kumar (2013: online) states:

> Amish found a gap between the scholarly versions of the epics, the middlebrow (Devdutt Pattanaik) and the square (Ashok Banker), writing in cliffhangers, making up plot details, including battle scenes, a tender love story, and a hero who seems to have walked right out of American popular cultures.

In all, though, it is the invocation of the past, of ancient India in particular, which presents as a recurrent motif in Bharati Fantasy, alongside the geography, the territory of Bharat (sometimes revisited in contemporary times) and various Hindu deities, *devas* and *asuras*. Bharati Fantasy is fiercely consumed by young Indians who wish to connect with Indian philosophy and heritage, and, on this, Sandipan Deb writes that 'young Indians want to connect with traditional Indian thought; they are more religious and more proud to be Indian than the previous generation' (quoted in Kumar's 'The Pied Piper of Meluha', 2013). Tripathi's narratives in particular offer a way for young Indians to do this and, furthermore, the marketing of his novels appeals to this demographic, with YouTube trailers of the books, a website and, initially, the handing out of first chapters free at bookstores in the metros. But his novels have been criticised for being 'too Hindu-orientated', even pushing Hindutva (Hindu autonomy) ideals and notions of Indianness. So prominent are the narratives of Tripathi, Sanghi, Choudhury, Bhanver, Nath and others anchored in Indian culture that it is questionable whether such works could be culturally translated into other literary markets despite all of these narratives being written in English from the outset. Bharati Fantasy, by the very nature of its overarching narrative style and anchorage in the Hindu epics, connects more concretely with the general observation of commercial fiction's ability to 'make a claim of local rootedness, of national resurgence' according to S. Gupta (2012: 50), an observation Gupta makes based on how commercial fiction in English is 'different from, and even resistant to, the established Indian literary fiction'; a premise that underpins my own study in *Reading New India* (2013).

2.2.4 Defining the Genre

A text carries less meaning without its social and cultural content – at its very base, its human content or its relation to humanity – and this is particularly noteworthy in relation to Bharati Fantasy novels where the language medium is familiar yet the content can be less familiar to the non-Indian reader. As I have stated earlier, the term Bharati Fantasy has been coined to reflect the fantastical reception that this fiction may evoke in its reader whilst the term also anchors the fiction in its Indianness through the term Bharati, as this fiction is inspired by (ancient) India, its traditions, practices, beliefs and peoples.

In the Western academy, James and Mendlesohn (2014: 1) highlight that 'fantasy is about the construction of the impossible whereas science fiction may be about the unlikely, but is grounded in the scientifically possible', to which Adam Roberts (2010: 5) concurs, stating that 'the grounding of SF in the material rather than the supernatural becomes one of its key features'. Mendlesohn (2008) highlights how fantasy 'relies on a moral universe: it is less an argument with the universe than a sermon on the way things should be, a belief that the universe should yield to moral precepts' (5). The fantasy that constitutes Bharati Fantasy is what Mendlesohn refers to as 'immersive fantasy' according to her taxonomy of 'portal-quest', 'immersive', 'intrusion' and 'liminal' fantasies. For Mendlesohn, 'the immersive fantasy is a fantasy set in a world built so that it functions on all levels as a complete world' (59) and, moreover, that 'immersive fantasy' does not need the dividing line between real and non-real (as other types of fantasy do – such as portal-quest, intrusion and liminal). But the genre term fantasy alone is problematic given that for some readerships the texts from which Bharati Fantasy draws its inspiration (such as the *Mahabharata*, the *Ramayana*) represent real narratives, that is, historical narratives; *itihasa*. The matter of reception and readership is central here given that social and cultural dimensions of the Bharati Fantasy narratives dictate a certain genre classification. Bharati Fantasy for readers who are not culturally conversant with the Hindu epics can easily appear as fantastical literature, when for other readers the narratives are real accounts or so much part of their sociocultural fabric that it may be accepted as a kind of historical fiction.

According to Jerome de Groot, 'historical fiction is written by a variety of authors, within an evolving set of sub-genres, for a multiplicity of audiences' (2010: 2), and de Groot goes on to say, 'the figures we meet in historical fiction are identifiable to us on the one hand due to the conceit of the novel form, in that they speak the same language, and their concerns are often similar to ours, but their situation and their surroundings are immensely different' (2010: 3). This characterisation of historical fiction speaks generally to Bharati Fantasy and for our purposes here, it is particularly well demonstrated in the eight novels analysed within Chapters 3 and 4.

Bringing together the two genres of fantasy and historical fiction, Schanoes (2014) writes that this partnership is not the clashing of two radically different discourses, rather she suggests that:

> Writers of historical fiction and of fantasy must engage in world-building, in constructing and familiarizing their readers with a world foreign to their own and yet fully realized *as* a world complete unto itself with its own mores, customs and tensions. (236)

Schanoes questions the function of historical narrative when she asks: '... is it to reproduce a lost historical viewpoint so as to illuminate how "these people" understood their world, or is it to explicate how we, looking back, understand what took place?' (238). But Sleight (2014) suggests that 'in the case of the fantasy of history, it may be that the writer feels certain ideas about our past and culture can only be made apparent by going beyond the facts and physics of the world we know' (256) and this is a point which will be explored in Chapters 3 and 4 where Bharati Fantasy authors narrate stories grounded in shared historical knowledge, only to embellish the 'facts' with novel technological, digital or scientific inventions (see in particular Nath and Bhanver in Chapter 3 and Doyle in Chapter 4).

Although Sleight offers his thoughts on the fantasy of history, he writes further on the fantasies of history *and* religion (2014: 248–256), which is of particular interest to the discussion here. The examples Sleight cites are fictional works anchored in Western contexts, making reference to Christianity rather than dharmic traditions. Sleight suggests that 'fantasies of religion often approach their subject obliquely or through misdirection' (250), a technique I suggest is far removed from how Bharati Fantasy authors treat their subject. Very often the protagonist is anchored in the religious narrative of the book – in the sense that they are drawn from the Hindu epic or text from which the story is inspired – and thus Bharati Fantasy authors foreground the 'religious' aspect of the novel by this very technique. Sleight goes on to suggest that 'in the context of fantasies of religion, this often means that the deity's existence or power is guarded by a secret society of some kind' (252). Although Sleight is making reference to Western fantasies of religion, his statement is also true of some of the Bharati Fantasy novels, evident in some of the novels discussed in this volume. Indeed, what lies at the crux of this discussion is the debate around reception and the degree to which the unknown and the strange present themselves. The reception of Bharati Fantasy is varied; one end of the spectrum reveals a reader of little or no knowledge of Hinduism and epic texts (such as the *Mahabharata* and the *Ramayana*), for whom the characters and plot lines (shape-shifting, teratology, longevity of hundreds of years, as examples) are most clearly of the fantasy genre, whilst the other end of the spectrum reveals a reader who knows the Hindu epics and believes in them – in terms of their spirituality and/or their *itihasa* status – and who therefore reads this new body of fiction outside of the fantasy genre, possibly reading it as historical fiction, as a mythology-inspired thriller or otherwise. As Sen (2007) reminds us: '[T]here can [also] be vast differences in the social behaviour of different persons belonging to the same religion, even in fields often thought to be closely linked with religion' (62).

To further explicate these issues of reception, a Hindu readership within India (as an example) might accept what I term as Bharati Fantasy as historical fiction or as the domestic market articulates, as mythology-inspired fiction; however, in cases where the author moves considerably away from the 'original' Hindu epic (or inspiration) or where contemporary sensibilities stretch the 'original' through technology or science (as examples), then such a readership may well consider the narrative as fantasy. A fine line exists in this debate, not simply in terms of cultural reception but also in terms of genre classification in how these narratives are actually crafted. This volume offers some insight into the crafting of such novels and their genre through the author interviews which appear at the end of Chapters 3 and 4.

To read Bharati Fantasy as historical fiction requires a shared historical and sociocultural heritage (or at least knowledge) with the worlds presented in the text and without this shared knowledge base, the works of this body of new fiction present themselves more as fantasy narratives than those of historical fiction. To better articulate this idea, we might reverse the circumstances, suggesting that an Indian (say, Hindu) readership of British historical fiction might read such fiction as fantasy, on the basis that the historical and sociocultural heritage presented in the text is 'unfamiliar' (as an example we might choose Philippa Gregory's *The Virgin's Lover*, 2004, or Hilary Mantel's *Wolf Hall*, 2009). Yet this argument is less convincing. The reception of Indian historical fiction in the West, at least of Bharati Fantasy if we are to consider it as historical fiction, is inclined to be received as fantasy according to how this genre has been defined and characterised in the Western academy to date. Given that Hinduism or Hindu-orientated practices and dharmic traditions feature significantly in the genre of Bharati Fantasy, it is worth exploring how this feature dovetails with the existing defining characteristics of the genre of fantasy according to the Western academy (Mendlesohn, 2008) – in particular, the features which construct a sense of wonder through the strange and the imaginary and, significantly, what Mendlesohn (2008) asserts when she says: 'Fantasyland is constructed, in part, through the insistence on a received truth' (7). The characters of the type of Bharati Fantasy discussed here are often ones having the ability to fly or to shape-shift, they hold extraordinary powers of strength or ability and are sometimes hybrid animal-humans. It is these very elements of Indian historical fiction (as Bharati Fantasy) which means that its reception in the West predisposes it to the fantasy genre and why a reversal of the circumstances as outlined earlier does not result in Indian receptions of British historical fiction being of a similar experience. There is also an important argument in suggesting that the impact of colonisation and the canon of British literature in India lessen the 'unfamiliarity' of such texts (although there is not space to take this argument forward here; see Dawson Varughese, 2012, 2013).

There are, however, elements of Bharati Fantasy that do culturally translate. Sunaina Kumar (2013: online) writes of the plots of Tripathi's works as: 'a tender love story, and a hero who seems to have walked right out of American popular culture'. This combination of a strong Indian (Bharat)-heritage narrative and an English-language medium with characters and plot lines that echo popular American TV culture results in Bharati Fantasy narratives being able to travel outside of the 'for sale in India only' restriction, providing distribution allows. I suggest that in their travel, these narratives will be received notably differently from the manner in which these narratives are received and consumed within India. Most likely, the narratives will be received outside of India and South Asia as fantastical, where ideas of shape-shifting, hybrid animal-humans, numerous deities and *vimana*[8] are not part of the general sociocultural fabric. Despite such manifest differences in cultural reception, fantasy fiction has an innate ability to transcend social and cultural barriers by nature of its 'otherworldliness' and, thus, curiously, despite its cultural anchorage, Bharati Fantasy has the ability to travel outside of its often regional distribution restrictions to move into global markets – Europe, the United States and otherwise. What is particularly interesting to our discussion here is the fact that Bharati Fantasy bucks the trend of the established identity and production of Indian 'literary fiction' as discussed in Chapter 1 of this volume; in this sense Bharati Fantasy to date has not needed endorsement or consumption from anywhere other than India in order to secure the prominent position it holds today.

2.2.5 *The Indian Scientific Imagination*

Earlier in this chapter, some discussion took place about ideas of science through both myth and cultural (religious) histories' *itihasa*. It is useful however to explore how science as a term and discipline is conceived of within the Indian imagination. Harder (2001: 105) writes, 'In the Indian context, the word "science" (together with its Indo-Aryan neologism *vijñāna*) rings different than in the West: less well-defined and at the same time more loaded with polarising connotations'.

The relationship between ideas of Indianness and science was a particularly problematic one in the 1800s when scientific authority invaded religion and society. Through colonial forces, Orientalist learning was under attack, and as Prakash (1997: 538) writes: '[A]s new technologies of governance – geological and land surveys, census operations, mining, telegraphs, railways, medical and sanitary establishments – emerged, they became modes of articulating science's authority'. With this celebration and revival of scientific cultures, science 'became a metaphor for rationality, modernity and power' (Prakash, 1997: 538) and in doing so, ancient scientific Hindu philosophy was reshaped for the purpose of the modern nation. Science therefore no longer signified experiments in laboratories or systematic, observational enquiry into behaviour, rather, science signified religion, culture and a sense of Indianness; in short, science was quickly recognised and celebrated as a Hindu tradition built on the ancient bedrock of Hindu sacred texts. Such a connection of the old and the new is seen as being fraught with issues, according to Prakash. He warns of the dangers in conceiving of a modern nation through the traditions of the past when he writes: 'The representation of a modern nation as the return of the archaic, then, constitutes a profoundly disjunctive process – a process that entails the evocation *and* displacement of the mythic past, a linear history, and a homogeneous people' (541).

This custom of harnessing and re-evaluating older and surrounding traditions, Ramanujan (1989: 189) argues, is what India has long enacted and yet, this process at its extreme may produce what Nanda (2003: 1) refers to as: '… prophets who, even as they march forward, keep their faces turned backward toward an imagined past of Hindu glory'. This volume recognises that Bharati Fantasy treads difficult ground anew as science and Hindu belief find themselves closely entwined within the storylines of the novels. It can be argued that both writers and readers of Bharati Fantasy (unwittingly) connect with old and new notions of Hindu identities as they engage with the storylines of the novels. This is a particularly interesting concept when we think how this engagement is being achieved through the vehicle of 'popular' fiction. As Chapter 1 in this volume discusses, the consumption of mythology-inspired novels is mainly by a middle-class, English-speaking (-reading) audience who may or may not be Hindu. Stratton Hawley (2001: 224) writes how the identity of contemporary middle-class religion is illuminated by 'a terrain of interlocking religious themata', of which he cites: '… a reframing of inherited rituals and theologies of science, an effort to connect urban realities with a remembered hinterland …'. These 'interlocking religious themata' that Stratton Hawley describes are demonstrated in many of the Bharati Fantasy novels and, furthermore, some of the novels analysed in Chapter 3 in particular echo what Stratton Hawley describes as having an 'overarching mood of *bhakti*' (224).

Nehru's vision at the time of independence was greatly shaped by modern science and the opportunities it offered to tackle poverty, illiteracy and even superstition (see Nandi, 2011: 77, and also Nussbaum, 2015) and now, against the backdrop of the 21st century, scientific developments in medicine, stem cell research, deep space exploration and technological warfare all feature as part of Indian research activity.[9] Although India began its outer space engagement with the launch of its satellite Rohini in 1980

(Abdul Kalam and Rajan, 2010: 7), India's outer space activity has developed significantly since the millennium, with the Hanle observatory being established in 2001, hosting a 2-metre-class (80-inch) telescope (Ananthaswamy, 2010: 276), and not least because of India's Mars Orbiter mission of 2013, also known as 'Mangalyaan', one of the most prestigious developments for the country's scientific community. Not only is India the first Asian nation to launch a craft to orbit Mars, it is also the first nation in the world to successfully launch such an orbit mission on its first attempt. Interestingly, the launch of Mangalyaan took place on a Tuesday (Mangalvaar), the day of the week which is associated with Mars. This choice of day was complemented by a temple visit near to the Indian Space Research Organisation by Chairman K. Radhakrishnan before the launch, seeking blessings for the craft's journey. As Patairiya (2013: online) comments: 'We [Indians] know how to embrace two ideas at once – tradition and science, frugality and innovation – just as we can deal with issues like poverty at the same time as taking a giant leap into interplanetary space'. If anything, the launch of the Mars Orbiter not only demonstrated India's scientific achievements, it also demonstrated that its achievements are somewhat rooted in a Hindu tradition of scientific endeavour.

As the analyses in Chapters 3 and 4 demonstrate, many of the Bharati Fantasy narratives make a connection with scientific theories and revelations embedded within Hinduism which have been revealed through its sacred and *itihasa* texts and this confluence of science and numinosity is manifest in both Bharati Fantasy and the weird. Moreover, the question of reception – which is at the heart of this book – also connects ideas of science with Hinduism, as readers with little or no understanding of Hinduism interpret the events or the people they encounter in Bharati Fantasy novels through the genre lens of science fiction or fantasy.

One of the most fertile grounds for the connection of science and belief is the theory of creation and, by extension, cosmology (which interestingly also features in Afrofuturism – discussed in the conclusions presented in Chapter 5). Yogashram (2015) suggests that the *rishis* of early Hinduism received (in the divine sense) scientific knowledge about the creation of the universe. Yogashram suggests, knowing that the people of the Puranic age would find such scientific fact very hard to understand, the *rishis* set about weaving this 'received' scientific knowledge into stories in order to convey the various scientific ideas to the people. One such story concerns creation. Yogashram writes:

> The story goes that before the creation of human beings, Brahma the Creator made himself into two – the male was Manu and the female was Shatarupa. This story shows how the neutron (Brahma) was split into the proton (Manu) and the electron (Shatarupa). The bigger one was the proton and the smaller was the electron. The Upanishad goes on to say that these two particles interplayed and produced the whole universe. (98)

Here Yogashram explains the creation of the universe through Hindu belief – knowledge, Yogashram asserts, which came from the Vedic seers (2015: 99). Capra (2010), likening the creation and destruction of particles to the cosmic dance of Lord Shiva, comments that 'modern physics has thus revealed that every subatomic particle not only performs an energy dance, but also *is* an energy dance; a pulsating process of creation and destruction' (244, original emphasis). Capra concludes that 'for the modern physicists, then, Shiva's dance is the dance of subatomic matter' (245). Furthermore, Malinar (2014) also reminds us of the overarching theme of sacrificial process when she writes that 'cosmology entails the creation of a new, diversified, but complete whole by splitting up a former, already existing whole into parts' (65). Other 'sacrificial' creation narratives of the *Rig Veda* include how the 'cosmic man' was dismembered and out of which the different elements of the cosmos came into being; his eyes became the sun, his mind the moon etc.' (see Malinar, 2014: 65). The *Poetic Edda* discussed earlier in this chapter (see Section 2.1.1) shares a similar cosmological creation narrative with the *Rig Veda*; the *Poetic Edda* talks also of a dismembered body, that of 'Ymir':

> From Ymir's flesh the earth was made,
> and from his blood, the sea,
> mountains from his bones, trees from his hair,
> and from his skull, the sky.
> And from his eyelashes the cheerful gods
> made Midgard for men's sons;
> and from his brain the hard-tempered clouds
> were all created.
> (Larrington, 2014: 54, *trans.*)

Also, the *Poetic Edda* describes the beginning of time, remembered by the Seeress in 'The Seeress's Prophecy' as she recalls:

> Early in time Ymir made his settlement,
> there was no sand nor sea nor cool waves;
> earth was nowhere nor the sky above,
> a void of yawning chaos, grass was there nowhere.
> (Larrington, 2014: 4, *trans.*)

This Old Norse depiction of the beginning of time is not unlike what appears in the tenth book of the *Rig Veda*; a 'creation hymn', known as the *Nāsadīya*. This hymn explores the beginning of creation in highly esoteric terms, it starts with:

> There was neither non-existence nor existence then; there was neither the realm of space nor the sky which is beyond. What stirred? Where? In whose protection? Was there water, bottomlessly deep?
> (Doniger O'Flaherty, 1981: 25, trans.)

And closes with:

> Whence this creation has arisen – perhaps it formed itself, or perhaps it did not – the one who looks down on it, in the highest heaven, only he knows – or perhaps he does not know.
> (Doniger O'Flaherty, 1981: 25–26, trans.)

This description of the beginning of time is simultaneously deeply scientific, philosophical and poetic, in particular through the manner in which the events are described, yet elements of this hymn reveal ideas that are akin to those theories of creation 'discovered' through 21st-century deep space exploration and theoretical physics. On this connection of the ancient and the contemporary, the East and the West, Capra (2010) writes:

> Eastern thought and, more generally, mystical thought provide a consistent and relevant philosophical background to the theories of contemporary science; a conception of the world in which scientific discoveries can be in perfect harmony with spiritual aims and religious beliefs. (25)

In these ways, the poetic and the scientific converge, for Capra (2010) there is little tension between the two given how 'the Eastern image of the Divine is not that of a ruler who directs the world from above, but of a principle that controls everything from within' (24). By extension, the Indian scientific imagination is caught up with ideas of change and transformation as integral elements of human life. This idea is seen as part of cosmic law and, thus, from life cycles and reincarnation to everyday events and objects, life is lived in flux; in the sense of Radhakrishna's words: '[L]ife is no thing or state of a thing, but a continuous movement or change' (1958: 369). It is through this same lens that 'history' is viewed meaning less a linear set of developments but rather a cyclical or ever-evolving aspect of human (sentient) experience. Cromwell Crawford (2003) reminds us of how integral the idea of non-linearity of human existence is in the Hindu world view when he describes the separation of self in the cycles of being reborn. He says: '[T]he great seers viewed this "coming" and "going" in a neverending sea of change as suffering, because it involved repeated separation of the self from the Self' (55). Thus, across all sciences – from medical science and ethics to physics and chemistry – the ideas of transformation and dynamism prevail, making for a particular relationship between science, rationality and the human experience. Das (2007) comments on how India has held steadfastly to its ancient traditions when he says: 'The Raj gave us modern values and institutions, but it did not interfere with our ancient traditions and our religion. India has therefore preserved its spiritual heritage and the old way of life continues' (15). This is clearly a subjective statement but it is possible to think of Das's claim as being manifest in the Bharati Fantasy novels' storylines given that they might be understood as venerating and upholding belief in 'ancient traditions'.

As some of the novels discussed in Chapters 3 and 4 demonstrate, the Indian scientific imagination is captured in both the ancient and the contemporary through ideas of creationism, nuclear power, airborne vehicles, chemistry, weaponry and technology as examples. The movement between ancient ideas of science and technology and contemporary ideas of the same is both fluid and complementary in these novels, depicting a shared and hegemonic understanding of science 'in' and 'of' Hinduism. On this complementary relationship, Capra (2010) writes: '[B]oth the modern physicist and the Eastern mystic have realized that all phenomena in this world of change and transformation are dynamically interrelated' (278). Not unlike ideas of science, *itihasa* (as discussed earlier in this chapter) lives on in contemporary times through the Vedas, the epic narratives of the *Mahabharata* and the *Ramayana*, as well as the Puranas. Embedded within these texts of 'history', science is found, anchored in the texts' ancient roots whilst (supposedly) simultaneously speaking to contemporary scientific advancements of the 21st-century age.

As part of this discussion, we should acknowledge that India's contemporary approach to science has been shaped by a particular Hindu movement, that of *advaita Vedanta*. This movement is most commonly linked to theologians Shankara and Ramanuja, the latter living during a time when Shankara's school of Vedanta was dominant. *Advaita* draws heavily on the Upanishads, the final iteration of the Vedas, where detachment and quest for liberation dominate the subject matter. Highly philosophical, the Upanishads offered fertile ground for *advaita* which refuted the ritualistic traditions that had preceded it and instead focussed on questions of Brahman and 'self'. Frazier and Flood (2014) write of Shankara: 'renowned for his defence of the extreme advaitic perspective that has been hugely influential on subsequent theological reflection and which, for centuries, was seen by the West as the main belief of Hinduism as a whole' (280). In addition to the Upanishads, the principal texts for *advaita* are the *Brahmasutra* and *The Bhagavad Gita* and, thus, in combination, bring together both *sruti* and *smruti* texts. This bringing together of *sruti* and *smruti* texts is interesting when we consider how an understanding of *itihasa* is formed and what can be regarded as being non-*itihasa* (see discussion earlier in this chapter). Desai (2014), in his enquiry into the authorship of *The Bhagavad Gita*, comments that 'even though it may be "personal, historic and original", it is because of this unique characteristic of having divine authorship that the *Gita* has become the best known and the most commented upon text over the centuries' (4). Its divine authorship and its non-*sruti* status, together with its compactness (thus, more easily translatable) made for an accessible introduction to Hinduism and, consequently, 'the reception of the Gita was part of the process whereby Indians recovered pride in their ancient culture' (Desai, 2014: 12).

The core concept of *advaita* Vendanta is as the Sanskrit states – 'non-duality' and, so, the concept of *advaita* Vedanta can be expressed as follows:

> [T]here is only one undifferentiated *Brahman*, and therefore cannot be any duality between the self (i.e. the human subject) and *Brahman*,

because *Brahman* truly is our self. Our aim in life must therefore be to realize that the self (*ātman*) is *Brahman*.

(Gosling, 2007: 38)

Given the spread and influence of *advaita* on contemporary Hindu identity, it is important to realise the connection that *advaita* naturally makes with science given that the non-dualistic approach to understanding self is inextricably linked to the cosmos (see preceding quote from Gosling). The Hindu Indian scientific imagination has therefore been shaped by this connection between the human, earthly existence and its inherent connection with the otherworldly and the numinous, namely Brahman. It is understood here that although *advaita* has been a dominant and far-reaching school of thought and practice within Hinduism, not all Hindus subscribe to this view. However, it is important to realise that *advaita* has generally been seen by the West to be 'Hinduism' per se and that much of *advaita*'s focus on the self has been adopted by the West, resulting in a plethora of meditation and yogic practices (as examples) to connect with the 'inner self' (in a bid to ultimately connect with a higher Self). Such is the difference between 'typical' Western ideas of self (and the self with/out 'soul') and Hindu ideas of 'self' (*atman*) as Brahman that the connection with the cosmos is significantly different in each philosophy. The Hindu worldview unites more readily with the cosmos in terms of its connection with humankind through the Supreme Being – Brahman – who is 'the life force that was covered with emptiness, that one arose through the power of heat' (Doniger O'Flaherty, 1981: 25, trans.), whereas Western ideas (again, this is to be read as 'typically' Western views) do not connect human existence so *intimately* with a Supreme Being. If the self is Brahman, then we are 'part' of that Ultimate Reality which in the beginning was 'the cosmic man 'whose eyes became the sun etc.' (see Malinar, 2014: 65). It is this connection between science, belief and *itihasa* – both scriptural and personal in its execution – that I explore in the analyses of the novels and through the author interviews in the next two chapters.

As this chapter section (Section 2.2) has discussed, the reception of Bharati Fantasy texts is complex given how the texts are anchored in ideas of *itihasa*, belief and culture, all of which are anchored in Indian and chiefly Hindu worldviews. The analyses of the novels in Chapters 3 and 4 seek to explore the reception of these novels against this background of difference whilst attempting to connect the albeit differing receptions through the genre term of Bharati Fantasy and, moreover, connecting the receptions with the overall genre term of the weird.

As we turn to analyse Bharati Fantasy narratives over the next two chapters, it is important to remember the backdrop of New India, framing the production of these stories. Juluri (2015: 119) writes of mythology-inspired novels, saying: 'They mark the beginning of a new journey in the modern Hindu imagination. They are rooted in the present, in the experiences of a new generation responding in the form of creativity and entertainment to very real, global, national, postcolonial concerns'.

Some of the authors of Bharati Fantasy novels are graduates of Institutes of Technology and Management (IITs, IIMs), others are variously trained in the sciences, commerce and finance, yet all are writing mythology-inspired fiction through which ideas of New India are explored. As a generation of Indians re-vision the now by drawing on previous Indias, Hindu belief and the Indian scientific imagination, narratives of belonging, in particular, emerge. For a Western readership, it is questionable if such narratives of identity and belonging are communicated through the novels' pages or whether these Bharati Fantasy stories simply represent other worlds, people and ideas. The analyses that follow in Chapters 3 and 4 aim to address such questions.

Notes

1. In this Routledge *Companion* 'the Weird' is considered as a sub-genre of science fiction.
2. That is not to suggest that Indian science fiction in English does not exist, see discussion of this body of fiction: Banerjee (2011), A. Gupta (2013) and Hoagland and Sarwal (2010) as examples and the various works of Anil Menon (www.anilmenon.com).
3. Personal communication with a Sanskrit scholar (January 2016).
4. Brahman is not to be conflated with Brahma, who is one of the *trimurti*: Brahma, Vishnu and Shiva.
5. I wish to stress here that this volume does not assert that all Hindus believe that *itihasa* represents that which historically, truthfully happened; it is a personal choice to believe the extent to which an *itihasa* text represents historical events. Rather, this volume respectfully appreciates that belief in *itihasa* (and its manifestation through the epics) as a representation of true, historical events is a notion that Hindus (and non-Hindus) believe in variously and to differing degrees.
6. From http://www.jofletcherbooks.com/, accessed September 2015.
7. Amazon.co.uk, October 2015.
8. Harder (2001: 106) writes that it is following the 'Arya Samaj tradition that for instance *vimānas* came to be identified with airplanes'.
9. See Saini's *Geek Nation* (2011).

References

Abdul Kalam, A. P. J. and Rajan, Y. S. (2010) *The Scientific Indian: A Twenty-First Century Guide to the World around Us*, New Delhi: Penguin Books India.
Ananthaswamy, A. (2010) *The Edge of Reason: Dispatches from the Frontiers of Cosmology*, New Delhi: Penguin Books India.
Arni, S. (2013) *The Missing Queen*, New Delhi: Zubaan.
Ashley, A. (ed.) (2008) *Subtle Edens*, Norwich, UK: Elastic Press.
Banerjee, S. (2011) 'Dystopia and the postcolonial nation', in Raja, M. A., Ellis, J. W. and Nandi, S. (eds.) *The Postnational Fantasy: Essays on Postcolonialism, Cosmopolitics and Science Fiction*, Jefferson, NC: McFarland & Co.
Capra, F. (2010) *The Tao of Physics: An Exploration of the Parallels between Modern Physics and Eastern Mysticism*, Boston: Shambala Publications.

Chaudhuri, A. (2001) *The Picador Book of Modern Indian Literature*, London: Picador.
Clute, J. and Grant, J. (1999) *The Encyclopedia of Fantasy*, London: Orbit.
Cromwell Crawford, S. (2003) *Hindu Bioethics for the Twenty-First Century*, New York: State University of New York.
Csicsery-Ronay Jr., I. (2012) 'What do we mean when we say "Global Science Fiction"? Reflections on a New Nexus', *Science Fiction Studies*, vol. 39, no. 3, pp. 478–493.
Das, G. (2007) *India Unbound: From Independence to the Global Information Age*, New Delhi: Penguin India.
Dawson Varughese, E. (2012) *Beyond the Postcolonial: World Englishes Literature*, Basingstoke: Palgrave.
Dawson Varughese, E. (2013) *Reading New India: Post-Millennial Indian Fiction in English*, London: Bloomsbury.
Dawson Varughese, E. (2016) 'Genre fiction of New India: Post-millennial configurations of Crick Lit, Chick Lit and crime writing', in Tickell, A. (ed.) *South Asian Fiction in English: Contemporary Transformations*, Basingstoke: Palgrave.
Dawson Varughese, E. (Forthcoming) 'Consuming post-millennial Indian Chick Lit: Visual representations of Chauhan's females', in Houlden, K. and Atia, N. (eds.) *Popular Postcolonialisms: Popular Cultural Forms and the Postcolonial Paradigm*, London: Routledge.
De Groot, J. (2010) *The Historical Novel London*, New York: Routledge.
Desai, M. (2014) *Who Wrote the Bhagavadgita?: A Secular Enquiry into a Sacred Text*, Noida: HarperCollins Publishers.
Doniger O'Flaherty, W. (trans.) (1981) *The Rig Veda*, London: Penguin Books.
Doyle, C. C. (2013) *The Mahabharata Secret*, Noida: Om Books International.
Frazier, J. and Flood, G. (eds.) (2014) *The Bloomsbury Companion to Hindu Studies*, London: Bloomsbury.
Frelik, P. (2009) 'Slipstream 100' http://www.sfra.org/sf101slipstream [accessed October 2015].
Glover, D. and McCracken, S. (eds.) (2015) *The Cambridge Companion to Popular Fiction*, Cambridge: Cambridge University Press.
Gosling, D. L. (2007) *Science and the Indian Tradition: When Einstein Met Tagore*, London: Routledge.
Gupta, A. (2013) 'Childhood's end: science fiction in India', in Sen, K. and Roy, R. (eds.) *Writing Indian Anew: Indian English Fiction 2000–2013*, Amsterdam: Amsterdam University Press.
Gupta, S. (2012) 'Indian "commercial" fiction in English, the publishing industry, and youth culture.' *Economic and Political Weekly*, vol. 46, no. 5, pp. 46–53.
Harder, H. (2001) 'Indian and international: some examples of Marathi science fiction writing', *South Asia Research*, SAGE, vol. 21, no. 105, pp. 105–119.
Hoagland, E and Sarwal, R. (eds.) (2010) *Science Fiction, Imperialism and the Third World: essays on postcolonial literature and film* Jefferson, North Carolina and London: McFarland & Company Inc,. Publishers.
James, E. and Mendlesohn, F. (eds.) (2014) *The Cambridge Companion to Fantasy Literature*, Cambridge: Cambridge University Press.
Joshi, S. T. (2004) *The Evolution of the Weird Tale*, New York: Hippocampus Press.
Juluri, V. (2015) *Rearming Hinduism: Nature, Hinduphobia, and the Return of Indian Intelligence*, Chennai: Westland Ltd.
Kelly, M. (2015) 'Foreword', in Kelly, M. and Koja, K. (eds.) *Year's Best Weird Fiction: Volume Two*, Canada: Undertow Publications.

Kincaid, P. (2014) 'American Fantasy 1820–1950', in James, E. and Mendlesohn, F. (eds.) *The Cambridge Companion to Fantasy Literature*, Cambridge: Cambridge University Press.

Kneale, J. (2006) 'From Beyond: H. P. Lovecraft and the place of horror', *Cultural Geographies*, SAGE, vol. 13, no. 1, pp. 106–126.

Koja, K. (2015) 'A home with the Weird', in Kelly, M. and Koja, K. (eds.) *Year's Best Weird Fiction: Volume Two*, Canada: Undertow Publications.

Kumar, S. (2013) "The Pied Piper of Meluha", *Tehelka*, February, issue 10, vol. 10. Web. Accessed 05 April 2013.

Larrington, C. (trans.) (2014) *The Poetic Edda*, Oxford: Oxford University Press.

Lochrie, K. (1986) 'Wyrd and the limits of human understanding: a thematic sequence in the "Exeter Book"' *The Journal of English and Germanic Philology* Vol. 85, No. 3 (July) pp. 323–331.

Lovecraft, H. P. (1973) *Supernatural Horror in Literature*, New York: Dover Publications Inc.

Lovecraft, H. P. (2009) 'Notes on writing weird fiction' http://www.hplovecraft.com/writings/texts/essays/nwwf.aspx [accessed October 2015].

Malhotra, R. (2013) *Being Different: An Indian Challenge to Western Universalism*, Noida: HarperCollins Publishers India.

Malinar, A. (2014) 'Hindu cosmologies', in Frazier, J. and Flood, G. (eds.) *The Bloomsbury Companion to Hindu Studies*, London: Bloomsbury.

McNish, I. (2004) 'Wyrd, causality and providence, a speculative essay', *Mankind Quarterly*, vol. 44, issue 3/4, spring, pp. 329–336.

Mendlesohn, F. (2008) *Rhetorics of Fantasy*, Connecticut: Wesleyan University Press.

Miéville, C. (2009) 'Weird Fiction', in Bould, M., Butler, A. M., Roberts, A. and Vint, S. (eds.) *The Routledge Companion to Science Fiction*, New York, London: Routledge.

Nanda, M. (2003) *Prophets Facing Backward: Postmodern Critiques of Science and Hindu Nationalism in India*, New Brunswick, NJ: Rutgers University Press.

Nandi, S. (2011) 'The "Popular" science: Bollywood's take on science fiction and the discourse of nations' in Raja, M. A., Ellis, J. W. and Nandi, S. (eds.) *The Postnational Fantasy: Essays on Postcolonialism, Cosmopolitics and Science Fiction*, Jefferson, NC: McFarland & Company.

Nussbaum, M. C. (2015) 'Nehru, Religion, and the Humanities', in Doniger, W. and Nussbaum, M. C. (eds.) *Pluralism and Democracy in India: Debating the Hindu Right*, Oxford: Oxford University Press.

Patairiya, M. K. (2013) 'Why India is going to Mars' http://www.nytimes.com/2013/11/23/opinion/india-must-go-to-mars.html?_r=0 [accessed October 2015].

Prakash, G. (1997) 'The modern nation's return in the archaic' *Critical Enquiry*, vol. 23, no. 3, spring, pp. 536–556.

Purohit, S. (2010) 'Why Indian pulp fiction is not as popular' *DNA*, March 21.

Radhakrishnan, S. (1958) *Indian Philosophy*, New York: Macmillan.

Ramanujan, A. K. (1989) 'Where mirrors are windows: toward to an anthology of reflections' *History of Religions*, vol. 28, no. 3, February, pp. 187–216.

Roberts, A. (2010) *Science Fiction*, London: Routledge.

Saini, A. (2011) *Geek Nation: How Indian Science Is Taking over the World*, London: Hodder & Stoughton Ltd.

Sanghi, A. (2012) *The Krishna Key*, Chennai: Westland.

Sattar, A. (2011) *Lost Loves: Exploring Rama's Anguish*, New Delhi: Penguin India.

Schanoes, V. (2014) 'Historical fantasy', in James, E. and Mendlesohn, F. (eds.) *The Cambridge Companion to Fantasy Literature*, Cambridge: Cambridge University Press.
Sen, A. (2007) *Identity and Violence: The Illusion of Destiny*, London: Penguin Books Ltd.
Sleight, G. (2014) 'Fantasies of history and religion', in James, E. and Mendlesohn, F. (eds.) *The Cambridge Companion to Fantasy Literature*, Cambridge: Cambridge University Press.
Smith, D. (2003) *Hinduism and Modernity*, Oxford: Blackwell.
Stratton Hawley, J. (2001) 'Modern India and the question of middle-class religion', *International Journal of Hindu Studies*, vol. 5, no. 3, December, pp. 217–225.
Thapar, R. (2014a) *The Past Before Us: Historical Traditions of Early North India*, Ranikhet: Permanent Black.
Thapar, R. (2014b) *The Past As Present: Forging Contemporary Identities through History*, New Delhi: Aleph Book Company.
Tripathi, R. (2014) 'Aesthetics of the *Mahābhārata*: traditional interpretations', in Chakrabarti, A. and Bandyopadhyay, S. (eds.) *Mahābhārata Now: Narration, Aesthetics, Ethics*, New Delhi: Routledge.
Yogashram, V. G. (2015) *The Science of the Rishis: The Spiritual and Material Discoveries of the Ancient Sages of India*, Rochester: Inner Traditions.
Vandermeer, J. (2008) 'Introduction: The New Weird "It's alive?"', in Vandermeer, J. and Vandermeer, A. (eds.) *The New Weird*, San Francisco: Tachyon Publications.
Weil, S. (1989) 'Grace under pressure: 'Hand-words', 'Wyrd' and free will in 'Beowulf', *Pacific Coast Philology*, vol. 224, no. 1/2, November, pp. 94–104.

3 Bharati Fantasy
Eternal *Bhāva*

This chapter examines Bharati Fantasy texts which engage in a celebration of ancient India, its folkloric traditions and legends. Unlike the Bharati Fantasy novels discussed in Chapter 4, where contemporary sensibilities significantly shape the storyline, the novels discussed in this chapter are anchored in ancient Bharat or, in the case of Arni's novel *The Missing Queen* (2013), in an undisclosed era through which Sita of the *Ramayana* is celebrated by way of a reimagining of her separation from Lord Ram.

This chapter begins by looking at Amish Tripathi's first novel in his 'Shiva Trilogy', *The Immortals of Meluha* (2010) and its connection to Bharat and celebration of the life of Lord Shiva. In his focus on Lord Shiva, Amish Tripathi engages with the 'eternal' storytelling of the *Mahadev* and the compassionate, reverential manner in which Amish depicts Shiva's early life as a tribal warrior creates a particular *bhāva* (mood) that some Bharati Fantasy authors adopt. Shatrujeet Nath's novel *The Guardians of the Halahala* (2015) pits three groups of people against one another: the humans, the *devas* and the *asuras*. Nath's novel is Book 1 of the 'Vikramaditya Trilogy', the Prologue tells of the fifth night of the Churning of the Ocean, how the elixir of life is released, only to be followed by the release of the *halahala* (a poisonous substance which threatens all life). In anchoring the story in the epic tale of the Churning of the Ocean, Nath narrates the eternal cosmic balance of good and bad, subjectivity and objectivity, themes that are also explored in Amish Tripathi's *The Immortals of Meluha* (2010). Out of the eight novels explored in Chapters 3 and 4, it is Nath's *The Guardians of the Halahala* (2015) which manifests as the most 'weird' according to Miéville's definition and Vandermeer's work (see Chapter 2, Section 2.1). Jagmohan Bhanver's novel *The Curse of Brahma* (2015) is also considerably 'weird'. The novel tells of the era before the birth of Sri Krishna, how Kansa's mind is infiltrated by the Dark Lord, Lord Brahma's former star pupil, and how the Dark Lord is banished to *Paatal Lok* by Lord Brahma himself in a fit of rage. The presence of the Dark Lord is both menacing and weird, as is the world of *Paatal Lok* and its inhabitants. The fourth novel to be examined in this chapter is Samhita Arni's *The Missing Queen* (2013). Despite the narrative's near-future setting, and consequently its speculative style, the story remains 'true' to the *Ramayana* in terms of its characters' names, places and journeys. Arni's novel, unlike Saket's *Urmila* (2016) discussed in Chapter 4, does not stray far from Valmiki's epic and thus sustains a certain connection with the 'eternal' storyline of the *Ramayana* whilst also with the tradition of 'many *Ramayanas*'. Arni's novel is discussed at the end of this chapter as it functions as something of a bridge from Chapter 3 into Chapter 4, where the focus turns to modern-day sensibilities in Bharati Fantasy novels.

3.1 Amish Tripathi: 'Shiva Trilogy Book 1': *The Immortals of Meluha* (2010)

As Chapters 1 and 2 in this volume have already indicated, Amish Tripathi was, alongside Ashwin Sanghi, one of the early novelists to break the genre fiction market with what has come to be known popularly as 'mythology-inspired' fiction. His first three novels constitute 'The Shiva Trilogy' (*The Immortals of Meluha*, 2010, *The Secret of the Nagas*, 2011, *The Oath of the Vayuputras*, 2013) and he has followed this collection with the 'Ram Chandra Series'. Book 1 of the Ram Chandra Series was published in 2015. The phenomenal sales figures that Amish's novels have attracted point towards an appetite for genre fiction with a moral edge; as Mishra says, '[T]he Shiva Trilogy becomes living inspirational scripture capable of providing spiritual direction in the modern world' (2013: 20), a point we will return to discuss later in this chapter. Ashwin Sanghi (*The Rozabal Line* in 2008 and *Chanakya's Chant* in 2010), publishing around the same time as the first book of the Shiva Trilogy came out, also drew on early Indian history and legend for his novels but unlike Amish, whose novels have focused on the lives of Hindu deities, Sanghi's novels have engaged with various aspects of Indian history and have been thrillers as well as mythology-inspired fiction (see Chapter 4, Section 4.1 and 4.5 for discussion of Sanghi's works).

Amish Tripathi's *The Immortals of Meluha* (2010) focusses on the life of Lord Shiva as he transitions from lead tribal warrior of the Gunas to become the Neelkanth ('the one with the blue throat'), thus a transition from human to the divine, becoming Lord Shiva. It is 1900 BC, at Mansarovar Lake at the foot of Mount Kailash (Tripathi, 2010: 1) and as Shiva fights to keep his tribe safe from the Pakratis, he considers the offer of moving over the mountains to Meluha, at the invitation of Nandi, the Meluhan. Shiva is sceptical and wonders why the Meluhans would offer to take him and all his tribe into their country, providing them with land and accommodation. But as the Pakratis kill Guna women and children as they complete their chores at the lakeside, Shiva decides that anywhere must be better than living in constant threat from the Pakratis. With this start to the novel, we are introduced to the protagonist, his position in society and the responsibility he has for the Guna tribe. Shiva is 21 years old at this point in the novel and already battle-worn as 'the numerous battle-scars on his skin gleamed in the shimmering reflected light of the waters' (1). To readers unfamiliar with Hinduism, Shiva may present as a warrior, fighting to save his people. The topographical context of the story for such readers may simply translate as a mountainous region where different tribes live, the mountain ranges dividing up the land, each tribe benefitting from that particular area's natural environment. This sort of description of the landscape and the various inhabitants of the regions makes easy connections to non-Indian Fantasy series such as Tolkien's 'The Lord of The Rings' or Brandon Sanderson's 'The Stormlight Archive' where regions, peoples and different 'races' clash, and where battles ensue as both parties pursue a coveted prize.

This landscape, however, has significant historic and religious meaning. For Shiva, it takes great courage to leave his homeland at the foothills of Mount Kailash for Meluha but as Shiva and his tribe cross the border into Meluha, they enter what Tripathi tells his readers is Kashmir:

> The melodious singing of the birds calmed the exhausted ears of Shiva's tribe, accustomed only to rude howling of icy mountain winds. 'If this is the border province, how perfect must the rest of the country be?' whispered Shiva in awe. (10)

This description of Meluha appears early in the novel and thus sets up the narrative of a utopian land. Inhabited by the Meluhans, otherwise known as the *Suryavanshis*, Meluha is posited as a society which always abides by its laws, meaning that all that takes place in Meluha is morally and ethically inclined. The cities in Meluha are carefully planned, drains run throughout and the buildings are well constructed, uncluttered and maintained. Royalty, although respected by Meluha's citizens, do not live ostentatiously, rather 'it seemed that special architecture was reserved only for structures built for the Gods or ones that were for the common good' (64). Above the city gates, a symbol is etched into the stone. It is the symbol of the *Suryavanshis* and is 'a bright red circular sun with its rays blazing out in all directions' (60). The sun motif (*surya* means 'sun') opposes the *Suryavanshis*' enemy, the *Chandravanshis*, whose symbol is the 'moon' (*chand* meaning 'moon'). In order to foreground how the Meluhans strive for high, societal ideals, the motto inscribed below the symbol of the blazing sun reads: '"*Satya. Dharma. Maan*": Truth. Duty. Honour' (60, original emphasis). As this chapter section discusses shortly, the two tribes are at war and are portrayed as opposites in lifestyle, beliefs and culture, although as Shiva comes to learn, difference does not necessarily have to result in hate for one another's way of life.

Given Shiva's transition from human tribesman to the divine Neelkanth, there are moments in the novel where Shiva is described as superhuman or for readers not familiar with Hinduism, as a man who has some kind of magical powers. We read of Shiva's extraordinary ability to dance and his practice of holding the *natraj* pose before he performs. The onlookers – Princess Sati, her maid and Sati's dance teacher Guruji – are in awe of his performance:

> Shiva was in his own world. He did not dance for the audience. He did not dance for appreciation. He did not dance for the music. He danced only for himself. Rather, it almost seemed like his dance was guided by a celestial force. (75)

Shiva's meditative posture which preceded his dance (the *natraj*) connects him with Mother Earth and all her energies. Shiva says that the *natraj* pose – standing on the right leg, slightly bent, the left leg held 'between the bearing of his right foot and his face' (74), his arms held gracefully as if holding a small drum (*dumru*) and the other palm uppermost – is the pose he must adopt in order to ask respectfully for the energy to dance to come to him. Shiva does not think that his dance skills are anything special whilst the onlookers are in awe of his lithe movements, especially given his warrior stature and muscular frame. For some readers, this ability to move so nimbly may be explained by Shiva's magical powers, whilst for readers familiar with Hinduism, Lord Shiva is known for his representation of both the male and the female. In this sense the *natraj* expresses the duality of Lord Shiva. Moreover, Lord Shiva's duality expresses the duality of the universe; the eternal struggle which keeps the universe in balance, a theme that runs through *The Immortals of Meluha*.

The manner in which Tripathi narrates the story of Lord Shiva highlights how, for Shiva, much of what we discover as readers, we are discovering *with* him. His awareness of being a god when for the past 21 years Shiva has been as human as his Guna tribesmen, is both slow and challenging. It is the physical changes that Shiva goes through which help him understand that he is actually a divine being and this realisation begins on arrival at Meluha, when the Gunas are given a special drink to consume. Expectedly, on the part of the Meluhans, all of Shiva's tribe become ill; the Meluhans monitor the Gunas, caring for them until they recover. Shiva's reaction to the special drink is different from his fellow kinsmen and women. His body starts to regenerate and his long-standing battle wounds begin to heal:

> His frostbitten right toe felt as if it was on fire. His battle scarred left knee seemed to be getting stretched. His tired and aching muscles felt as if a great hand was remoulding them. His shoulder bone, dislocated in days past and never completely healed, appeared to be ripping the muscles aside so as to re-engineer the joint. (17)

The 'magical' drink Shiva is given not only heals his injuries, it brings out something that had previously been invisible: his blue throat. Complaining of a cold neck, Shiva speaks to Doctor Ayurvati to see what might be done. The doctor is awestruck and, stunned, she asks herself 'why had she not noticed it before? She had never believed in the legend. Was she going to be the first one to see it come true?' (22). The doctor's thoughts foreground the unbelievable, suggesting that Shiva's blue throat is something fantastical. However, as her eyes see the change from human to divine through the transformation of Shiva's throat into an iridescent blue, Doctor Ayurvati suddenly believes that which has circulated as legend. Through the presentation of this short scene, questions of truth versus legend are raised and Tripathi uses the character of Doctor Ayurvati to demonstrate how one's beliefs and faith might be put to the test.

The novel is interspersed with what appear to be instances of Lord Shiva in a dream-like state. Tripathi reveals that Shiva is haunted by a childhood memory and that when he smokes his *chillum*, he forgets. His scientist friend Brahaspati warns Shiva of the harmful effects of a marijuana habit, saying 'And worst of all, it even harms your memory, causing untold damage to your ability to draw on past knowledge' (164). Shiva considers his friend's words and replies: '"That is exactly why it is good, my friend. No idiot who smokes this is scared of forgetting". Shiva lit up his *chillum*, took a deep drag and continued, "They are scared of *not* forgetting"' (164). In this scene, Shiva reveals the human side of his character, lamenting his past and the childhood memory that has come to haunt him. He remembers as a young boy witnessing the sexual assault of a woman by what appeared to be a monster in the forest near his home. Shiva is consumed by guilt as he did not act on the injustice he saw, rather he ran away from the scene in fear.

Shiva comes into contact with Hindu priests (*pandits*) at several points in the novel. It is unclear if these meetings are due to Shiva's *chillum* habit and the dream-like state he enters or whether these meetings are 'real'. Each time, the *pandit* knows Shiva's innermost feelings and the first time he meets a *pandit*, at the Lord Brahma temple in Meluha, the *pandit* questions Shiva's belief in the gods that are represented as idols – in this case, Lord Brahma. Shiva, taken aback by the *pandit*'s insight, admits that he believes that the real gods are all around us, in the natural world (45). This questioning nature of Lord Shiva is elucidated by Kishwar (2001), who writes that 'Pauranic descriptions of Shiv show him as the least domesticated and the most rebellious of all the gods, one whose appearance and adventures border on the weird' (305). Indeed, it is this very facet of Shiva's character that Amish explores, foregrounding how 'different' Shiva is both as a foreigner in Meluha and as the Neelkanth amongst humans. Throughout the novel, the reader wonders if these mysterious men (*pandits*) really do appear to Shiva or whether he simply imagines them, and if they are 'real', what is their interest in his life? Near the end of the novel, Tripathi reveals that the *pandits* are Vasudevs. As each avatar of Lord Vishnu leaves, a tribe, the Vasudevs, are left in his place and are entrusted with the task of helping the next *Mahadev* as and when he appears. The question of how 'real' these men are remains, despite the explanation of their provenance and their mission. As is common in Bharati Fantasy novels, reality and otherworldliness collide as the reader adjusts to different levels of truth and possibility.

In *The Immortals of Meluha*, it is the 'magical' drink that Lord Shiva and his Guna tribe consume that brings together the divine and the scientific. Referred to as '*Somras* the *drink of the gods*' (79, original emphasis), the reader is informed that this potion, when taken at the defined times, 'not only postpones [our] death considerably, but it also allows us to live our entire lives as if we were in the prime of our youth – mentally and physically' (79). Its invention is attributed to 'the greatest Indian scientist that ever lived' (79), who Tripathi reveals to be 'Lord Brahma' (79). Known as the Creator (see Chapter 2, this volume), Brahma is one of the *trimurti* of Hinduism, the other two being Lord Vishnu (the Protector) and, interestingly (for our discussion here), Lord Shiva (the Destroyer). Shiva quickly forms a close bond with Meluha's chief scientist Brahaspati, and looks for an opportunity to quiz him over how the *Somras* works; specifically, Shiva wants to understand how his blue throat has appeared after consuming the liquid. Furthermore, and more pressingly, Shiva wants to know Brahaspati's own opinion on the coming of the Neelkanth. Shiva hesitates asking Brahaspati in front of the other Meluhans because 'their faith is overwhelming' (134), so it is only in the company of the scientist that Shiva finally asks his question:

> 'I believe in science. It provides a solution and a rationale for everything. And if there is anything that appears like a miracle, the only explanation is that a scientific reason has not been discovered as yet.'
> 'Then why do the people of Meluha not look to science for solving their problems?'
> 'I am not sure,' said Brahaspati thoughtfully. 'Perhaps it is because science is a capable but cold-hearted master. Unlike a Neelkanth, it will not solve your problems for you. It will only provide you the tools that you may need to fight your own battles.' (136)

It is here in this scene that Shiva and Brahaspati unpick how science and belief may come to coexist. Shiva's questioning nature sits uncomfortably in the Meluhan culture where law and order are maintained through unwavering adherence to ritual and faith. Shiva seems to inhabit the interstitial spaces between belief and the rational, and Brahaspati is therefore a welcome friend. Curiously, though, when Shiva discovers how the *Somras* is manufactured, belief and science merge again in a very particular concoction. The chief scientist eloquently explains how the *Somras* works on the body *scientifically* but what he is unable to explain (as of yet) is why only water from the Saraswati river can be used to process the drink. He simply states that 'water from other sources doesn't work' (132). Clute and Grant (1999: 338) recognise such a declaration as a definition of fantasy, writing: 'when set in an otherworld, that otherworld will be impossible, though stories set there will be possible in its terms'.

In the spirit of the questioning Shiva, Tripathi's novel poses questions about the writing and documenting of the past. From the outset, Shiva, albeit unwittingly, aligns himself with the *Suryavanshis*. He learns about the region he moves to, the customs, the moral and ethical codes from the *Suryavanshis* (the Meluhans) and in doing so, forms opinions about the *Chandravanshis* – the so-called enemies of the Meluhans – from the outset. Tripathi's presentation of 'right' over 'wrong' manifests in the Meluhans' strict moral code, urban planning and the culture's portrayal of their own lifestyle as the ideal. Shiva struggles with aspects of the Meluhan code and is somewhat vocal about this, however, he does overall accept that the *Chandravanshis* are a threat to the Meluhans. There is a moment in the novel where Shiva is reading a book whose storyline pits two groups of people against each other, thus depicting a situation not unlike the one between the *Suryavanshis* and the *Chandravanshis*. 'It was an interesting manuscript about the terrible war that was fought many thousands of years ago, between the *Devas*, the *gods*; and the *Asuras*, the *demons* and eternal struggle between opposites: good and evil' (Tripathi, 2010: 123). And later, we learn that the book is called 'The Righteous War against the Asuras' (137), aspects of which 'troubled' Shiva (137), namely the fact that 'Lord Rudra, though personally a great man, seemed to ignore the indiscretion of the Devas in the interest of the larger good' (138). It is at the close of the novel that Lord Shiva realises he has been imprudent, reluctant to critique the culture in which he has been living. It is a meeting with the *pandit* that makes Shiva consider that the *Chandravanshis* may not be as evil as the *Suryavanshis* have made them out to be, as the *pandit* says: '[A] difference of opinion between two dissimilar ways of life gets portrayed as a fight between good and evil' (385). Shiva laments: 'But I was not beyond biases. I was convinced that the Chandravanshis are evil. Maybe what Anandmayi says is right. Maybe I am naïve, easily misled' (385). The *pandit* reassures Shiva, explaining that the Neelkanth was always going to be an outsider – neither *Suryavanshi* or *Chandravanshi* – how else would he be able to know both sides?

3.2 Shatrujeet Nath: *The Guardians of the Halahala* (2015)

Out of the eight Bharati Fantasy novels discussed across Chapters 3 and 4 in this volume, it is Shatrujeet Nath's novel *The Guardians of Halahala* (2015) that strongly demonstrates the majority of the definitions of the Weird that Miéville and Vandermeer put forward (see Chapter 2, Section 2.1). The numinous as a threatening force, 'weird' presence and revolutionary teratology all feature in Nath's novel, drawing on established fantasy traditions as well as substantially on Indian epics and folklore.

Nath presents a narrative which pits three groups of people against each other; the humans, the *devas* and the *asuras*. The *devas* and *asuras* feature in the Indian epics but are most commonly known for their joint appearance in the *samudra manthan*, often translated as 'the churning of the ocean', where they work together (as they are actually arch enemies) in order to release the elixir of life, *amrita*. In Nath's novel, which is Book 1 of the 'Vikramaditya Trilogy', the Prologue tells of the fifth night of the Churning, how the elixir is released, only to be followed by the release of the *halahala*, 'the primordial poison, which, if not trapped in a vacuum, could destroy all creation' (2015: 4). Lord Shiva arrives to save all from imminent destruction as 'Shiva was the only force in the three worlds capable of destroying the Halahala' (5). In drinking the *halahala* Shiva saves the three worlds from annihilation but as the novel's Prologue tells us, Shiva knows that the *halahala* has not been totally destroyed and that the curse of this poisonous liquid has only just begun. Nath's novel then jumps to 'Many Thousand Years Later …' (7), the era through which the rest of the story is narrated. The idea that the *halahala* has not been completely consumed by Lord Shiva is a departure away from the original story of the Churning (as it is widely understood) and although Lord Shiva nearly died consuming the poison, he did contain it, in the sense that no *halahala* was left. For a readership acquainted with the story of the Churning, this detail reimagines the story and, combined with the protagonist, popular folkloric character Vikramaditya, the story of the *halahala* takes on a new and something of a fantastical direction.

Lord Shiva appears only once again in Nath's novel; he arrives in the guise of a sadhu at King Vikramaditya's palace. Gaining entry into the king's chamber, Shiva (as a sadhu) bequeaths a dagger to the king. He stresses the importance of keeping the dagger away from those that desire it because the dagger is the most powerful weapon in the three worlds. King Vikramaditya disbelievingly examines the blade of the weapon and the sadhu says: 'Its power rests not in its blade, but in its hilt' (73). As the king holds the hilt up to the light, he sees a strange light: 'It was a light coming from *within* the inky blackness of the hilt, iridescent blue, speckled with gold and silver motes, pulsating with light' (74). The sadhu tells the king that what he sees in the hilt of the dagger is a tiny amount of the *halahala*. The king is shocked and questions who the sadhu standing before him really is. The king blinks and 'in that moment, as the cosmic beat of the *damaru* roared in his ears, Vikramaditya saw the white, crescent moon adorning the sadhu's matted locks, and noticed the tinge of blue iridescence around his throat' (78). The king 'knows' it is Lord Shiva and quickly apologises for questioning his identity, consequently he seeks his blessings. Lord Shiva's decision to leave the dagger in human hands is taken because he knows that the '*devas*' – often translated as 'divine' – and the '*asuras*' – often translated as 'malevolent' – cannot be trusted with such a powerful potion.[1] Even the *devas*, Lord Shiva says, cannot be sure to use such a potent, powerful force for the good and so he decides that a human should guard the *halahala* even in the knowledge that both the *devas* and *asuras* have special, superhuman powers that could overwhelm the humans if enabled. Nath, however, chooses King Vikramaditya to be the human to guard the dagger.

Vikramaditya in Indian cultures (he is chronicled in various Indian languages) is said to have communicated with ghost-like beings (*vetala*) and in contemporary culture, circa 1985, a Doordarshan series called 'Vikram aur Betaal' explored such stories. It is disputed as to whether Vikramaditya is a historical figure although it is reported that he lived in the first century BCE. This connection to history as well as to *itihasa* is a curious performance here as Nath extends the ideas of Vikramaditya's (supposed) reign concurrently with the epic tale of the *samudra manthan*, taking both narratives in new and yet connected directions (Nath discusses this in some detail in the author interview in Section 3.6). This choice allows readers unfamiliar with the *samudra manthan* to engage with the story given that no prior knowledge of the story is needed in order for the narrative to make sense as a whole, whilst those readers who know the story of the Churning are invited to read Nath's fantastical interpretations and extensions of certain aspects of the tale.

Given that Nath employs fantastical tropes, *The Guardians of the Halahala* includes both *deva* and *asura* teratology as the three parties – *deva*, *asura* and human – fight over possession of the dagger. Given the context of conflict, the teratology is both menacing and threatening whilst simultaneously numinous as the creatures described in the novel belong to those species of 'god' worlds. The creatures who belong to Devalok (the world of the *devas*) are portrayed as intelligent as well as mighty on the battlefield. A 'garuda' (in Hinduism this is often referred to as the mount of Lord Vishnu) is described as transforming from a bird of prey, namely a kite, into a lion. The garuda is a scout for the *devas* and he returns to the palace in Devalok to report on what he has learned. Later in the novel, as King Vikramaditya's palace is under siege, the 'brotherhood of devas' is seen 'breaking and growing' (231) as the king's archers attempt to shoot the *devas* on their approach. Nath writes how the *devas* went about the battlefield, killing off the soldiers who were mortally wounded. The palace looks on in horror as:

> The devas rammed the blades in with brute force, choking and gurgling as their lifeblood ebbed away from them. [...] as [they] went about their ghastly chore, they seemed to grow in size, their bodies swelling and distorting and stretching sideways, as if being pulled in opposite directions by enormous, invisible forces. (230)

It is the king's councillor, Vetala Bhatta, who proposes that the cavalry is being controlled as 'one common mind' (238) and thus proposes to use a spell to 'enter that mind and try and control it' (238). Vetala Bhatta, in entering the 'common mind', hears only messages of destruction and sees flashing images of annihilation of the palace and the surrounding town and its people. He is unable to control the 'one mind' and as he struggles to exit the enthralment, the Wielder of the Hellfires enters the battlefield and the horsemen disperse. Vetala Bhatta survives his brush with the 'one mind' of the *devas*.

The teratology of the *asuras* is more about might than intelligence. The monstrous beings are huge, beast-like and demonic. They appear as *rakshasas* which, according to the epics, appear as ghosts or ogres. Here, Nath classifies the *rakshasas* as *asuras* (he provides an index of the major characters at the front of his book) and it is the blind *asura*, Andhaka, who Nath describes thus: 'gray scaly skin, the membranous webbings that covered large parts of its body, and the bulging head with its slanted reptilian eyes and sharp, pointed horns' (193).

Diti's seven sons are also described as beasts with horns, specifically as *maruts*. Nath tells us that these seven creatures are *asura* by birth but *deva* by allegiance. He writes: 'the beast had a human body, but was much larger and heavier, with eyes that shine like moonlight. It also had four horns on its head' (359). In this example, Nath takes information from the epics that he then imaginatively expands in order to create his own storyline. In suggesting that the *maruts* are adopted by Lord Indra, he is able to turn the creatures against their mother, Diti; a complete move away from the original telling(s).

The Guardians of the Halahala creates awe at strangeness through its portrayal of inventions and weapons. Some of these inventions are fantastical and adhere to Mendlesohn's (2008) definitions of fantasy, and many of them are anchored in the Indian epics wherein such inventions or weapons are mentioned: the *urumi* (Nath, 2015: 188) and the *chakram* 'fashioned out of iron, its outer edge wickedly sharp' (Nath, 2015: 376). Nath has also extended the inventions through his own imagination, such as mention of the *suryayantra* whose description is somewhat steampunkish: 'The soldiers stood around a *suryayantra*, a large contraption full of levers and cogwheels and mechanical arms, to which were fitted tin alloy mirrors of various sizes' (170). The machine is used to communicate messages over large distances by using the sun and the mirrors on the heliotrope (173), communicating one machine to another, which are positioned on the tops of hills or on raised ground. This example of invention blurs the boundaries between 'ancient science' and Nath's own fantastical imagination. Unlike in other Bharati Fantasy novels where invention and science are often attributed to ancient Vedic science or practice, Nath does not seek to qualify the invention of the heliotrope in the same way; Nath simply celebrates an aspect of his characters' technological abilities by showing how they were able to invent such a machine.

One of the more fantastical scenes in the novel is where a potter and his son are distracted from their work by the appearance of a huge rainbow which stretches over the desolate plain where they are working. Nath writes:

> At the point where the rainbow touched the ground, a vaporous portal shimmered – and through it emerged a horde of helmeted horsemen bearing bronze shields and longbows. The steeds were large, black beasts snorting powerfully and stamping the ground in impatience, and there was something menacing about the riders as they spurred their horses forward. (191)

Here, a sense of the weird and a sense of a menacing numinosity are created through Nath's description of the rainbow portal and the 'strange' beasts emerging from the sky. The boy and his father look on from the safety of the clay pit in which they are working, the boy is described as 'dazed', and his father, unable to fully explain to his son what they have just witnessed, says: '… they're definitely not human. And something tells me they are here to cause trouble' (192). To foreground the idea that the cavalry is not of the human world, the rainbow portal is described as vaporising, diffusing and gradually disappearing 'once the entire cavalry was firmly on Avanti's soil'

64 *Bharati Fantasy*

(192). As Nath's novel is set in ancient India, scenes like the one described above do not use complex real-world models to subvert traditional fantasy (one of the definitions of the New Weird – see Chapter 2, Section 2.1) but such scenes do employ fantasy tropes. Another example of the use of fantasy tropes is the battlefield scene where the Hellfires are unleashed on the approaching horsemen who are attempting to attack the king's castle. We read that a lone horseman leaves the castle gates and rides into the enemy. The enemy holds back, thinking that the horseman has been sent as a courier to seek a truce but soon the lone horseman 'began flourishing his swords in broad, sweeping moves, the flames on the blades tapering and growing in length and intensity with each successive movement of his arms' (236–237). The swords that the horseman holds are magical, charging with more fire as he wields the blades, the blades of fire finally detaching from the swords to whip across the battlefield, killing and injuring the enemy. 'As the devas started in amazement, the whips magically entwined to form three gargantuan, fire-breathing *churails*. Waiting and screaming, the fiery banshees lunged at the flanks of the cavalry, spewing green flames from their horrendous black mouths' (237).

In drawing on traditional tropes of the fantasy genre, Nath's storyline, although anchored in the Indian epics and folklore, allow for readers who are not familiar with such narratives to access the story. Nath's use of poetic licence means that a reimagining of the epics takes place through contemporary fantasy tropes such as the 'Hellfires' and 'screaming, fiery banshees' but, moreover, Nath's novel demonstrates that his storylines move beyond any reimagining of the epics, rather they create fantasy storylines and plots per se.

Throughout *The Guardians of the Halahala* there are characters who exude something akin to a weird presence. Their existence in itself is weird because of what they are able to perform, be it casting spells, predicting future events, healing or the ability to read minds and enter other (ghoul) worlds. Amongst the humans there is the Mother Oracle who, belonging to the Wandering Tribe, is able to discern from the natural elements that which threatens the peace of the land. We are introduced to her when a member of the king's palace, who is also the Mother Oracle's granddaughter, seeks her advice on current events. The Mother Oracle tells her:

> 'The winds from the west won't blow this way for at least a week, if not more,' the hag said at last. 'But let me listen to what the migratory birds have to say. They may have something that your king might find of value.' (67)

As the *devas* and the *asuras* look for new ways to penetrate the king's palace in order to steal the dagger (in whose hilt resides the *halahala*), King Vikramaditya pleads with Mother Oracle to stay at the palace to help forewarn the king and his army of imminent threats. She eventually agrees and is thus given a room in the palace. One day, she calls for the king.

'I am happy to hear the queen is better,' she repeated. 'But beware of the stranger in the palace, wise king.'

The samrat knitted his brows. 'Do you mean the Healer, mother?'

'The breeze blowing through the palace speaks of bad intentions,' the Mother Oracle replied obliquely. 'Be on your guard.' (338)

The Healer has managed to infiltrate the king's palace by suggesting that he can heal the king's long-ailing wife, Queen Vishakha. He has been sent by the *asuras* and is gathering information about the king and his entourage whilst he supposedly 'heals' the queen. He says little about his identity, only that he hails from 'the misty valleys through which the mighty Lauhitya flows before it enters the kingdom of Pragjyotishpura' (316). Unlike the Mother Oracle who consults the natural world for her divine knowledge, the Healer uses six pieces of human vertebrae to reveal information about situations and people around him.

> Using a pinch of vermilion, he drew a *mandala* on the marble floor, before cupping the bones in his hands and shaking them as he uttered a mantra. Throwing the bones inside the *mandala*, he leaned forward and began studying the pattern, trying to divine something more about the man who had just paid him a visit. (328–329)

The Healer's practices are distinctly 'Indian' – the vermilion, the *mandala*, the mantra – whilst simultaneously otherworldly and thus fantastical and weird. This combination allows for readers to interpret the Healer according to their own cultural preconceptions of such a character. It is this space for interpretation which allows readers to engage variously with Nath's novel. The book taps into universal fantastical tropes whilst carefully allowing such tropes to be manifestly of a particular culture or era, but not so demonstrably that they might occlude engagement with the storyline.

Finally, there is Vetala Bhatta, another character who resides in the king's palace (he is mentioned earlier). Vetala Bhatta is 'human' but has the ability to read minds and is able to take the king (through the portal of his own mind) to the Borderworld, employing what Nath calls a 'death-sleep'. We first understand Vetala's powers when he offers to read the mind of the queen, who is unwell and bedridden:

> … Vetala Bhatta stood at the foot of the bed, eyes closed, one hand gripping the spear, which was adorned with two human skulls near its sharp, pointed tip. His other hand was rolled into a fist and was pressed against his chest. The raj-guru moved his lips in whispers, the incantations barely audible in the heavy, loaded silence. The skulls on the spear burned a dull red, light emerging from their cavities, as if lit from the inside. (162)

Vetala Bhatta's powers mean that he is able to inhabit the Borderworld (that of the dead) and the Earth world (that of the living) and thus acts as a bridge between the two. His relationship with the king is one of immense trust given that the king relies on Vetala to facilitate his movement in and out of the Borderworld through the 'death-sleep'. If the death-sleep is ever interrupted by a sudden noise or by violent movement in the Earth world, there is a risk that the king will never be able to return. As the king arrives in the Borderworld he looks up 'at the wan, dying sun [...] What he was witnessing was nothing but Creation caught in the transition between life and death' (350). This particular depiction of the Earth world in the future could be a reference to the ages or *yuga* of Hinduism. At the end of *Kalyug*, the age that followed the Mahabharata War until the present, an apocalypse will take place and the description of the Borderworld is symbolic of such:

> ... the eternal realm of the undead ghouls, the gloaming separating the world of the living from the world of the dead. The bridge over which everything that had been created had to pass when going from a state of existence to a state of destruction. A mirror world where things already existed in their doomed, decomposing state ... (350)

For a reader with little or no knowledge of Hinduism, its *yugas* and its worlds, Nath's description of the Borderworld makes other mythological links such as those with Greek mythology and the realm of Hades, the waterway of Styx which formed a boundary between the Earth and the Underworld. These references to European mythology allow readers to formulate schemas to understand the story without having to access Hindu referents.

Once in the Borderworld, the king has no idea as to how and where he will locate the Ghoulmaster but 'strangely enough, even though he had no way of finding his bearings in this featureless desolation, the king's feet instinctively knew where to lead him' (Nath, 2015: 370). This strange, unexplainable ability to find his way across the Borderworld suggests that the Ghoulmaster and the king might be linked in some way, how they may already share an understanding and a bond. As he finally arrives at the cremation grounds and meets the Ghoulmaster, King Vikramaditya is warmly received because we are told that the Ghoulmaster owes his existence to Samrat Vikramaditya. He gladly takes on the responsibility of the dagger and the *halahala* (384), meaning that, at last, the poison is safe. Vikramaditya has managed until now to satisfy Lord Shiva's command.

3.3 Jagmohan Bhanver: *The Curse of Brahma* (2015)

Jagmohan Bhanver's novel *The Curse of Brahma* (2015) is set in Bharat, ancient (pre-)India and tells the story of a time preceding the birth of Sri Krishna. The anchoring of the story in the ancient past and in the life of

Brahma and his 'star pupil' Amartya Kalyanesu resonates with other Bharati Fantasy novels. Like Nath's *The Guardians of the Halahala* (2015), Bhanver's novel is manifestly 'weird' according to the definitions presented in Chapter 2, Section 2.1 of this volume. Bhanver's novel foregrounds the numinous as a threatening force through the protagonist the 'Dark Lord'. The world in which the Dark Lord lives is strange and menacing. Its inhabitants are monstrous and thus the novel includes many instances of teratology and the creation of a 'weird presence'. Although the story takes place in ancient times, the presence of fantasy tropes blurs real-world possibilities with ancient practices, many of which take their inspiration from (sacred) Hindu texts (namely, the *Mahabharata*, the *Ramayana*, the *Harivarsha*, the Vedas).

Of the three worlds, the Dark Lord lives in the lowest, *Paatal Lok*, which, as a world, has seven planes of existence. The bottom plane, the seventh, is called *Tamastamah Prabha* and is 'the most feared plane of existence' (Bhanver, 2015: 225). Although such ideas of numerous worlds – and levels of worlds – within a universe is familiar within dharmic thought, such a description of 'worlds' in non-dharmic traditions is understood as being fantastical or pertaining to the mythological. Described as a world of hells, *Paatal Lok* is not a hell of the Abrahamic tradition – once banished to *Paatal Lok* it is not mandatory to remain there for eternity, although normally the time spent there can be thousands of years (or longer). This is the case of the Dark Lord as we learn that he was banished from *Swarglok* (the world of righteous beings) by Lord Brahma to live in *Paatal Lok*.

As Brahma's star pupil whose abilities exceed even those of the *devas* (130), the Dark Lord, known previously as Amartya Kalyanesu, is ordained to the order of the *Brahmarishi* because Lord Shiva tells him: '[T]he very fact that you have learnt all there is to learn about life, death, karma and dharma in so short a time shows how different you are' (131). Amartya's extraordinary abilities are powerful, whether he resides in *Swarglok* or in *Paatal Lok*. Once banished to the 'dark side' Amartya becomes the Dark Lord and although he initially spends seven days without his 'powers', they return to him and he adjusts to his new surroundings. We do learn how Amartya is banished to *Paatal Lok*; Bhanver writes that Amartya is witness to his six brothers mocking Lord Brahma, he questions one of his brothers and chastises him for his insolence; Lord Brahma does not see Amartya's actions. In a rage, knowing that the boys had been mocking him in a clear display of disrespect, Lord Brahma's anger is directed at Amartya who he believes is simply looking on (and endorsing) such impertinence. Caught up in his emotions:

> Brahma's fury was terrible to behold as he glared at the young man. His curse was quick and the youth paled as he heard Brahma mutter the shocking punishment that would banish him forever from the place he had always thought of as home. (50)

The use of the *Brahmashira* was so strong, it not only sends Amartya to *Paatal Lok* but it also burns off half of his face. 'Amartya felt himself being pulled through different planes of existence of the three worlds. And then just as he thought that he was trapped in the air bubble for eternity, he saw the landscape around him change dramatically' (225). Lord Brahma regrets his action as soon as he banishes Amartya but he can do nothing about it as the curse cannot be undone.

It is in *Tamastamah Prabha* that the narrative presents in particular as 'weird'. The description of the seventh plane is not only dark and eerie; it is also threatening. Bhanver writes: 'He [Amartya] couldn't make out anyone else's presence, but he was certain that there were others besides him, and not too far from where he stood' (227). Throughout the novel, *Tamastamah Prabha* (and in turn *Paatal Lok*) is described in strange terms through its depiction of a strange force, of 'death' as a numinous presence and through the monstrous beings that inhabit the seventh plane. Like Nath's novel, the tropes of the fantastical and the weird lift the storyline out of cultural specificity and the backdrop of Hinduism (Brahma and his star pupil) are lost to the more menacing aspects of the Amartya's banishment.

Bhanver describes the ground of *Tamastamah Prabha* as alive with serpents whose 'eyes gleamed yellow' (227), feeding on corpses and who 'appeared almost human in the way that they looked at him [Amartya]' (228). On Amartya's arrival, it is a *bhuta* which threatens the life of Amartya in the 'hell of hells' (229) that is *Tamastamah Prahaba*. 'Bhutas were considered the most dangerous creatures in Paatal Lok and their hunger and thirst were impossible to quench irrespective of how much they ate or drank' (228). Described as a 'human-like creature' (228), the *bhuta* 'had sunken eyes, mummified skin and narrow limbs. [...] The creature had a host of maggots coming out of its ears and nose' (228). The creature, biting off bits of flesh hanging from Amartya's face, stops to listen to an increasing roar of sound. He flees the scene as thousands of snakes make their way to attack the *bhuta*. The *bhuta* is able to flee quickly, his feet barely touching the ground as he glides away. Amartya recalls how, whilst in Brahma's ashram, he learnt that *bhutas* would avoid all contact with the ground as 'it depleted them of their supernatural strength' (230).

The *bhuta* is not the only kind of demon monster that appears in the novel. Bhanver explains that there are many types of *asura* and it is Narada, a sage close to Lords Brahma, Vishnu and Shiva, who travels through the three worlds to gather information, who tells that many kinds of *asuras* are being mobilised by a powerful force, forming a large army. Narada speaks of: 'daityas, rakshasas, pisacas, danavas, bhutas, pretas, dasyus, kalakanjas, khalins, nivata-kavacas, paulomas ...' (48). The Dark Lord instructs a *pisacas*, a *kalakanja* and a *bonara* (not mentioned in this list here) to assassinate Devki, daughter of Kind Dev. In failing to carry out their mission:

> ... an eerie green light emanated from the pointed limbs of each of the three creatures. It travelled upwards and seemed to culminate at the point above the ground, where the three of them were focusing their energies. [...] there was a flurry of wind where each of the

three creatures stood, and what appeared to resemble a mini-typhoon hauled the swirling figures of the three monsters up into the air and disappeared along with them. (81)

Where dark or evil magic is performed, it is a green light – such as that above – which symbolises the malevolence. The Dark Lord's eyes turn green as he uses his powers and even Kansa's eyes – a prince of half-*asuran* origin – start to turn green as he begins his move over to the dark side at the behest of the Dark Lord. This trope is commonly found in fantasy or science fiction and, consequently, the reader does not need to reply on knowledge of Brahma and Hinduism to understand the characters being described here. True to the trope, it is the presence of blue light that symbolises peace and life. As Amartya is initiated as a *Brahmarishi* blue light appears as he bonds his mind with Brahma's. Despite his banishment to *Paatal Lok*, the Dark Lord does not lose the life-giving energy that was imbued in him by Brahma; when the Dark Lord kills a *bhuta* in order to show his extraordinary powers to other *asuras*, he magically revives him: 'a cloud of blue light enveloped the dead monster's body and the incredible power of the Brahman energy could be felt by all present …' (207). Thus the power of Brahman,[2] even when wielded by the Dark Lord, prevails over darker forces and the reader is reminded of the Dark Lord as Amartya, Brahma's star pupil. As part of Amartya's initiation to become a *Brahmarishi*, we read that Brahma must bind his mind with his pupil's, we are not told how this is accomplished, rather we read only that:

> … Brahma focused on the innermost root of his own consciousness and released at once the entire knowledge of Brahman from his mind into Amartya's consciousness. There was a sound like the clap of thunder as the knowledge of Brahman travelled from the guru to the disciple. (139)

Amartya is the only one outside of the *Saptarishis* and the Lords Brahma, Vishnu and Shiva to receive 'the knowledge of Brahman' and is therefore singled out as unusual from the start. Having extraordinary abilities is a common feature of fantasy or weird fiction and thus the reader is able to engage with the character as being 'exceptional' when he is using his powers for both good and bad deeds (readers familiar with *Star Wars* might make links to the character of Darth Vader).

The fact that the Dark Lord comes to *Paatal Lok* after having lived in the higher worlds creates a sense of numinosity in the narrative. He is both trained in the (benevolent) numinous world of the three Lords (Brahma, Vishnu and Shiva) whilst he latterly oversees the training of others through a destructive numinosity with the focus on assassinating Devki, turning Kansa to the dark side and facilitating the infiltration of the higher worlds with *asuras* from the lower world (*Paatal Lok*). In order to bring Kansa over to the dark side, the Dark Lord uses what Bhanver calls *svapnasrsti*. He writes:

> Svapnasrsti was the ability to enter a person's mind and create a dream that would seem so vivid that the person dreaming it would be haunted by the reality of it, even after waking up. Frequent doses of svapnasrsti administered to a person could make them lose sight of what was real and what was imagined. (213)

Kansa's mind is infiltrated by the Dark Lord in this way and over time, Kansa starts to lose sense of reality. Kansa begins to suffer from seizures and these happen whilst Kansa's mind is under *svapnasrsti*. Having been told that it is a son of Devki that will be the one to end his life, Kansa vows to himself that any sons born to Devki will have to be killed. Readers with knowledge of the birth of Sri Krishna make the connection with the epics (this appears in the *Harivarsha* and the *Mahabharata*) and know that Devki gives birth to Sri Krishna. In Bhanver's novel, Devki gives birth to sextuplets and Kansa, in a moment of *svapnasrsti*, smothers the six babies, murdering them all:

> As Kansa looked at them through the haze of his pain, it seemed to him that they were no longer laughing with him. They now appeared to be laughing *at* him. Their raised arms seemed to point accusingly at him as they continued to laugh at him. The sound of their laughter threatened to split open his head. (356, original emphasis)

With a heightened sense of sound and the intensity of the babies' 'supposed' laughing inside his head, a seizure begins to take over Kansa and it is in this very moment that he is able to kill the infants. The infiltration into Kansa's mind is reminiscent of the Weird tale. The numinous Dark Lord controls the minds of others in the novel too, most notably kings and people in positions of power, and so as readers we are aware of both the manifest and the invisible forces of the Dark Lord, the latter creating a feeling of the strange and the threatening throughout the novel.

Bhanver's novel explores magical and fantastical happenings through unexplained scientific interventions. There are several examples of where science and medicine meet the fantastic in Bhanver's novel. As Kansa fights off an *asura*, he is struck in the abdomen and scratched down his arms. Kansa is returned to the palace where a doctor versed in Ayurveda, referred to as a *vaid*, is summoned to treat him. The *vaid* is shocked by how quickly Kansa is recovering from his injuries. The internal bleeding has stopped and 'the scratch marks on the prince's arms seemed to be vanishing before their very eyes. It was almost as if the skin surrounding the scratch marks was closing over to shroud the cuts, healing them completely' (84). As the prince's father praises Lord Shiva for this incredible recovery, the *vaid* is concerned, he shivers involuntarily in the knowledge that 'no mortal could have healed as fast as Kansa had just done!' (85). Whilst Kansa's family are happy to believe in the divine intervention of Lord Shiva, the *vaid* – a practitioner of Vedic medicine all the same – will not accept such an explanation.

The *vaid* suspects that Kansa is 'no longer' mortal but he is unsure of what kind of immortal he has become – divine or otherwise.

As Lord Brahma learns of the Dark Lord's destruction, Lord Brahma goes to speak to Lord Shiva for advice. Knowing the story of how Amartya was banished to *Paatal Lok*, Lord Shiva counsels Lord Brahma on how best to handle the current situation. As their conversation comes to a natural end, Lord Shiva tells Lord Brahma that he should return to him when things don't go to plan. Lord Shiva begins to disappear in front of Lord Brahma and he realises that 'he had been talking to Shiva's projected image all this while. Shiva had never been here. He had just used his immense powers of concentration to create a holographic image' (97).

It is the creation of Sri Krishna in Bhanver's novel which totally reimagines how Krishna, the son of Devki, survives Kansa's murderous intent. Narada, the wise and well-travelled sage, gives Devki's maid Mandki a 'sterilized packet' (358) in which she places a hair plucked from Devki's head and a hair from Devki's husband's head. She returns the now-sealed packet to Narada. Lord Brahma is given the packet by Narada who in turn hands it to Lord Vishnu. The packet containing the hairs of Devki and her husband are taken to the 'pratiroop kaksh (cloning room) surrounded by all manner of lab equipment' (373). Here, Lord Vishnu removes the two hairs: 'Put together, he would be able to isolate all the vita; properties from both Vasudev and Devki's DNA. *But that won't be enough*, he smiled, as he plucked out one strand of his own hair and kept it under the scanner' (373).

Some readers of this novel will understand that through the *pratiroop kaksh*, Bhanver is 'creating' Sri Krishna, who is the eighth avatar of Lord Vishnu, as Lord Vishnu donates his DNA to Sri Krishna's biological mother and father. Bhanver writes:

> The last seven times that he [Lord Vishnu] had cloned himself, it had been easy. He had simply separated the few characteristics that were required and recombined them to form a partial clone. The situation in the mortal world was so dire that a partial clone would not help. The clone would need all his representative genes. (373)

Knowing that Kansa will kill a child that is born of Devki, it is Vasudev's brother's wife Yashoda who is to carry the child. Lord Vishnu explains that the capsule must be taken orally and that it will find its own way into the womb (375). We are not told as readers *how* this capsule will find its way to the womb or, indeed, how the DNA inside it will produce 'a saviour', who will be born 'at midnight, nine months from tomorrow. He will be the foremost warrior in all three worlds!' (375). Lord Vishnu announces that his name will be Krishna and that he will save *Mrityulok* (the middle world) from the suffering it is undergoing at present.

The Curse of Brahma is a Bharati Fantasy novel which, although anchored in the ancient Indian epics, reimagines the era before the birth of Sri Krishna through fantastical and weird tropes. Even for readers familiar

72 *Bharati Fantasy*

with the story of Kansa and the birth of Sri Krishna, the departures away from the more traditional tellings of this story are significant. In this manner, Bhanver's novel is similar to that of Nath in terms of creating fantasy worlds above and beyond the established epics and folkloric imagination. The manner in which Lord Vishnu 'creates' his seventh avatar (Sri Krishna), the manner in which *Paatal Lok* and the various types of *asuras* are depicted, the idea of infiltrating the mind of Kansa and the 'magical' healing that even the *vaid* cannot make sense of, all take the narrative in newly imagined directions. Of interest here is that these new departures do not rely on the reader knowing the story from which the novel takes its starting point (or inspiration), rather, the frequency of fantastical or weird tropes mean that a reader can engage with the novel *within* that very genre, rather than having to fit the storyline to an existing story schemata. Given that both Nath and Bhanver's novels enact this technique, Chapter 5 discusses the technique and its effect on reader engagement in some detail.

3.4 Samhita Arni: *The Missing Queen* (2013)

Samhita Arni's novel *The Missing Queen* (2013) creates a sense of 'weird' presence from the outset. The setting of the novel feels contemporary but the characters' names, places and cultural references seem to place it in an older age whilst other narrative features place it in a near future or speculative era. Saran (2013:33), however, suggests that it is more 'earth bound, with more political and social moorings than fantastical connections to birds and monkeys or fish'. *The Missing Queen* is driven by the quest to find Sita, the eponymous 'missing queen'. Anchored in the story of the *Ramayana*, the characters of Lord Ram, Sita, Lakshman, Hanuman, Kaikeyi, Ravana, Urmila and others are familiar names, that is, to those readers for whom the *Ramayana* is a cultural cornerstone, however, the epoch in which Arni crafts *The Missing Queen* is both familiar whilst being concurrently strange. One character in the novel references 'an old film strip' (Samhita, 2013: 7) she has seen many times, 'Ram and Sita entering the city in a Cadillac, waving to admiring crowds' (7), and later in this same section Arni writes: 'television is the mouthpiece of the New Ayodhya. Ayodhya is booming, Ayodhya is shining. Images flash on screens in every household, speaking of progress and development. Ayodhya is poised to take the world by storm' (11). Through indirect references to New India, the post-millennium television and satellite boom, its relentless news reporting and its booming economy, Arni crafts a recognisable India whilst rendering it strange through motifs of utopia and fantasy worlds. A further example of this technique is found in a scene where buildings etch out time and era:

> On my way home, I pass an art-deco styled cinema, and the ancient, faltering neon sign proclaims that an old classic is playing: *The Demon King*. A crumbling hoarding displays a fiendish villain, who bears a

striking resemblance to the late Ravana, despite the addition of bulging muscles, curving horns and talons. (20)

The palimpsestic nature – specifically through the layering of 'time' – of *The Missing Queen* is particularly well captured in this quote as Arni, whose reader is already submerged in a near-future or weird contemporary moment, further destabilises the narrative through the description of the cinema as 'an art-deco styled cinema' and the 'ancient, faltering neon sign', the 'old classic' and 'the addition of bulging muscles' to an original depiction of Ravana. This layering of eras connects with the novel's pursuit of 'truth-telling' whilst also connecting with the idea of A. K. Ramanujan's essay 'Three Hundred Ramayanas'. In an early section of the novel, Arni states that the story of Lord Ram, Sita and Ravana is the 'only one worth telling in Ayodhya' (21) and that 'it's the greatest tale ever told, and better still, it's true. Real' (21, 22). Furthermore, she says: 'It has crossed over the boundaries of the merely real, and been spun into fantasy. It is a fairy tale now' (22). In this short passage, Arni explores the idea of *itihasa* in relation to the epic tale of the *Ramayana*. Adopted by Ayodhya as 'the only one [story] worth telling', the position of power that the *Ramayana* holds is both powerful and destabilising. Here, in this passage, the *Ramayana* is projected as 'real' in the sense that it is *itihasa* (see discussions of this in Chapter, Section 2.2) and thus, by extension, it is suggested that such a story can only venture into the realms of fantasy by virtue of being real in the first place. This claim renders *The Missing Queen* yet more layered given that Arni's own telling of (aspects of) the *Ramayana* is couched in the speculative genre and thus manifest of fantasy-like tropes and motifs. The challenge here is thinking about *itihasa* as fantasy per se due to the years, authors and versions that this literary (and cultural) monolith has been shaped by and, consequently, the suggestion that the *Ramayana*, in a certain sense, is no longer *itihasa*.

Without a doubt, *The Missing Queen* focusses on the idea of 'truth' and its telling, and this is foregrounded, not only through the search for a woman (Sita) who is missing (what is the truth surrounding her disappearance?), but also through the meta-text of the narrative, as demonstrated in the novel's Prologue:

> 'You'll go back and write that piece, like all the other reporters, like Valmiki, painting me as some beguiling siren who ruined Dasaratha and Ayodhya. Sex, revenge, jealousy, vindictiveness – it will all be there …' Her voice rises. 'But do you want the truth?' (5)

The reporter alluded to here is the novel's protagonist, a young, female journalist, based in Ayodhya, the homeland of Ram. It is ten years since the fall of Lanka, a war which Ram won, a war triggered by the kidnapping of his wife Sita by Ravana of Lanka. Sita was kept for ten years, living in Ravana's palace until finally being rescued by Hanuman and Ram's men. Ayodhya, the novel tells its reader, 'is shining' and Lanka is now ruined and desolate. The enmity between the two nations runs deep and Ayodhya's contemporary history by which this discord is charted *is* the *Ramayana*. In an early section of *The Missing Queen*, Arni describes how the journalist goes about preparing for an interview she is conducting with Ram and how she comes to consult the *Ramayana*:

> ... I start to prepare for the interview, pulling out my copy of Valmiki's weighty tome – every hack's handbook to Ayodhyan contemporary history (and the only authorized biography), *The Story of Ram*, authored by Ayodhya's most famous journalist. Ram fills the cover, larger than life. (19)

The position of the one and only story of a contemporary nation haunts the narrative, setting up uncomfortable, dystopian ideas of hegemonic cultural identity and recent history. Ayodhya is juxtaposed with Lanka, a nation which is destitute yet 'free' of any imposing national narrative. Ayodhya shines outwardly yet it is tarnished from within, and motifs of a 'weird' presence are developed out of this particular anxiety. It is the Washerman, a shadowy and spectral being, who haunts the storyline, appearing in person on only a few occasions, sending instead his 'men' to keep those who wish to ask (unwanted) questions at bay. The Washerman (or his men) show up at various points in the narrative, dressed in pure white and often appearing as if out of nowhere. This emphasis on such a weird presence is underscored by the uncertain timeframe of the story as it reads as a near-future story which is quickly subverted by the constant anchoring of the narrative in *itihasa* and thus in an older India.

The motif of 'searching' in the *Ramayana* and the journeys that are embedded within the original story – namely those from Ayodhya to the forest, to Lanka, then back to Ayodhya via the forest – are found layered throughout the novel. There is the search for the 'missing queen' which explores those individuals who are of the *Ramayana* narrative; there is also the search for Sita that the journalist enacts herself, a journey which traces the footsteps of the *Ramayana* from Ayodhya to Lanka and back; there is a film showing of a part of the *Ramayana* titled *The Demon King* at a cinema in Ayodhya that the journalist decides to watch as part of her search for Sita and, finally, I suggest that there is a suggestion of a cyclical narrative in the story of current-day Ayodhya itself – caught up in the tropes of happiness, sadness, struggle (war), sadness, to happiness (to sadness) – whereby Ayodhya which is 'shining' may not always shine and will inevitably know sadness and war anew. By extension, the final scene of the novel is apocalyptic in that many of the main characters are lost to what reads like a natural or 'god'-invoked disaster.

The idea that Ayodhya might be 'rewritten' is embodied in the suggestion that the author of Ayodhya's most well-loved story, Valmiki, can simply write an 'epilogue' (129). Arni explores this idea in a bar scene between the journalist and an old colleague of hers:

A few 'mocktails' later, on my tab, he whispers, 'Valmiki's coming out with a new edition.'
'Why?'
'Updating the story, making a few changes, mentioning Sita's disappearance. An "epilogue", as he calls it.' (129)

And when the young journalist pushes to know why such a new edition is necessary, her colleague makes a case for the use of story in nation-building, saying:

'What Ayodhya needs is a story. A story that you can believe in. Something that makes us feel good. Ram and Sita separating – it becomes a sad story. Not an uplifting tale of heroism, conquest, love. It becomes a tragic romance. It will undermine us. It will make us doubt ourselves, what we've done. Doubt our manifest destiny as an Empire, bringing light to Mithila, Lanka and so many other nations.'
'Ayodhya needs a story, and you are going to twist the truth to provide it?' (130)

Given that the search for truth is foregrounded throughout *The Missing Queen*, the subversion of truth is an equal partner in the narrative. An example of such subversion is most evident in Arni's exploration of silence. Often imposed, often coupled with violence and even death, silence in *The Missing Queen* drives the narrative forward. The protagonist experiences directly what it is to break silence, speak out and ask questions that have been deemed inappropriate and distasteful. As a consequence of her actions, she spends time in prison, has her life threatened and attempts are made on her life. After interviewing Ram live on air where she asks the question she should never have asked (where is Sita?), the young journalist returns to her office to be confronted by a raging editor.

'... The powers-that-be are not pleased!'
'Who are the powers-that-be? Ram?' I pause and think. I don't believe he would ask for my resignation. Ram is just too damned honest.
'No. Not Ram.' My editor is weary. 'You should go away, somewhere else, lie low for a while.'
'Who are the powers-that-be?'
He doesn't answer.
'If it's not Ram, then who? Who runs this goddamned show? Who tells us what goddamned questions we should and shouldn't ask? Who runs this country, this empire in Ram's name? Tell me!'
He walks away. (27)

It is such passages of text which create a strange and threatening presence. If Ram – the king of Ayodhya – is not in charge of the state, then who is? The journalist muses that such a king could not be human anyway (Arni, 2013: 39) and in doing so, Arni further challenges the idea of Ram as virtuous and righteous, a challenge which goes against the core notions of *itihasa* and the *Ramayana* wherein Ram is portrayed as the ideal in all his relationships and dealings. As Kishwar (2001: 303) writes: 'It is a common sentiment among Indian women (and men) that ideals set in bygone ages are still valid and worth emulating, though they admit few people manage to follow them in today's world'. As a deviating loop around such a contentious topic – the questioning of Ram's morals and virtues – Arni crafts the sinister figure of the Washerman. We find out that the Washerman takes his name from a more ancient practice of surveillance. Here again we encounter the layering of time, referents to an older India and moreover, to the 'original' context in which the *Ramayana* would have been penned by Valmiki. A colleague of the young journalist tells her:

> 'In the old days, in Dasaratha's time, there were none of these new-fangled gizmos for gathering information. But there was a network of informants – people who could go anywhere and everywhere, who had wide access. Dhobis, ironing women, vegetable sellers. They infiltrated homes, picked up gossip and scraps of information and pieced it together.'
>
> (Arni, 2013: 131)

Curiously, Arni reveals something of the Washerman's identity whilst continuing to conceal who 'the' Washerman really is. He is both known and unknown, linked to the 'original' text whilst belonging to the contemporary moment. Arni alludes to the Washerman's competencies for modern-day surveillance when she writes 'there were none of these new-fangled gizmos for gathering information' (131), suggesting that the Washerman is dangerous in contemporary (technological) and maybe unknown ways.

It is during her time in Lanka that the journalist meets Surpanakha, Lanka's leader and the sister of Ravana. The journalist is brought into a darkened room, lit only by a lamp, full of smoke and the smell of oil and perfume. Here the journalist finally casts her eyes upon the once-beautiful Lankan, a woman she finds ruined, cut and haggard:

> She turns the light brighter, and now, bereft of shadow, her face is truly grotesque. Demonic. It may have been beautiful once, but now her nose is just a bloody slit. What is left of the nose – a hunk of flesh – is puffy and red, and when she breathes the sound is monstrous. (66)

The grotesque description of Surpanakha's face is coupled with the story of how she came to befall such a tragedy. But the journalist presses her on the account. In Valmiki's version the events are described differently, to which Surpanakha replies: 'Who do you believe? Ram and Lakshman? Or me? No one else was there' (67). The journalist muses 'There is something to what she says, I have to admit, even if she is guilty of twisting the truth' (67). The severity of Surpanakha's facial mutilation is beyond received norms of disfigurement (if such mutilation can be thought of as having 'norms') which stray into the realm of the weird and fantasy. If Surpanakha's nose is nothing but a 'bloody slit', it seems implausible to think that she could survive such an injury or, in surviving it, that no surgery has been performed to improve her condition. As sister of (the evil) Ravana, Surpanakha is portrayed as grotesque in appearance as well as in her Lankan morals (she says 'we believe in the right of the individual to create the rules that bind them' [65]). She asserts that her brother Ravana took Sita 'from the narrow confines of the circle where she stood' (65), a circle drawn around Sita by Lakshman, Ram's brother, to protect her. Surpanakha's vision for society and for women to be free of the protection of their male family members is perceived by Ayodhyans to be grotesque, a dystopian vision of society which can only bring about unease and unrest; her facial features are a symbol of such as well as a manifest reminder of the war with Lanka.

In Arni's novel, we read very little of Hanuman, who, in Valmiki's 'original' *Ramayana*, was responsible for rescuing Sita from Ravana on Lanka. In Valmiki's narrative, Hanuman is depicted as strong, superhuman and creative in his military strategy. In *The Missing Queen*, Hanuman is General Hanuman, the Army Chief, described thus:

'A decade after the war, he is still gigantic. Muscles threaten to burst the seams of his tight-fitting uniform. His simian features, beloved and so familiar, decorate many a young boy's bedroom and his face adorns army recruitment posters' (114). Given that the novel is written in a speculative style, Hanuman as a character is surprisingly not developed within this particular framework. Arni signals to the reader that Hanuman has 'simian features', that he is muscular and 'gigantic' but none of these features are developed further and so the reader understands this description to be one which works within a normative frame of human depiction – he does not look simian per se, rather he has some simian features, he is tall, 'well-built' and muscular, but Hanuman has, after all, been in the army all his life. Arni's avoidance of developing the character of Hanuman in her novel through speculative tropes is significant. His depiction falls somewhere between human and superhuman and as such a balanced description, Hanuman can be either to the reader. When elucidating on how Hanuman arrived into Lanka to rescue Sita, Trijatha says: 'I knew it the day that Hanuman parachuted in to reconnoitre the city and locate Sita' (89). Here the word 'parachuted' has both the semantic of actual parachuting (using a parachute) as well as 'rushing in to save a situation' as one might do for an emergency. The manner and specifics of how Hanuman rushes in to this situation is purposely vague. The fact that Arni restricts information about Hanuman which contains the more speculative-leaning aspects of his being as told in the *Ramayana* (such as how Hamuman lifts a mountain from the Himalayas to bring a particular medicinal plant to Lakshman on the battlefield in Lanka) means that Hanuman does not distort Arni's carefully crafted near-future, delicately speculative novel.

It is rather the apocalyptic scene at the end of *The Missing Queen* which develops the speculative genre of this story. As Ram meets Sita at what Arni calls the 'Shining Palace', he approaches her and the journalist. Watching from afar, she witnesses Ram ask Sita something, to which Sita shakes her head. As Sita turns away, Ram calls after Sita but she does not turn back. As Ram goes to follow Sita, the earth trembles and cracks appear across the floor of the palace; the earth is beginning to split in all directions. Arni does not offer an explanation as to why the earth should begin to quake and, eventually, as the tremors increase and the earth splits further, Sita's life is taken. We do not read of her recovered body or of her funeral pyre; she disappears from the narrative and the next paragraph reads that Valmiki's body is being carried, on its way to be cremated.

Arni's *The Missing Queen* raises questions about truth-telling and representations of truth. It is a pointedly layered novel, and this very layering echoes the complexity involved in truth-telling and representation. The speculative genre acts as an overlay to these already multiple layers of interpretation of truth, and the weird presence that Arni creates, most notably through the spectre-like Washerman and the slippage in terms of era, further accentuates the complexity around understanding truth, *itihasa* and narrative as a shared cultural experience. As a symbol of this complexity, *The Missing Queen* closes as the journalist watches over Valmiki's funeral pyre. She hesitates but is sure she sees the ochre sari that Sita wears, 'standing apart from the crowd' (178) and, so, as the flames burn, Valmiki and Sita both dead, the story of 'The Missing Queen' hangs in the air, complete yet unfinished.

3.5 Interview with Author Amish Tripathi

Author biography: Amish Tripathi was born in October 1974 in the city of Mumbai in India. His father is an engineer and mother a homemaker. The family originally hailed from the holy city of Kashi (Benaras). The children in this household were brought up in an atmosphere of deep religiosity and liberalism with a major focus on education and reading. Due to the nature of his father's job, the family moved to various parts of the country. What remained constant was the steady flow of books and reading material on different subjects which everyone in the family read voraciously. Amish's passion for books (especially history) began during his school days. He read at least four to five books a month, and he continues to read at that pace even today.

Career opportunities were limited in India 25 years ago. Since Amish came from a family of limited means, he made pragmatic choices on his

education and career front, rather than professionally pursue his passion for history and mythology. He graduated in mathematics and went on to complete his MBA at one of India's premier institutes, IIM Calcutta. He spent the next 14 years in the world of financial services, rising quite high in the corporate ladder to become the youngest senior management committee member of an MNC Life Insurance company subsidiary. It was during his professional career, around 2004, that an idea struck him on a very philosophic theme, which was to explore 'the nature of evil' and what it means to different people. Thus, what began as an intensely deep and philosophic thesis eventually took the final form of a fast-paced novel with Lord Shiva, the Destroyer of Evil, as its main protagonist.

After having been rejected by most publishers, Amish decided to self-publish the book (with his book agent). He subsequently spent months creating marketing plans for the book (effectively using the new-age social media and traditional media) in a strategic fashion. *The Immortals of Meluha* (2010) hit its mark with readers in a manner Amish could never fathom. The Shiva Trilogy finally went on to become the fastest-selling book series in Indian publishing history. With the trilogy's subsequent titles *The Secret of the Nagas* (2011) and *The Oath of the Vayuputras* (2013), The Shiva Trilogy has 2.7 million copies in print with gross retail sales of over Rs 75 crores. These books have been translated into sixteen Indian and international languages. His latest book, titled *Scion of Ikshvaku*, the first book of the Ram Chandra Series, released in June 2015, has already grossed Rs 22 crores and was the highest-selling book of the year.

Forbes magazine has listed Amish amongst the 100 most influential celebrities in India four years in a row, and he has been selected to be an Eisenhower Fellow, a prestigious American programme for outstanding leaders from around the world. Amish is now a full-time writer, having resigned from his job when his second book, *The Secret of the Nagas*, was well received. He lives in Mumbai with his wife Preeti and son Neel.

E. DAWSON VARUGHESE: Amish, could you please say a bit about how you came to write what is commonly referred to within India as 'mythology-inspired' fiction.

AMISH TRIPATHI: I was always interested in mythology, spirituality and philosophy. My grandfather was a pandit in Kashi (Benaras) and a teacher at Benaras Hindu University. Both my parents are deeply religious so I grew up in a deeply religious family. I read a lot as well; at least 4–5 books per month, often more. I have been reading at this pace for decades. I mostly read non-fiction and among my favourite genres are spirituality, mythology, history and philosophy. So I guess it's obvious that if I had to write (which was not a foregone conclusion when I was young) I would write in an area that combined mythology, spirituality, philosophy and history.

EDV: Thinking about the genre label of 'mythology fiction' – to what extent would you agree with this genre categorisation? Is there a different label that you would use to describe your fiction, if so please say what it is and why?

AT: I don't much care for genre labels. They don't necessarily help. Every book has its own journey. Having said that, the word mythology has different connotations in different parts of the world. These stories were never called 'mythology' in Indian languages and the English word 'mythology' is often conflated with a Hindi word 'mithya', which means untruth. Indians would not call such stories 'untruth'. They were either called *Itihasa* or *Kaavya* or *Pauranik katha* and in the Indian way, the purpose of these stories was to primarily learn philosophical lessons for life; to learn about the many 'Truths' that exist, and find the one that is most relevant to you. Having said that, this is not something that I am deeply emotional about. I don't use the word 'mythology' when I am speaking in Hindi. But when I speak in English, I use the word since it readily conveys what I am speaking about to a Western or a Westernised audience.

EDV: There is a revival of sorts as tales of ancient (pre-)India are explored through contemporary fiction, and your novels have been key in bringing about this renaissance. What are your thoughts on this movement and this rise of pride in the 'ancestors' or in a celebration of 'older Indias'? How do you understand India's own sense of modernity, independent (or not) from Western ideas of modern life? And where does belief or Hinduism in the sense of *sanatana dharma* feature in all this?

AT: Mythology has always been the most popular genre in Indian languages like Hindi, Tamil, Marathi, etc. However, it may not have been so in the Indian English language publishing industry till the recent past. Till 10 to 15 years ago, the Indian readers who read in English were the old elite and they were very Westernised. Is it that they did not want to read mythology from ancient India or is it that the Indian English language publishing industry did not supply such books? One can debate that. Today, however, due to increased education, there are many non-Westernised Indian readers who have also started reading in English and their tastes reflect the tastes of the real India, i.e. the traditional love of our mythology. So the 'revival', if at all, is more in the area of English language publishing in India rather than anything else.

EDV: I'm interested to talk to you about the relationship between science and Hinduism. How do you conceive of these two and could you say how both 'appear' in your fiction (in both demonstrative and subtle ways)?

AT: In the traditional Indian way (or frankly, the way of most of the ancient cultures), science and religion were never in conflict with each other. In fact, most of the great scientists were also deeply religious. What we see today, in terms of a conflict between science and religion, is a leftover from the conflicts in Europe between scientists and the Medieval Church. Why did this conflict not take place in most ancient cultures like India, Egypt, Mesopotamia, South East Asia, China, etc.? I think in these ancient cultures the habit of questioning was encouraged within religion which puts it in consonance with the core spirit required for scientific inquiry. In ancient Sanskrit, for example, there is no translation for the English word 'blasphemy'; they did not have that word at that time because there was no concept of blasphemy in ancient India. Nobody was beyond question, not even God. So you could be deeply religious and yet nurture a questioning spirit within you; I believe that automatically gave you a scientific approach as well.

EDV: Unlike other 'mythology-inspired' fiction, your novels have been intimately connected to Hindu deities and, moreover, to renowned Hindu deities (Shiva and, latterly, Ram). Could you talk about how you approach a novel knowing that you are writing a narrative anchored in *itihasa* and also knowing that for some readers that very *itihasa* is a 'truth' in terms of historic events?

AT: In the traditional Indian way (and again, in the way of almost all ancient cultures), there is no one Absolute Truth. There are many Truths possible, and each of us sees the Truth that is meant for us, depending on the facts that we have before us at that point of time, and of course, coloured by our own pre-existing biases. I am a believer, so I write about my Gods with respect. And yes, I believe they exist. But I am not forcing that point of view on anyone else. If someone does not want to believe, it's their choice. Everyone has a right to believe what gives them peace.

EDV: I'm interested to explore your understanding both as a Hindu and as a novelist of 'mythology-inspired' fiction around science and belief. How does Hinduism and how does the type of fiction you write interface with 21st-century ideas of scientific discovery, creation theory and space exploration?

AT: Remember, theories explain the facts as we see them today. New theories may emerge in the future and some scientists in the future may laugh at the theories that we believe today, just as many of us science-lovers

82 *Bharati Fantasy*

today laugh at the theories believed in 200 years ago. Now, I am not saying that we should move away from science. Of course not. I am a lover of science and according to those who follow the ancient way (Hinduism is one of the few surviving ancient ways), science is one of the paths of knowledge that leads to God. It's called *gyan yoga*. There are other paths to God as well, like the path of *karma* or action; the path of bhakti or love/devotion. What I do advise against is in any arrogance due to the knowledge that one possesses because there is always a lot more to learn and arrogance can stop you from learning more, and hence stop your spiritual development. There is a beautiful hymn in the *Rig Veda* called the *Nasadiya Sukta* which exemplifies this ancient Hindu spirit that nobody can really know everything. The hymn initially asks various questions about how creation could have happened, then posits some theories, but the beauty is in the last lines. The English translation of the last lines are as below:

> But, after all, who knows, and who can say
> Whence it all came, and how creation happened?
> the Gods themselves are later than creation,
> so who knows truly whence it has arisen?
>
> Whence all creation had its origin,
> He, whether He fashioned it or whether He did not,
> He, who surveys it all from highest heaven,
> He knows – or maybe even He does not know.

This was the spirit of scepticism in ancient India, which allowed science, atheism and religiosity to coexist peacefully with each other.

EDV: Amish Tripathi, thank you.

3.6 Interview with Author Shatrujeet Nath

Author biography: Shatrujeet Nath has sold ice creams, peddled computer training courses, written ad copy and reported on business as a journalist and assistant editor at *The Economic Times*. In 2009, when he was very much at the top of his game, Shatrujeet quit journalism to write fiction. His first book, *The Karachi Deception*, was a spy thriller, published in 2013. His next book was *The Guardians of the Halahala*, the first volume in the Vikramaditya series, with *The Conspiracy at Meru*, the second volume in the series, released in 2016. Shatrujeet is also the co-founder of JokerStreet, a content creation company. He divides his time between writing fiction and poetry, reading, playing with his daughter – and dreaming of buying a small castle in Scotland. Till that happens, he plans to continue living in Mumbai.

E. DAWSON VARUGHESE: Shatrujeet Nath, there is a prevailing notion that history is taught through books, formal education and in some cultural contexts, by the fastidious learning of 'key dates'. What are both your thoughts and experiences of this notion of learning history? Has your experience impacted the manner in which you conceptualised *The Guardians of the Halahala* and the storylines, the characters within it?

SHATRUJEET NATH: One of the biggest problems that I have experienced with the way history is often taught is that the subject is presented to pupils more as a chronology of important events than as a deeply interwoven narrative of human nature and evolution. The accent on 'key dates', as you put it, is a direct fallout of this approach to teaching. The problem with this approach to inculcating history is that what students take away with them are 'factoids' – disjointed and aseptic nuggets of information, with none of the subtle glue that holds all of it together and helps us make sense of the bigger picture. I do understand that history, in its totality, is very large and unwieldy and diverse, but a storytelling approach to the subject is better suited to understanding how the mechanics of so many different and small events spread across a large geography have influenced and changed the outcome of collective human history.

To take just one example, students everywhere routinely study about how the Spanish and Portuguese armadas explored and 'discovered' the Americas and India in the late 15th century. What they hardly ever learn about is the capture of the Byzantine capital of Constantinople by the Ottoman Turks in the mid-1400s, which blocked the overland trade routes between Europe and Asia, and forced powers like Spain and Portugal to look for an alternate trade route to India. In many ways, the fall of Constantinople paved the way for the eventual colonisation of the Americas and large parts of Asia. A war between two powers had such far-reaching consequences, yet students almost never learn of it. Why? Because the focus is all on the important milestones and in the memorising of the dates, as opposed to a contextual understanding of how the world we live in has come to be. The really important and interesting bits frequently fall in the interstices between milestones.

History is an elaborate, sprawling narrative of human ambition and initiative, a point that is so often missed in this obsession with milestones and dates. Take the *Ramayana* and the *Mahabharata*, the two epic narratives of India. Both have been termed as 'myths' by Western scholars because there is practically no documented evidence attached to the events that occur in either narrative. But, in some ways, these are deeper histories because they are 'remembered and shared histories' or histories documented in the mind. In these epics, less importance is attached to dates and timelines, and more to human motivations and the political and societal outcome of these motivations. Yes, there is likely to be exaggeration in these histories, there will also be conjecture, but which historical account is truly immune to bias, exaggeration and conjecture?

While conceptualising *The Guardians of the Halahala* – and the larger Vikramaditya series that the book is a part of – I was clear that I would not be bound by the pressure of history. Historical accuracy was anyway not the purpose of the series. It helps that this is a fantasy series centred on a legendary king, still there were obvious questions like what era the series would be set in, would the events in the series precede or succeed the *Ramayana* and the *Mahabharata*, how true will I be to what is known of ancient Indian society and politics et cetera. My objective with this story was not to present a historically accurate picture, but to narrate a human tale of survival against all odds.

EDV: There is a revival of sorts as tales of ancient (pre-)India are explored through contemporary fiction in India; *The Guardians of the Halahala* is part of this renaissance. What are your thoughts on this movement – might such a revival somehow combat a sense of engulfing 'Westernisation'? Or is India's own sense of modernity, independent from Western notions/influences of modern life enough to stem the flow of such Westernisation (if this is indeed the case)?

SN: Indeed, there is a general revival of interest in ancient India – or Hindu India, if I may use the phrase. This is quite in keeping with the new Hindu assertiveness that is prevalent in India these days. However, I must add that when it comes to fiction writing in India, authors writing in Indian languages – be it Tamil, Marathi, Malayalam or Kannada – have always drawn inspiration from the tales and legends of ancient India, and they have always enjoyed readership in their chosen languages. It is only now that Indians writing in English have started exploring the myth-based fiction sub-genre, so it feels like a new trend in contemporary Indian fiction.

Coming back to your question, many Indian authors writing in English are naturally drawn to the tales that they heard from their mothers and grandmothers as children. These are typically tales from our past, tales that are probably no longer as commonly narrated in families as they once were due to the gradual phasing out of the joint family system and its replacement with an increasing number of nuclear families. These tales present a ready catchment of ideas for authors, and there is a ready and receptive audience that can be appealed to, provided these tales are retold nicely. To my mind, the contemporary Indian author's desire to repackage old myths and legends for Indian readers is not very different from a Western author's decision to repackage a vampire-and-werewolf narrative or a quasi-Medieval epic saga or an alien/zombie invasion tale for Western readers. The vampire-and-werewolf narrative, the Medieval epic and the alien / zombie threat are all a part of Western mythology, so to speak. That said, I do not see the celebrating of ancient India in contemporary Indian fiction through the prism of the East-versus-West debate. For one, in many instances, the inspiration for telling or retelling these Indian tales comes from reading the works of Western authors. Most contemporary Indian authors have grown up reading Western authors, idolising them. Their works have, in many instances, served as a template and springboard for Indian authors. Yes, it is possible that some Indian authors may have decided to tell or retell an Indian story after reading something elsewhere – something like 'but we have a story here in India that is as good as that one, so let me write it'. The inspiration for my own Vikramaditya series sprang, in part, from the Arthurian legend. I have always been fascinated by the Arthurian myth, and when I sought to replicate the myth in an Indian context, I had a ready-made king in Vikramaditya, who is quite the Indian version of King Arthur. The other reason why I believe this current trend is not a reaction to 'engulfing Westernisation' is that the authors of these contemporary narratives are choosing to tell these stories in English, a language handed to us by the British, our erstwhile colonial masters. Our readers too are comfortable with the language, and harbour no fears of being swamped by Westernisation. I do not see this as an 'us-versus-them' scenario. Instead, I see these narratives as a synthesis – age-old narratives being given new form in styles that have been inspired by Western storytelling techniques.

EDV: Shatrujeet, I'd like to explore the relationship between mythology, *itihasa* and history with you. How do you conceive of both history and the contemporary moment as vehicles of intellectual and cultural enquiry?

SN: There is a fair degree of debate in India over what is mythology and what is *itihasa*. The Western-educated, scientific-minded, left-liberal is prone to terming the epics as mythology. The more conservative, neo-nationalist Hindu sees the epics as *itihasa* – or an oral documentation of history. So while the former dismisses concepts like the *vimana* (an airborne vehicle) and the *brahmastra* (an all-destroying weapon) as products of the imagination, the latter sees them as evidence of planes and nuclear warheads having existed in ancient India. I shall not pretend to have all the answers, but when put under the microscope of scientific enquiry, it does become hard to defend the epics as *itihasa* – or a faithful recording of history. At the same time, I would not put the epics down as pure creative concoctions of balladeers. I do think the epics are historical narratives at their core, with legions of poets and storytellers adding their own creative two bits down the ages.

If we were to take the *Ramayana*, there is broad consensus that Sage Valmiki was the original writer/archivist of the events mentioned in that narrative. It is believed that he was a contemporary of Lord Rama, and that he put down what he saw happen. The interesting bit is that Valmiki never refers to Rama as god – he only uses the term 'nar' or human. And there are many incidents missing in his original version of the epic – the most prominent of them being Lakshmana drawing the *lakshmanrekha* to protect Sita in the forest – which were added on in later versions by later poets and authors. So the evolution of the *Ramayana* narrative clearly shows later embellishments. What does that make it – mythology or history?

What I find interesting about the epic narratives of India is that they have been constantly adapted by their narrators to suit the prevailing sociocultural climate of their times. So, in a way, our epics are palimpsests – or malleable, constantly evolving histories. They are not a collection of cold facts, but a part of an ongoing discourse, existing in many versions, shaped and kept fresh and relevant through independent enquiry and narrative. In many ways, each version of our epics mirrors a historical time that reflects that particular era or geography's sociocultural mores and attitudes.

EDV: In *The Guardians of the Halahala*, 'ancient weaponry', 'teratology', 'seers' and 'strange technology/science' are all key aspects of the storyline. It is through these aspects that truth, *itihasa* and belief are all brought into question. How does the poetic licence that fiction offers help narrate these ideas and where do you stand in presenting such ideas as 'truth' or 'non-truth'?

SN: Creative licence is the bedrock of storytelling – without that, even cold facts would simply wither and die. As Somerset Maugham famously put it, 'The faculty of myth is innate in the human race. It seizes with avidity upon any incident, surprising or mysterious, in the career of those who have at all distinguished themselves from their fellows, and invests a legend to which it then attaches a fanatical belief. It is the protest of romance against the commonplace of life.' Poetic licence is very much the protest of romance against the commonplace of life. Speaking for myself and the Vikramaditya series, the use of concepts like ancient weaponry, teratology and 'strange technology' were not key elements to forward any philosophical point of view – they were simply narrative devices to add to the charm of the story. So, for instance, when I make a mention of the *suryayantra* or heliotrope that is used as a military signalling system, I am not conjecturing or implying that heliotropes were invented or used in ancient India. I have used the heliotrope merely as a device to show how clever my fictitious characters are in a fantasy tale. Similarly, the purpose behind beasts like the *vyalas* or the serpent-dragon Ahi in *The Conspiracy at Meru* is only to add fantasy elements and raise the stakes against my heroes.

However, there is an entirely fictitious legend that I have conceived and incorporated into *The Conspiracy at Meru* vis-à-vis the relationship between the *garudas* and the *vyalas* – two hitherto unrelated mythical beasts in Hinduism. The legend I have created goes like this:

The first *garuda* and the first *vyala* were twins born to Ayanemi, the immortal Mother Bird. Ayanemi first gave birth to the *vyala*, and the agony of childbirth made her scream. The scream became a part of the *vyala*, deforming it, making it ugly. But when the *garuda* was born, she felt no pain and her joy made the *garuda* beautiful. Ayanemi despised the sight of the *vyala* and grew partial towards the *garuda*, so when the time came for her to pass on the gift of immortality, she chose to give all of it to the *garuda*, ignoring the *vyala* entirely. Then, fearing that the *vyala* would steal her blessing from the *garuda*, she sent the *garuda* into the skies and cast the *vyala* into the fires of Naraka. Filled with rage and hatred, the accursed *vyala* swore that it would have its revenge on its sibling whenever their mother's scream fell on a *garuda*'s ears. That is why the *vyalas* are always screaming, and that is why the *garudas*, who had never heard such a fearsome sound before, died of fright.

For me, this little parable is a lesson in parental partiality, and the deep scars such partiality leaves on children. Poetic licence enabled me to tell a cautionary tale that to me holds a deep truth. Again, if you look at the premise of the entire Vikramaditya series, you will find a philosophy that is contrarian to the set religious/ethical discourse of good ultimately triumphing over evil. The underlying philosophy in the Vikramaditya series is about cosmic balance – which manifests in the need for good and bad to coexist. As Lord Shiva tells Vikramaditya in *The Guardians of the Halahala*, 'The universe is all about balance … The forces of light and the forces of darkness are there to keep a check on one another. If one becomes too powerful and starts overrunning the other, that balance will be upset. The tyranny of virtue is as unbearable as the stranglehold of vice.'

I am quite fascinated by the concept of Yin and Yang and harmony. I am equally drawn to the concept of Ardhanarishvara – the Hindu concept of Shiva and Parvati synthesised into a unity of all the opposite forces of the universe. Today, we as humans are perpetually seeking balance in our lives. For me, at a philosophical level, this story is not about good (traditionally associated with the *devas* in Hinduism) overcoming the bad (traditionally associated with the *asuras*), but about the tug of war between opposite, and the forces these opposites exert on the human being. Whether it is work–life balance, the mind versus the heart, materialism versus spirituality or even two voices of the conscience, the battle is eternal and it is for man to strike the right balance between the opposing sides. This is my kernel of truth, couched in a sweeping story.

EDV: I was taken by your 'Author's Note' which details how you 'have taken many liberties in the telling of this tale'. Could you expand on this idea for me please?

SN: I have taken all sorts of creative liberties in this story. In fact, the very premise of the story – the existence of the *Halahala*, the all-destroying poison – is a creative leap. According to legend, Lord Shiva consumed the *Halahala* that emerged during the churning of the Ocean of Milk, thus saving the universe from the poison's destructive powers. My book's premise, however, postulates that Shiva did not consume all the *Halahala* – a small portion of the poison remained, and that portion is what the *devas* and *asuras* want to get their hands on in their ongoing battle for supremacy. Again, according to one Hindu legend, Diti (the mother of the *asuras*) conceived a baby and undertook a hundred-year penance to make the growing embryo infallible in war. The objective of this penance was to eventually get the baby she delivered to destroy Indra, lord of the *devas* and arch enemy of the *asuras*. However, Indra came to know of Diti's plan, and according to legend, he used his thunderbolt to kill the foetus in Diti's womb. But the foetus was so strong that the thunderbolt was only able to break it into seven pieces (in some accounts it is even a hundred pieces), and from each of these, a *marut* (a minor deity) was born. These seven *maruts* later went on to become Indra's servants, and manifest as storm clouds. What the legend says nothing about is how the seven *maruts* born to Diti (an *asura*) became the helpers of Indra (a *deva*). So I took the liberty of creating an entire myth of my own of how Diti forsakes the seven *maruts*, and how Indra finds them and adopts them, poisoning their minds against the woman who gave birth to them and abandoned them.

The asuras and the devas have a common progenitor in Sage Kashyapa – which makes them cousins, if not brothers. Yet, there is very little in legend to tell us how the devas and asuras fell out, and what made them such bitter rivals. This is again something that I have addressed in my books. What I have really done in most instances is fill in the blanks with my own interpretation of what might have happened. As I have mentioned in my Author's Note, '... the very notion of "established myth and legend" is flawed, for mythology is a wellspring of possibilities, where many versions of the same myth can coexist in harmony. This is the way mythology always has been, told and retold by bards and balladeers, each teller giving the story a new spin. It is my firm belief that this is what keeps myths alive. This ever changing, ever evolving narrative is the beauty of myths' (Nath, 2015: 'Author's Note').

EDV: I'm interested to know your thoughts on how your novels are categorised and marketed. Your novel has been described as 'fantasy' in some reviews. *The Guardians of the Halahala* is published by Jaico and I wonder how important a consideration the genre classification of your novels really is and if this plays a part in choosing a publisher for your work?

SN: It is pertinent that you raise this point, for the decision to label the Vikramaditya series as 'an epic fantasy' was primarily mine. The series cannot be clubbed under 'mythology' for the obvious reason that I have taken many departures from existing/known myths and legends. While the series borrows events and characters from myth and legend, its texture and treatment are closer to fantasy. Had I stayed true to mythology by, say, retelling the *Ramayana* or the *Mahabharata* or Indra's story, it could have been tagged as mythology, but that was not the case. However, going by general feedback from the market, I think in readers' minds, the series broadly straddles the emerging 'mytho-fiction' space. Having said that, these tags are probably limiting at one level. I have had one reader tell me that she is poorly inclined towards reading mythology, and that she picked the book up only because a friend of hers strongly recommended it. She went on to read the book and loved it. So, in this case, the 'mythology' association almost harmed my chances of getting her to read the book. Inversely, a genre tag helps readers find books, and improves the chances of the book being picked up by lovers of that particular genre.

About your question on whether a book's genre plays a part in choosing a publisher ... well, the truth is that in India, right now, I don't think that is even a consideration. The reason for this is that all publishers in India publish a variety of books across genres, so for an author, it is more a case of which publisher you are most comfortable working with, which publisher offers you the best deal, and things like that. Having said that, Jaico is one publisher who has built its reputation on the back of a lot of self-help books ... or books that traditionally fall into the 'mind, body and soul' space. So yes, if your work is in that genre, Jaico would probably be the first port of call. For the Vikramaditya series, I think it was the excitement that Akash Shah (Jaico's CEO) displayed for the concept that clinched the deal.

EDV: What kind of reading has shaped your ideas about the topics explored in *The Guardians of the Halahala* – such as science, philosophy, belief? Could you cite any specific texts that have particularly shaped your thinking and writing over the years?

SN: As I state earlier here, the primary inspiration for the Vikramaditya series stemmed from a desire to create an Indian version of the Arthurian legend. When I started developing the idea of a brave and noble Indian king, I realised that I already had a prototype in Vikramaditya. There are so many tales and legends already associated with Vikramaditya that he is quite a popular folk hero – all I had to do was give him epic scale. The other important element that went into the creation of the series was my fascination with an aspect of Greek mythology – the fact that the gods themselves are envious of man. I found this quite intriguing, so I incorporated that aspect into my story as well by way of the *devas* and *asuras* hankering after something (the *Halahala*, in this case) that is the possession of a human king.

However, I think the real philosophical inspirations came from the old Hindu myths and legends themselves. One of the things that I have always liked about our mythic tales is our ability to see our gods as fallible. There are plenty of stories where Hindu gods behave in a petty and myopic manner, and where even *asuras* have good and desirable qualities. Indra, for instance, is lionised in the *Rig Veda*, but later stories show him to possess devious and weak character traits. Ravana, for all his villainy, was acknowledged for his wisdom – his ten heads are at times interpreted as a metaphor for his wisdom. Our willingness to look at the good and the bad in our mythic characters amazes me. It shows the degree of maturity that the previous generation of storytellers and their audience possessed. In fact, I sometimes fear we are progressively losing that maturity and are becoming increasingly narrow-minded in the way we look at and represent our gods and goddesses and epic villains.

EDV: Shatrujeet Nath, thank you.

3.7 Interview with Author Samhita Arni

Author biography: When she was eight, Samhita Arni started writing and illustrating her first book. *The Mahabharata – A Child's View* went on to be published in seven language editions and sell 50,000 copies worldwide, winning the Elsa Morante Literary Award, and receiving commendations from the German Academy for Youth Literature and Media and The Spanish Ministry of Culture. Samhita's second book, *Sita's Ramayana*, a graphic novel developed in collaboration with Patua artist Moyna Chitrakar, was on the *New York Times* Bestseller list for graphic novels. *Elle* magazine named Arni as one of twenty young upcoming South Asian writers to watch out for. Her latest book, *The Missing Queen*, is a speculative fiction mythological thriller and has been published by Penguin (Viking) and Zubaan. Samhita is an alumnus of the United World College in Italy and has a double major in religion and film studies from Mount Holyoke College (South Hadley, Massachusetts). Samhita spent six months in 2013 in Kabul, Afghanistan, working as head scriptwriter at Tolo TV. In 2014, Samhita was the writer-in-residence at FIND, the Foundation for India-Europe dialogues in Zagorolo, Italy, and was selected for the Charles Wallace India Trust Writing Fellowship at the University of Kent for 2015.

Samhita's personal biography: As an Indian child growing up in Karachi, Pakistan, I was drawn to the *Mahabharata*, an epic that told the story of two warring factions of cousins, disputing the right to rule over a kingdom. When I returned to India in 1994 at the age of eight, I retold the epic, returning to its anti-war message, exploring its shades of grey that, I believed, mirrored the ambiguities of the situation in 1994. Ten years later, I returned to India after studying in Thailand, Italy and the US. Again, I found myself drawn to another Indian epic – the *Ramayana* – an indissoluble part of conversations on the role of women, the Indian state, politics and identity. This fascination with the *Ramayana* led to two books: First, *Sita's Ramayana* that explored other, oral, feminist traditions of the epic – versions that are being whitewashed and forgotten today, when increasingly, one monolithic version of the story dominates. And second, *The Missing Queen* which drew upon my experience as a journalist in India and used the *Ramayana* as a means to explore the growing nexus between the media, corporate India and the Hindu Right. I am fascinated by the way that such narratives are used politically, and how conflict and politics, in turn, shape the best-known versions of these narratives. As a writer, I'm also eager to see how narratives can positively influence and inform society – and that desire led me to Afghanistan, to a job working as a script writer at an Afghan TV network, on a TV series created with the hope of changing perceptions and instigating cultural transformation. As a storyteller, I believe that my work cannot but reflect the world I live in. My job is not just to entertain but to use the means that fiction gives me to critique, provoke, inspire and question.

E. DAWSON VARUGHESE: Samhita, in *The Missing Queen*, there is a palimpsestic experience of 'time'. You layer what seems to be a contemporary or near-future moment with more ancient times as well as older 'contemporary' moments through references to a Cadillac, TV and an 'art-deco styled cinema'. Could you say a little bit about how you approached the crafting of time in your novel and why it is such a significant part of your narrative?

SAMHITA ARNI: I think the best way to talk about the concept of time, and why it is relevant when it comes to thinking about and exploring mythology today is to start off with an anecdote. A couple of days ago I was having lunch with a colleague of my father, Nitin Pai, who heads a public policy think-tank, the Takshashila Institute, in Bangalore. He was talking about Fareed Zakaria, who, when he came to India, happened to say in an interview that the difference between Indians and Americans – this is according to Nitin's paraphrasing – could be explained simply: Americans will ask 'where are you going?' whereas Indians will ask 'where are you coming from?' I think this is quite true and illuminating. I would extend Zakaria's observation into the realm of literature. I'm a big fan of writers like Asimov, and it seems to me, that in attempting to portray – as he does in his Foundation series – a society yearning, struggling to be a Utopia, exploring the ideas of good governance, he projects a political idea onto the future. And yet at the same time, his Foundation series, with its idea of 'manifest destiny', the economic empire built by the Traders, the relationship between Trantor and the Foundation, he is undoubtedly influenced by his own time – particularly by the circumstances of the Cold War. [Even his robot series – the Naked Sun and The Caves of Steel – explore the ideas of Plato's Republic (the titles refer to the Allegory of the Cave) and that of the Philosopher-King.] And in this, I would dare suggest that his fiction, at least when it comes to the Foundation series, is an illustration of Ursula Le Guin's insight – 'Science Fiction is not predictive, it is descriptive.'

Whereas, the interesting thing about Indian literature is that one could suggest that we haven't been quite as successful as the West has in producing science fiction, or even fantasy. I have often thought about this, and it seems strange to me – particularly when our own epic literature has such wonderful fantastical elements. Such imagination. Astras. Flying Monkeys. Bridges that cross the ocean. The Pushpak Vimana. And it is precisely these epics that have captured the political imagination – we map, we project our ideas of utopias, of good governance, onto the past – and not onto the future. We look to reimagine a golden age, an ideal time. And so we map our present onto the past, whereas Asimov and other Western science fiction writers – I would suggest – map the present onto the future. I think I follow the Indian trend, into bringing the past into the present or near future – and I use the epics not to imagine a Utopia, as most do today, but to suggest the frightening possibility that by invoking the epics as we do in mainstream discourse, and creating a Hindu Nationalist identity, we will actually create a dystopia – which is my great fear.

EDV: I'd like to explore the relationship between mythology, *itihasa* and history with you.

SA: That's a tough question and I think I've touched a little upon it in the last answer. We tend to blur mythology and history in this part of the world, our mythology becomes history and starts to have political ramifications. And yet, at the same time, the distinction between mythology and history is a Western one. I'm very interested in the work of Jung and Joseph Campbell and the sort of correspondence one can see between mythology and psychology. Is mythology a way of programming our subconscious? Or do these reoccurring patterns suggest that this is the way our minds work? And then, there is the question of history. Why is history relevant? My cousin, who is a history teacher, provides the following answer to this question – history in some ways is a study of the Self. It can make us or help us understand what it is to be human. We observe patterns, cause and effect. The Jains think of the study of history as the study of collective karma – I do not see these ideas as incompatible; both are the study of cause and effect. Mythology, too, if you look to these myths as explaining the subconscious patterns and impulses of the mind – is also the study of the Self, of patterns, of cause and effect. So these two things – mythology and history – often coalesce and overlap.

EDV: And by extension, I'd like to ask how do you conceive of both history and the contemporary moment as vehicles of intellectual and cultural enquiry?

SA: It could be argued that perhaps the reason we have a more 'backwards' view of time and history is possibly because, culturally, we have a more non-linear, circular understanding of time than in the West. And given this understanding of time, given the lack of distinct emphasis on the individual – mythology and history blur. Should we discard this circular view of time? I have found great solace in it, personally, even though it is non-linear, perhaps even non-rational. The linear narrative of time and evolution suggests that the world, and the human, are improving, evolving into something better. We have tended to map this idea of the great improvement onto our past – if things are better today, they must have been worse in the past. This is certainly the sort of concept of time and history that many in India struggle with, especially in regard to modernity and our discomfort with it, and how it has ruptured our sense of time and identity. And while I find this idea of harking back to a golden age problematic, there is, even for me, when I delve into the history of say, the 8th-century Cholas of Tamil Nadu, that they seemed to have a far more progressive attitude towards women and sexuality than the prevalent one today. For example, in the 8th century, the Chola king upholds the decision to make a woman the head of a Jain university/monastic centre, with a population of four hundred. So which narrative, or which view of time?

EDV: I'd like to focus on the idea of 'truth-telling' here as I feel it runs like lifeblood through your novel. This aspect of your work, like 'time', is layered and is also web-like in its appearance: it appears through the protagonist as a journalist and her ethics of 'telling the truth', through those who are 'hiding' Sita, through those who know of Sita's last movements (but not necessarily where she is), through the State and Ram's 'leadership', through the various anti-Ayodhyan groups (Lankans, Sam Bhoo Kha) as well as other more nuanced aspects of the storyline.

SA: I guess I view truth as subjective and not objective, that it depends on perspective, that there is always another side to the story. I think the debate over A. K. Ramanujan's essay, on many *Ramayanas*, that explores the various iterations of the *Ramayana*, to me explores this idea, that there is not one singular version of the story, or any story. Nabaneeta Dev Sen's essay on 'When Women Retell the Ramayana' also posits a tension between the oral traditions and textual traditions – with the oral traditions, the disenfranchised and the marginalised voice their very different take on the *Ramayana*. To me, there is a striking parallel between that difficulty in accepting multiple versions of one story, and our own difficulty, when it comes to the conflict between the state's view and the dissident view, and all the views in between, when it comes to issues such as Naxalism, Separatism (like United Liberation Front of Assam (ULFA), for example, the inspiration for Sam Bhoo Kha).

EDV: The role of the Washerman in *The Missing Queen* sets up an eerie and unsettling narrative of surveillance. Could you say how you came to craft the character of the Washerman, why it is that he appears as a spectral figure and how this characterisation dovetails with the speculative genre through which *The Missing Queen* is told.

SA: The novel is so long ago now that I have a hard time recalling writing it! There is a Washerman in the Valmiki Ramayana, he's the one Ram listens to and sends away Sita.

I thought it would be interesting to imagine the Washerman partly as a whitewashing PR rep, always interested in appearances and perception and projection – and the idea of bleaching dirty laundry – was a nice one to go along with that. And also, more sinisterly, as a cross with the head of an intelligence agency, who has to monitor and control perception and threat.

But he is symbolic more than real – that's why I kept him 'spectral' – I wanted my readers, who I imagined to be familiar with the Ramayana, to catch the reference to the washerman of Valmiki's Ramayana, and too much realism with this character could detract from that.

Speculative fiction is similar, or more encompassing, than science fiction. Speculative allowed me to explore some of what science fiction writers do, writing fiction that is more descriptive rather than predictive, but mapping this onto the past, rather than on the future. That dislocation, in some ways, I think enables us to use fiction, or the genre, as a mirror for our own time. The properties of the mirror, and thus the genre, allows us to skew or heighten the contrast, so as to bring out our issues, in greater relief.

EDV: Your biographical note often mentions your love for the epic narratives and the books that you have written echo the same: *Sita's Ramayana* and *The Mahabharata: A Child's View*. Could you share with me some of the key reference texts you consulted whilst writing *The Missing*

Queen and what kind of reading has shaped your ideas about the topics explored in it?

SA: Ramanujan's essays were enormously helpful when it comes to thinking about the epics, and identity, literature, folktales, etc. Paula Richman's anthologies on the Ramayana – many *Ramayanas* as well as *Questioning Ramayanas* – were of great help. So was Doniger's essay on Shadows in the Ramayana (I forget the exact title). As was Nabaneeta Dev Sen's essay 'When Women Retell the Ramayana'. There are, of course, a vast number of versions of the *Ramayana* that I read – from *Bhavabhuti*, to the *Adhmatya Ramayana* to C. N. Sreekantan Nair's *Kanchana Sita*.

EDV: Samhita Arni, thank you.

Notes

1. The manner in which *devas* and *asuras* have been depicted and defined through the epics over the centuries has changed significantly and although it is too simple to suggest that the former represents all things 'good' and the latter all things 'bad', this portrayal is fairly commonplace. This portrayal of 'good' and 'bad' is particularly true in genre fiction where the two groups are pitted against one another – see Choudhury's *Bali and the Ocean of Milk* (2011) as an example.
2. See Chapter 2, this volume, for a differentiation of Brahman and Brahma.

References

Arni, S. (2013) *The Missing Queen*, New Delhi: Zubaan.
Bhanver, J. (2015) *The Curse of Brahma*, New Delhi: Rupa Publications India.
Clute, J. and Grant, J. (1999) *The Encyclopedia of Fantasy*, London: Orbit.
Kishwar, M. (2001) 'Yes to Sita, no to Ram: the continuing hold of Sita on popular imagination in India', in Richman, P. (ed.) *Questioning Ramayanas: A South Asian Tradition*, Berkeley: California University Press.
Mendlesohn, F. (2008) *Rhetorics of Fantasy*, Middletown, CT: Wesleyan University Press.
Mishra, L. (2013) 'Ethical wisdom and philosophical judgement', in Amish Tripathi's *The Oath of Vayuputras Linguistics and Literature Studies*, vol. 1, no. 1, pp. 20–31.
Nath, S. (2015) *The Guardians of the Halahala*, Mumbai: Jaico Publishing House.
Saran, M. (2013) 'So many Ramayanas', *Biblio*, March/April.
Tripathi, A. (2010) *The Immortals of Meluha*, Chennai: Westland.

4 Bharati Fantasy
Modern-Day Sensibilities

This chapter looks at Bharati Fantasy texts which engage with modern-day sensibilities. This engagement is achieved variously – through the alternation of chapters from ancient to modern times as in Ashwin Sanghi's *Chanakya's Chant* (2010) or through a contemporary story prefaced by the life of Sri Krishna – *The Krishna Key* (2012) – or in the case of Pervin Saket's *Urmila* (2016), where the narrative connects India and Dubai in what reads like the recent past. Like Sanghi's novels, Christopher C. Doyle's *The Mahabharata Secret* (2013) also visits the ancient past. Although the narrative is set chiefly in the present day, there is a focus throughout the novel on the exploration of ancient science and how this scientific knowledge may be harnessed for use in contemporary times. Whilst Choudhury's *Bali and the Ocean of Milk* (2011) situates the narrative in ancient India, references to the modern day appear throughout, most notably through the performance of contemporary speech patterns and through reference to 21st-century technology.

4.1 Ashwin Sanghi: *The Krishna Key* (2012) and *Chanakya's Chant* (2010)

Sanghi's novel *The Krishna Key* (2012) is anchored in the life story of Sri Krishna, an avatar of Lord Vishnu and a widely admired Hindu deity, his life popularised through TV serials, calendar art and song in contemporary popular culture (Bhanver's novel discussed in Chapter 3 explores the time leading up to the birth of Sri Krishna). In the extracts of *The Krishna Key* discussed shortly, elements of the Weird – namely 'the numinous', 'awe at strangeness' and 'the subversion of traditional fantasy' – are presented through the analysis of extracts from the novel. Through extracts of another of Sanghi's novels, *Chanakya's Chant* (2010), teratology and the role of 'history' in narrating the present are discussed in some detail as well as 'timelessness', superstition and notions of predestiny. Vandermeer reminds us that defining the New Weird is ever evolving given that 'in some countries it has already mutated and adapted as an ever-shifting "moment"' (2008: xv). This statement is particularly helpful to the discussions here given that the body of post-millennial Indian fiction we're concerned with is itself new and evolving.

4.1.1 The Krishna Key

Complementing a map of the Mahabharata era, an excerpt from the *Rig Veda* prefaces *The Krishna Key*:

> Who really knows, and who can swear,
> How creation came, when or where!
> Even gods came after creation's day,
> Who really knows, who can truly say
> When and how did creation start?
> Did He will it? Or did He not?
> Only He, up there, knows, maybe;
> Or perhaps, not even He.
>
> *Rig Veda* 10: 129

Sanghi's *The Krishna Key* foregrounds the modern world, its preoccupations with science against a backdrop of Hindu numinosity and the final avatar of Lord Vishnu, namely Kalki. *The Krishna Key* is intersected with maps, mathematic expressions, diagrams and symbols and its narrative oscillates between modern and ancient worlds; we witness murders as the re-enactment of Sri Krishna's own death, revisit the lost city of Dwarka and learn how the Shiv lingam may be an example of an ancient form of nuclear power. Just as the novel opens with a citation from a Hindu holy text, each section of Sanghi's novel begins with an extract from the story of Sri Krishna's life. Sri Krishna is an avatar of Lord Vishnu.

It is not a coincidence that there are 108 sections to this 465-page novel. The number 108 is significant as 108 names are attributed to the Almighty, and the chapter sections work as an echo of this religious detail. The extracts which appear in the novel are taken from the *Bhagavata Purana* which chart the birth of Sri Krishna and his early years, and also from *The Bhagavad Gita* which tells of his time with Arjuna as part of the great war and thus this aspect of his life is also found as part of the *Mahabharata*. The structure of the novel – the 108 sections, each prefaced by a short paragraph about Sri Krishna's life – has a significant effect on the way the reader approaches and engages with the novel. The life of Sri Krishna portrayed through these spiritual texts foregrounds a sense of the numinous throughout, and this in turn dovetails with the contemporary storyline that Sanghi crafts as the main text. The numinous also appears in the main narrative (that is, the contemporary storyline), however it does not appear as benevolently as the numinous presence of Sri Krishna does in the prefacing paragraphs; in the main text, the numinous is dark and threatening.

The contemporary storyline revolves around a set of murders which are carried out in order for the perpetrator, Taarak Vakil, to seize four ancient seals. At each murder scene, Taarak imprints one of four symbols of Lord Vishnu on the victim's forehead using a rubber stamp – the four symbols being a discus, a lotus, a conch shell and a mace. After knocking his victim unconscious, Taarak kills his victims by thrusting a scalpel into their left foot; the scalpel remains in the foot, the blood draining gradually and the victim dies a slow death. This scene re-enacts the death of Sri Krishna, who, whilst meditating in the forest, is inadvertently shot in the left foot by a hunter's arrow. The work of Taarak is complete when, using the blood of the victim, Taarak inscribes a *shloka* (verse) in Sanskrit near the body – usually on the wall or floor near the corpse. The sense of a threatening numinosity is created by the religious symbols involved in the killings as well as through the 'invisible' commander that orders Taarak to carry out the murders. Initially, the reader knows only of a mysterious 'Mataji' who Taarak phones to report that the four victims have 'fallen'. Once the information has been reported, the remainder of the phone call is spent chanting as Taarak repeats after Mataji all 108 names of the Almighty (Sanghi, 2012: 19).

The numinous is further developed when we discover that the murderer is more than a mere human servant of Mataji – at least, that is, in the murderer's mind. The main protagonist of the story, Ravi Mohan Saini, a university professor, 'decodes' Taarak Vakil's name and an illustration in the novel depicts Saini's 'decoding' as arrows from Taarak's name link its letters to another name below, and an anagram is revealed: 'When jumbled up, the letters contained in the name TAARAK VAKIL now spelt out a name that every theologian in India would be familiar with. Kalki Avatar – the tenth incarnation of Vishnu' (96). So the name TAARAK VAKIL becomes KALKI AVATAR and thus the connection between the murderer and the numinous becomes clear – he believes that he *is* Kalki, the tenth avatar of Vishnu, the avatar to follow Sri Krishna.

There are moments in the novel where Sanghi creates a sense of awe through the mysterious and the supernatural. One such moment is when the protagonist Saini and his accomplice Radhika Singh travel to Mount Kailash in the Himalayas, looking for clues in their search for 'the Krishna key'. Mount Kailash is revered by Hindus as a holy place, where, it is said, Lord Shiva can be found in a state of perpetual meditation. The mountain is not easily accessible in terms of terrain but also geopolitically as it forms part of present-day Tibet. As the helicopter flies over the revered and sacred mountain, Saini is in awe of what his eyes take in; Saini does not simply see the mountain rising out of the great valley, Saini sees the gods – Lord Shiv and Lord Vish:

> Saini was able to see in reality that the six-pointed star symbolism of Mount Kailash was very much true. As he gazed at the mountain, he thought of the Sri Yantra, a symbol of energy used by Hindus around the world in their homes. (302)

For Saini, this symbol, the Sri Yantra, evokes an image of awe, a powerful response to an unchanging scene which links the ancient past to the everyday. At other moments in the novel, Saini and Radhika are met by three spectre-like figures, each one an aesthetic or a priest. At the Taj Mahal they meet a fakir, at Mount Kailash a sadhu, and at the Somnath temple, a pujari. These encounters are depicted as 'visits' and it is not clear if these men actually exist. Each of the three aesthetics bring the same message: 'the philosopher is more important than the stone' – a phrase that one character in the novel declares as 'spooky'. The three figures Saini and Radhika meet on their quest to solve the mystery of the murders are, like Mount Kailash, a bridge between the ancient and the present. Each man embodies a religious, philosophical tradition and these men are motifs for the search of the meaning of life (and death). They are strange in their spectre-like manifestation, yet their presence in the novel underscores the timelessness of human nature, the quest for meaning and the importance of living in harmony with the natural world.

It is whilst Saini and Radhika are on Mount Kailash that they become trapped in a freezing cave. The cave, however, is not a 'usual' cave, rather, this cave is known as the Saptarishi cave where it is believed ancient *rishis* gathered (see also my discussion of Nath's *The Guardians of the Halahala*, this volume Section 3.2). The cave is therefore, to those readers who may make this cultural connection, something of a mystical cave, possessing divine powers. Whilst trapped in the Saptarishi cave, Radhika is hit by falling debris and as the cave begins to close off, Saini, attempting to revive her, is unable to find a pulse; he surmises that she is dead. However, Sanghi writes how Saini remains hopeful: 'What Saini hoped was that Radhika was in forced hibernation – more commonly known as suspended animation. It involved the sudden halting of chemical reactions in the body due to lack of oxygen combined with freezing temperatures' (298). This rationalisation for an otherwise impossible prospect is expressed through ideas of science and belief. Sanghi writes how Saini had read research which had shown how it is possible to survive such forced hibernation. He recounts discussions with colleagues at the University of Memphis and 'documented cases of humans who had been successfully revived after spending hours without a pulse in extremely cold conditions' (299). Radhika survives the ordeal although we are not told exactly how this happens. Sanghi writes: 'He [Saini] briefly closed his eyes and opened them again as soon as he heard a sound. She was shivering and incoherently mumbling something' (300). The Saptarishi cave and its divine powers remains a quiet backdrop to this event – as readers, we are left wondering if indeed it is science that saves Radhika or the divine powers of the Saptarishi cave.

The interface of science and belief (Hinduism) appears in other parts of the novel. Invariably, each instance suggests that ancient civilisations have generated theory on significant scientific phenomena in advance of our contemporary era. Such examples include considerations on the 'Big Bang', land reclamation (70), surgery, medicine, genetic cloning (189) and even nuclear power (189). On this latter topic, the mysterious Mataji exclaims to Taarak:

> Oppenheimer, the father of the atom bomb is said to have quoted the Bhagwad Gita after witnessing the first successful test of the atom bomb in 1945. His words? I am become death, the destroyer of the worlds Oppenheimer had learned Sanskrit specifically with the intention of being able to understand the Gita [...] The clues to an ancient nuclear age are right before us in the ancient Hindu scriptures, my son! (42)

It is not only in Sanghi's *The Krishna Key* where science and belief are explored, *Chanakya's Chant* also features such discussion. Unlike *The Krishna Key* though, *Chanakya's Chant* also includes teratology. One of the characters in the novel is the *vishakanya*, and of the creation of this 'poisoned maiden', Sanghi (2010) writes:

[...] Chanakya has personally supervised the creation of an entire army of such maidens. His secret service would identify young and nubile girls whose horoscopes foretold of widowhood. These beautiful damsels would be sequestered at an early age and fed a variety of poisons in graduated doses, making them immune to their ruinous effects. By the time each of Chanakya's vishakanyas reached puberty, they were utterly toxic. A simple kiss with an infinitesimal exchange of saliva was lethal enough to kill the strongest bull of a man. (3–4)

Sanghi reasons how the creation of the *vishakanyas* comes about, as he explains the Vedic astrology behind their existence:

> The ancient seers of Magadha had observed that birth under specific positions of the moon made certain women extremely unlucky for the longevity of their partners. Girls born on Tuesdays during the seventh lunar day of Vishaka possessed unfortunately potent horoscopes that guaranteed that any man they cohabited with would die. (2010: 383)

Here, Sanghi offers a 'logical' explanation as to how some women are born to be 'poisoned maidens' (*vishakanyas*) and, in doing so, disputes any idea that the *vishakanyas* are borne out of superstition. It is 'the ancient seers of Magadha' who have studied the phenomenon and therefore know that certain women are predestined to become widows.

4.1.2 *Chanakya's Chant*

As we read above in the discussion of *The Krishna Key*, elements of *Chanakya's Chant* – and, indeed, other Bharati Fantasy – probe the thin line between 'truth', in the sense of reality (or coincidence) and ideas of astrology, predestiny and superstition. These worlds exist concurrently in this novel not simply through the juxtaposition of the two historical periods, arranged in their alternating chapter structure but, rather, embedded more deeply across the time periods in the actions of both the ancient people of Bharat – namely Chanakya – and Gangasagar, a man of 21st century India.

The 'chant' of the novel's title suggests both a timelessness and something of the magical. It is suggested that the recitation of the chant can bring about the realisation of a woman leader for India but the chant's instructions make clear that unless the chant is observed 400 times a day for over 4000 days, it will not result in actualising a woman leader, of the kind of powers and strategy that Chanakya held. The result of Chandini Gupta becoming the nation's prime minister might be understood as emanating directly from Gangasagar's observance of the chant, or, rather, it might be coincidental that Chandini Gupta becomes prime minister – she is after all groomed and educated by 'Uncle Ganga' (Gangasagar) to those ends; the power of the chant, it might be argued, is irrelevant.

Given that the ideas of astrology, predestiny and superstition run across the two eras of *Chanakya's Chant*, debate on the role and value of such philosophy in modern New India is evident, albeit quietly displayed throughout the narrative. Sanghi weaves in references to some of the modern-day cultural and societal issues of the noughties but instead of presenting this in the 'present-day' chapters, Sanghi presents these issues through the chapters set in 340 BC. This technique of joining the mutual concerns of two societies, set apart by over two millennia, results in the powerful message of the universal challenges of politics and society in general. Sanghi's narrative technique demonstrates how the issues of the Bharat people are still alive today; people and culture are still struggling with many of the same issues, two millennia later. Just as we see in *The Krishna Key* through the Saptarishi cave or through the unchanging natural world embodied in Mount Kailash, the bridge from the ancient to the present is manifest in the black granite tablet upon which the chant is inscribed. Furthermore, the novel extends the connection from past to present to future through the character of Gangasagar, who is so dedicated to making change happen for the better that he recites the chant 400 times a day for over 4000 days.

In linking the past and present, Sanghi explores societal debates from identity (and questions of Indianness), to farmer suicides and even war. Sanghi (2010) links these topics across the two millennia thus:

> 'It's unfortunate that the concept of Bharat – the common abode and cultural heritage of us Indo-Aryans – has been subjugated by petty rulers and kingdoms. Our scriptures, traditions, culture, prayers, and deities are common. Why is it, then, that we refer to our homes as Magadha, Gandhar, Kashi, Kosala, Mallayrajya or Panchala? Why don't we say that we're citizens of Bharat? It's this fundamental divisiveness that will bring about our downfall in the future.' (43)

> 'How many more farmers have to commit suicide because the tax inspectors of Dhanananda loot their grain? How many more soldiers must die in battle because their armour has been compromised to make wine goblets for the king's pleasure?' (7)

> 'Correction. In order to become a master, a ruler must profess to be a servant of the people.'
> [...] 'Acharya, is war the only solution to political differences?'
> 'Wise pupil, politics is war without bloodshed and war is simply politics with bloodshed.' (45)

Through the structure of the chapters in *Chanakya's Chant*, namely through the alternation of ancient times and contemporary times as well as through the exploration of common themes being as manifest in the present day as in the ancient past, Sanghi takes real-world problems, exploring them through fantastical tropes which, in turn, provide a complex narrative around the idea of history repeating itself, and the idea of Indianness, as India, in its 21st century avatar, evolves once again, at pace. Sanghi's *The Krishna Key*, on the other hand, raises darker questions around threatening forces, misguided belief and the killing of innocents in the name of God. Both novels, however, narrate their stories from the interface of science, history (and *itihasa*) and belief, and in doing so these narratives demand various receptions both within and outside of India. Sanghi's 2016 novel *The Sialkot Saga* is described as a 'business thriller with a historical twist' (see Sanghi's biographical note in Section 4.5).

4.2 Pervin Saket: *Urmila* (2016)

Pervin Saket's novel *Urmila* (2016) begins with an arresting scene. Urmila's artwork is causing riots outside the flat where she lives with her in-laws. Urmila has painted what her lawyer suggests should be described as a 'naïve nature scene' (10). It is a painting set in a forest with three figures lying sleeping amidst grass and flowers. It is a reimagining of the exiled Ram with his wife Sita and Ram's brother Laxman. Saket writes of the painting:

> The woman's shape and flowing sari produce a distinct 'S', her hair and garments following the breeze. A dark man faces her asleep, their hands clasped together even in slumber. But the willful loose end of her sari falls on the face of the other man who lies some distance behind her. (9)

As this depiction of Urmila's painting appears so early in the book's narrative, the image of the three people who are related either through blood or through marriage carries a powerful symbolism forward into the rest of the novel. Urmila creates this image and so is part of its construction but she remains *outside* of its very being; she is part creator, part observer, empowered yet disempowered all in the same moment. This complex and layered portrayal of loyalty and love both reciprocated and unreciprocated is the focus of the book.

Saket's novel reimagines the life of Urmila through seven key movements, each movement framed by a wedding vow as per the Hindu wedding tradition and the seven movements around the fire. In an echo of this timeless tradition, Urmila lives in an era that we recognise as contemporary, although it is difficult to identify how contemporary this moment really is. The narrative makes little reference to contemporary life as we might expect it to do – there is a curious absence of the Internet, mobile phones appear only a handful of times, although the TV advertisements, availability of Viagra, the Indian rupee sign – ₹ – selected in 2010, playing Ludo and Shree's journey to Dubai with his brother and sister-in-law are part of the storyline, thus situating it in something of the present day. Despite the (intended) ambiguity of era, 'time' structures and drives the narrative. We are told: 'Four years and counting' (26), 'Eight years and counting' (200) and 'Eleven years and counting' (218) as she waits for her husband to return from Dubai. Urmila tells us that she has mistrusted time from when she was very young: 'The day I learnt to mistrust time was slippery and with cunning. I was plumper than I was tall, a tot in oily pigtails with a handkerchief pinned to the pinafore' (101). This deep-seated, problematic relationship with 'time' haunts the novel until she is able to break free of its bondage, a separation which is linked to the breaking free of her husband, that is, the 'waiting' for her husband to return to her. As the years pass Urmila by, she comments on how she exists in this vacuum of time: 'Time played games with me – and not just the seconds and minutes. Whole hours, days and weeks would trick and tease me, until I learnt that it was capricious by nature' (105).

A key turning point in the novel is when Urmila lights her father-in-law's funeral pyre – a request made by the deceased in his will. In the absence of his sons (who do not return from Dubai to attend his cremation, something he anticipates ahead of his death), someone must light the pyre and as unorthodox as it is for a woman to carry out such a duty (women are not normally allowed to even *attend* a cremation), it is even more unorthodox for a father to stipulate that it is his daughter-in-law who should carry out this responsibility. Even in this scene, 'time' troubles Urmila as the priest tells her: 'Move anticlockwise [...] In death, everything is reversed. Use your left hand' (239). Urmila wishes to tell the priest that she is left-handed by nature but she resists; this detail of her nature links her to the idea of time reversal and thus we see later in the novel how Urmila goes about undoing all the years lost in waiting for her husband to return to her from Dubai by attending a fertility clinic in order to conceive a baby.

As Urmila learns how to deal with 'time', she learns how to deal with her non-existent marriage. It is a slow realisation and the narrative is peppered with moments whereby Urmila searches out possible reasons for why her life is unfolding as it is. Superstition stands in the way of truth and the novel explores this idea through key moments depicting irrational belief. On a pilgrimage to Rameshwaram with her in-laws, a trip to Dhanushkodi is arranged and the three of them – Urmila and her in-laws – find themselves at the edge of the Indian Ocean, looking across the sea to Sri Lanka. Saket writes:

> The spot where history, legend and mythology churned together, where one half of a couple embarked on a journey to find a beloved in a foreign land. Where a bridge once possibly stood, marking a union, however brief, a hope, however lost, and a love, however doomed. (36)

Through the references to the *Ramayana* and Ram's search for Sita, Saket finds an echo in the life of Urmila whose husband is away in a foreign land. However, as the novel reveals later in its telling, despite Urmila's hope, her love *is* doomed, her love *is* lost. In Saket's novel, it is only the character of Urmila which carries over a name from the epic *Ramayana* but the characters of Shree, Puroshottam and Vanita are manifestly representations of Laxman, Ram and Sita, respectively; this link is easily made with Ram, given that the name appears in Saket's text as 'Puroshottam' (which translates as 'the most ideal of men'). On the other hand, the word 'Shree' can be used to denote the short form of a name and more significantly, it can represent the everyday man – Shree as 'Mr' – but it can also be used as an epithet for some Hindu gods, thus the very opposite of being a 'Mr'. To Urmila, her husband is revered by her in the early stages of their marriage but as he distances himself from her, he becomes nothing more than an everyday, unremarkable 'Mr'.

A scene early on in the novel plays with the naming of the young women; having consulted a pundit with regard to Puroshottam's marriage, it is said that his marriage will be more successful if his wife's name begins with the letter 'S'. Here, Saket plays the contemporary narrative alongside the ancient one, referencing Sita through the idea that the marriage would be more successful if only Vanita's name was not Vanita but rather a name beginning with 'S'. It is Puroshottam and Urmila who openly reject such an idea whilst Vanita and Shree are in agreement with 'tradition' and thus in agreement with Shree's (and Puroshottam's) parents. Urmila's father-in-law states: 'Puro, Urmila, it's not all mumbo-jumbo. It's scientific. Chhotu, as per your horoscopes, your marriage will be more compatible if your wife also has a name beginning with 'S'. It will bring in lots of prosperity […] Harmony, peace, two children within a few years …' (72).

As the novel progresses, 'harmony, peace' and 'two children' are hard to come by for Puroshottam and Vanita, and consequently the novel revisits the idea of superstition and its part in not only their destiny but also the role of superstition in the destiny of Urmila's marriage. Even Urmila, whose position throughout the novel is chiefly disbelieving when it comes to matters of superstition, weakens on the night her husband leaves her to follow his brother to Dubai. She questions: 'Was there some truth in the horoscope reading? [...] Had the astrologer foreseen this? Would I have lived a different marriage if I had been a Sunanda or Savitri?' (78). Urmila recalls the preparation for her marriage and how her mother had taken her to get her ears and nose pierced so that she could wear the full extent of wedding jewellery possible on the day. She muses on the nose stud she now wears:

> On the wedding day, it was a Brahmani nath, with bosra pearls and rubies. Later I stuck to a thin gold band. Then I chose a diamond stud instead of the dangling metal. And now, a plain gold dot rests on my left nostril. (114)

The adornments have changed over time, lessened as the years have passed by and now the simple gold stud she wears symbolises the state of mind she is in with regards to her marriage. She muses that 'the last stage of hope is the abandonment of symbols. The symbols adorn me, simultaneously providing a mockery of my marriage and the collage of a dream. [...] For now, the rings, bindis, necklaces and sindoor act as substitutes' (114).

In keeping the name 'Urmila', Saket forms a connection with the past, with the epic tale of the *Ramayana*, yet simultaneously disturbs the original narrative enough to craft not only modern-day sensibilities therein but to thoroughly re-vision some of the story's central themes. The retelling or, indeed, reimagining of the *Ramayana* from Urmila's perspective deeply disrupts the epic's original text through an imaginative yet significantly unorthodox reformulation of Urmila's separation from Laxman (the character 'Shree' in Sakat's novel). More broadly, Saket's principal vehicle for disrupting the narrative of Ram, Sita, Urmila and Laxman is through the presence of the 'fertility clinic'. This trope appears in both women's lives but through very different circumstances. Vanita and Puroshottam visit the clinic in Dubai because Vanita suffers a series of miscarriages. In a loving relationship with Puroshottam, the couple is bereft at not being able to conceive and the money they earn in Dubai finances a string of fertility treatments. Finally, Vanita delivers a baby boy, the first grandchild of the family. Urmila visits the fertility clinic for a different reason. In the knowledge that she will not want to see her husband again – if he would ever return from Dubai – Urmila decides to go through fertility treatment in order to have a baby of her own. It is this decision that Urmila takes in Saket's novel that destabilises the novel's relationship with the *Ramayana*. Moving into a flat that she purchases with the profits from her artwork sales, Urmila is essentially embarking on the journey of a single mother, and mindfully so. This decision, even in contemporary India, is a bold one to make and the fact that the baby's father is unidentified further underscores how courageous Urmila is in taking such a decision. In a further echo of the *Ramayana*, albeit it a distorted one, Urmila delivers twins, just as Sita did in the epic. However, Urmila does not deliver boys, rather she delivers girls, a further twist to the already complex relationship between Saket's novel and Valmiki's *Ramayana*.

When Urmila meets Shree for the first time – they are introduced by the two families at Urmila's parents' house, where Urmila serves tea and snacks – it is Urmila's mother who sings her praises, telling Shree how she can cook wonderfully, sew and how she 'sings like a koel too!' (21). Urmila, embarrassed at such clear elaboration of the truth, stares at her mother who then 'whispered one truth, "She dabbles in art once in a while"' (22). Urmila's artwork is a key element of Saket's novel as it is a vehicle of personal expression as well as a form of personal income that allows her to move out of her in-laws' house once she decides not to wait any longer for Shree to return. This relationship between the deeply personal and the emancipatory 'practical' is a curious detail to the novel's storyline and yet functions as an echo of the character Urmila; she is both deeply sensitive to life, others around her and her own sense of fulfilment, yet she is practical in her day-to-day activities and in her approach to living without Shree. This combination of the emotional (and expressive) alongside the practical is revisited in my discussion later in the chapter. Urmila's artwork is described as specialising in 'Epic Art' (108), as 'distinctly feminist' (108) and drawing on 'Indian myths' (108) and is thus an echo of the novel itself. This layering of the reimagining of the *Ramayana* is made ever more urgent when Saket describes the paintings that Urmila creates within the novel's chapters. Urmila's artwork, in tandem with Saket's narrative, not only reimagines but re-visions the story of Urmila in the *Ramayana* by inscribing her experiences by way of both word and brushstroke. Through these vehicles of expression, Urmila is doubly manifest, each medium expressing the different facets of Urmila's character and importantly, of her situation. Her internal state of mind is captured on her canvases whilst the words of Saket's novel tell of her existence at her in-laws, the waiting she endures in the hope that Shree will return and the details of her day-to-day life, caring for her father-in-law, the duties of the house and her relationship with Vanita. It is the cessation of painting that Saket writes of in the closing pages of *Urmila*. Vanita asks Urmila how she is managing on her artist's salary, to which Urmila says, 'I get by ... and I conduct art classes too' (284). In fact, since Puroshottam, Vanita and Shree have returned from Dubai, Urmila has not created a 'half-decent canvas' (284). Her studio is stocked with the paintings she created in the years of Shree's absence, of which she says: 'now they don't speak to me; they are just heaps of dye and tangles of strokes. At one time, the pictures implored me ahead, charted my desires, but now they are quiet as a sunset' (285).

Out of the eight Bharati Fantasy novels discussed across Chapters 3 and 4 of this book, Saket's *Urmila* is the least 'weird' fiction if we use the definitions of the Weird according to Miéville and Vandermeer (discussed in Chapter 2, Section 2.1). *Urmila* does not include any revolutionary teratology, any awe at strangeness or even the creation of a 'weird presence'.

Rather, *Urmila* creates a sense of the weird through its anchoring in the old Indian epic of the *Ramayana* and its presence in the very contemporary moment. Unlike other Bharati Fantasy novels that move between the old and the contemporary in very manifest ways such as Sanghi's novels, Doyle's or Choudhury's (these latter two follow in this chapter), Saket's novel does not connect to the two eras in such a marked-out fashion. Nor does *Urmila* use the speculative to the extent that it is used in Arni's novel *The Missing Queen* (2013). Instead, Saket creates an era that is familiar enough to make sense whilst drawing on enough of the old epic in order for the storyline to make that important connection to the *Ramayana*; the result is a strange and surreal account of a woman and her relationship with, and to, her husband.

The strangeness that Saket creates lies in the juxtaposition of the old and new but this can only be found at the level of detail. The overarching themes of longing, disappointment, love and lament are all very visible across the narrative whilst at the small level of detail, the novel emerges as strange. The detail of the everyday – from making tea, caring for her father-in-law, hosting a *bhishi* (kitty) party, carrying out the responsibilities of the household with Vanita – is somewhat misplaced for a woman who is a successful artist and someone who goes on to buy her own flat and 'arrange' her own babies by fertility treatment. This curious situation is foregrounded by the surprising amount of time that Urmila spends *inside*, be it at her in-laws' home or at her parents' home.

In focusing on the relationship between Urmila, Shree, Vanita and Purushottam, Urmila's world is made small and it is the relationship that Urmila has with the world outside this sphere that renders the novel strange. There is a disjuncture between Urmila as the 'relative' (sister, sister-in-law, daughter, daughter-in-law, wife) and Urmila as a woman, independent of her familial connections. Interestingly, there is no tension in this disjuncture; Urmila is not portrayed as 'unhappy' living with her parents-in-law; in fact, that particular relationship is not simply exemplary in terms of respect, it is also a loving and warm relationship and it is aspects of the storyline such as these that destabilise the reader. The novel sets up a certain expectation for drama; the disappointment of a defunct marriage, the fact that Urmila remains living with her in-laws although her husband has left, the fact that she is unable to paint due to Shree's actions and, finally, the fact that this 'situation' with Shree goes on for years. The fact that Urmila is not presented as an 'angry young woman' in present-day India is significant in how this novel's strange presence is formulated (indeed, we are told early on in the novel by Urmila's mother that Urmila is not your usual woman – 'Our daughter is a little shy, don't mind. Nowadays, girls are so outspoken …' [21]). In disrupting a more typical or expected plotline, the reader is destabilised and questions how such a novel might be contemporary and, for readers outside of an Indian frame of reference, how such a character can be 'believable' (in the narratological sense of the word).

It is this destabilising of the reader's expectations, coupled with the novel's preoccupation with 'time' that results in a strange, slightly speculative narrative. The detail of Urmila's day-to-day life reveals a very slow and unhurried existence; she is after all, waiting. Time therefore manifests at growing levels as the novel progresses; in minutes as the urgency of the rioting outside the flat demands new levels of security, in days as she prepares to marry and following the wedding ceremony, in more days as she waits for Shree to accept her, to love her. This waiting turns into months and, then, as Shree follows his brother to Dubai, Urmila's waiting turns to years. Near the end of the novel where Urmila decides to seek fertility treatment, her waiting turns inward and she waits only for herself – to be ready for the treatment – and then for her baby to arrive. This movement from an external to an internal state of waiting culminates in the delivery of new life, thus a manifest, tangible outcome of waiting. Moreover, the arrival of this new life signals the advent of the marking of time through developmental, progressive events (crawling, walking, talking, etc.), all of which are activities outside of Urmila herself, yet, unlike those external events she has known through her marriage to Shree, her babies' developments are positive and full of hope.

4.3 C. C. Doyle: *The Mahabharata Secret* (2013)

C. C. Doyle's *The Mahabharata Secret* (2013) opens with a 'Prologue' which sets the context for the rest of the novel through its mention of Emperor Ashoka and a secret 'that could destroy the world' (xii). There is also mention of this secret being buried within the *Mahabharata* and at the close of the Prologue, there is a scene from 2001 where a description of the Bamiyan Buddhas being destroyed by the Taliban is given. The novel then moves to the present day where a man, Vikram Singh, is murdered – by decapitation – in his home, 130 km from New Delhi. The intruders swiftly disable his super-sophisticated security system, constructed to keep out those that would eventually come calling for him. Despite the intruders' swift manoeuvres, Vikram has enough time to send on 'information' via email to his nephew Vijay in the US; he sends five emails and the information in them is both cryptic and brief. The first email simply says '9!', the second email points the nephew to *The Bhagavad Gita*, the third mentions the edicts of Ashoka the Great, the fourth email tells him to 'seek out the Nine' and to 'follow the path of truth and you will find your way through any illusion' (8) and the final email simply tells him to talk to 'Greg White'. Thus, as with other Bharati Fantasy novels (such as Sanghi's) the novel's opening pages read like a thriller although the reader does not have to wait long before 'weird' aspects begin to appear on the page.

Police inspector Homi reveals the nature of Vikram's murder to Vijay, explaining that his uncle Vikram was not simply decapitated – there was no trace of blood on the floor – rather the autopsy had revealed that the blood vessels in the neck had been sealed at the moment of the murder. Homi says: 'It is as if they'd been cauterised at the same time that they had been cut, without a single drop of blood being spilt. A physical impossibility; yet, there's no denying it' (14). This statement embodies much of Doyle's approach to the storyline of *The Mahabharata Secret*, specifically in terms of truth-telling and 'truth-knowing'. We learn later in the novel that Vikram is killed by a *Sudarshana Chakra*, a spinning disc made up of two plates with 'a hairline joint between them' (247). We are told that 'all that everyone's seen are artists' impressions, which invariably show the *Chakra* severing heads with blood flowing like a fountain' (246). Here we see that the legitimacy of how the *Chakra* 'really' works is compromised through the way (contemporary) culture has represented it. This disjointed understanding of the ancient weapon and the contemporary representations of it are captured in the following sentence spoken by one of the main characters in the novel, Maharaja Bheem Singh, as he describes the *Chakra* as being: 'quite advanced for a weapon that is thousands of years old' (246).

There are other points in the novel where similar instances of 'truth' and 'reality' do not seem to jointly configure. It is through such exploration that the story of 'The Nine Unknown Men' (also known as 'the Nine') is brought out of its mythical status, posited to be 'true' according to 'evidence' found in a German anthropologist's notebook by the Maharaja Bheem Singh. Bheem Singh shares the notebook with a historian, Greg White, who is taken aback by what he reads. The anthropologist's entries unveil Sanskrit inscriptions (which he has presumably copied whilst out in the field – at The Temple of The Tooth, 200 miles from Lhasa, Tibet, we are told) revealing information about a 'secret brotherhood called the Nine Unknown Men' (18). Greg White, whose special academic interest is in the Magadha empire, reads through the notebook with enthusiasm, exclaiming: '"So it *is* true," White could hardly believe it. "The legend of the Nine isn't just another myth"' (18).

It is the (non-)existence of the Nine that dominates the storyline of *The Mahabharata Secret* and the questions around the existence of the Nine are anchored in belief, truth-telling and 'history' (in both Western and Indian senses of the word, thus also *itihasa*). It is the character of Bheem Singh who reveals the true purpose of the Nine when he says: 'It is believed that Asoka, having renounced violence, wanted to ensure that the scientific advances made by mankind were not put to military use or to cause destruction and death' (55). As Bheem Singh continues to give details about the Nine's activities – its research in cosmology, psychological warfare, chemistry – it is Colin Baker, Vijay's American friend (they met at MIT as students) who questions the legitimacy of the Nine and their work. This moment in the novel sets up what Banerjee (2014: 15) writes of as the 'inherent concerns with fundamental epistemological and ontological questions that often separate Indian and Western societies'. Indeed, as a non-Indian, Colin Baker is the one person in the group to question what is being presented to him, to Vijay and to the others. Bheem Singh is careful in his response, stating that he doesn't believe in the *legend* of the Nine. Greg White clarifies that Vijay's uncle actually 'believed in the *existence* of the Nine, but not in the legend of the nine books written by them or any other fantastic stories about them' (Doyle, 2013: 56, original emphasis). Here, Doyle layers ideas of truth, history and legend and to make the matter of the Nine even more cryptic, Bheem Singh suggests that 'all the other myths and stories about the Nine were fabricated to conceal this great secret from inquisitive minds and prying minds' (57). The notion that stories are fabricated to conceal great truths further layers the ideas of truth and history, feeding into the idea of 'the secret' at the heart – and in the title – of Doyle's book.

Evident also, as we read earlier in Sanghi's *Chanakya's Chant* the idea of (ancient) history repeating itself, *The Mahabharata Secret* uses the contemporary moment of 'terror' and Islamic militancy to fulfil this same narrative technique. Just as Vijay is looking for the secret of the Nine following his uncle's brutal murder, a shady character called Farooq enters the scene. Having belonged to Al-Qaeda, and more latterly Lashkar-e-Taiba Farooq is looking for the secret in order to galvanise his terrorist activities. Harnessing the Nine's secret scientific knowledge for terrorist endeavours goes against everything the Nine was (supposedly) set up to do – to protect scientific knowledge from those who would use it to wreak harm and destruction. As part of the storyline, Farooq uses one of the 'ancient weapons' he has already found in his pursuit of the Nine. He uses it to blow up a vault door. Doyle (2013) writes of the weapon Vijay sees Farooq's men handling:

> [T]o his amazement, he saw three of them carrying a metal pedestal with a heap of metal piled on top of it into the truck. Was it the contraption they had seen? But that had been seven feet tall! It was almost as if they had been able to fold it into something that was not more than two feet tall. And they carried it as though it was not too heavy. (73–74)

It is only later in the novel that Farooq reveals the details of the weapon that Vijay had seen being loaded into the truck:

> 'One of the original weapons,' Farooq beamed. 'Not one of the replicas we built. Imagine it. A weapon thousands of years old, still in pristine working condition. And amazingly lightweight as well. That metal – we couldn't figure out its composition – was lighter than aluminium or even carbon fibre.' (262)

The weapon that Vijay sees is actually viewed through the car's rear-view mirror as he is driving away from the men who are in pursuit, the weapon he sees is described through the language of conjecture and surprise. The viewing of it through an indirect means, the rear-view mirror of the car, further adds to the uncertainty and to the speculation. Vijay's disbelief that such a weapon could exist is countered by Farooq's description of the weapon later in the novel. Farooq describes the weapon in concise and celebratory terms; the short, clipped sentences highlighting awe at the fact such a weapon exists. Yet Farooq's description also depicts the weapon as surreal; after all, no one can 'figure out its composition' (262) and it is not identifiable by any known lightweight metals such as aluminium or even carbon fibre.

In allowing the scientific knowledge to make its way into the hands of Farooq, Doyle's storyline suggests that the Nine's scientific knowledge is available to anyone who has the capacity to 'decode' it. The storyline, however, is somewhat controversial when we realise that those wishing to access the secret are not only acting with ill intent but are also acting as terrorists, killing mercilessly in order to follow their goals. This contemporary connection with Islamic fundamentalism is made all the more challenging when we think that it is through the knowledge of (supposedly) ancient Hindu scientific discoveries that Islamic terrorists are able to destroy and murder innocent people in the present day.

As Chapter 2, Section 2.2 ('Bharati Fantasy: *itihasa*, myth and the Indian scientific imagination') has already detailed, the popularity of *The Bhagavad Gita* within and outside of India is due to its divine authorship, together with its compactness (thus being more easily translatable) and its accessibility as an introduction to Hinduism. The same divine text is invoked in Doyle's storyline as Vikram's second email to his nephew instructs Vijay to 'study, the *Bhagavad Gita*, it is the source of much knowledge. The subject of the Gita, though mixed up, is a mark upon us for our future lives and will lead you through the door to knowledge, which you must unlock' (7). In anchoring the storyline in *The Bhagavad Gita*, Doyle connects the search for the 'secret' with the *Gita*'s philosophy for life which is known by the five basic truths of *Isvara, Jeevas, Prakriti, Samay* and *Karma*. Once again, the narrative is layered in terms of truth-telling, truth-knowing and *itihasa* and as a result, it is only Vijay and the other Hindus (we know this by their character names at least) that eventually 'unlock' the truths. In the cryptic email, it is Vijay who spots '*Karma*' in the words 'A mark' (as an anagram) and it is Radha who decodes 'Study', pointing out that Vikram is asking his nephew to 'look deeper within', which Radha does by looking deeper within the email itself, focussing on the word 'study', noticing the comma that follows it and arriving at the idea that 'study' is most likely being used as a noun and not as a verb. The group return to Vikram's 'study' where they quickly unravel further clues. It is this layering of hidden meanings, by extension (supposed) truths, that render Doyle's novel somewhat fantastical. Doyle subverts traditional fantasy through his choice of a real-world 'thriller' context, employing fantastical tropes through the search for utopian truths (this is enacted mainly through the anchoring of the story in *The Bhagavad Gita* and the *Mahabharata*) and through the inclusion of fantastical weaponry.

The depiction of celestial weaponry (used by Farooq and his allies as well as by Bheem Singh) is significant in terms of its fantastical inclination as well as by the fact that these weapons are directly attributed to *itihasa* texts. Farooq uses such a weapon in order to access a vault where he believes a disc that he needs urgently is being held. The intelligence officer, Imran Kidwai, consulting a forensic report, says to his chief:

> 'They couldn't identify the explosive residue. [...] But eyewitness accounts say that it wasn't a bomb that went off there.' [...]
> 'Several people described the attackers as possessing a large contraption that was used to fire a projectile at the vault door; a contraption in the shape of a bow. In fact, one eyewitness even called it Lord Shiva's bow.' He snorted. (87)

Later in the novel, the same intelligence officer, Imran Kidwai, investigates the activities of Bheem Singh and discovers that Singh is planning to wipe out the leaders of the G20 countries in order to control the most economically powerful countries in the world (225). Holed up in Bheem Singh's subterranean vault, Imran is shown an array of 'celestial weaponry'. Bheem Singh announces:

> 'Look around you. What you see are some of the so-called celestial weapons from the Mahabharata: ancient designs used to create modern weapons in modern factories. Whatever the truth behind the Mahabharata and its historical authenticity, those weapons existed ...' (226)

In marrying the ancient with the modern, Bheem Singh and Farooq foreground the idea that war appears as 'timeless'. Across the eras, wars have been waged, military campaigns fought for and land, power and knowledge fought over with many and varied consequences. In *The Mahabharata Secret*, Doyle's storyline goes as far as to suggest that Farooq's plan of terror can only be enacted with information from the past. Having developed an 'invisibility shield', Farooq reveals to Vijay that 'our prototype is not completely invisible. We've missed something vital in putting it together; which is why we need the original shield or the blueprints of the technology to put it together again' (310).

It is Vijay and his friend Colin who discover 'invisibility' in the passageway that allegedly leads to the Nine's cavern in the hillside. Following a row of suspended stone pillars, the men step on to 'nothing' to find that their feet hit a hard surface – a bridge. Doyle writes: 'Colin found it and stepped on to it. He looked down at his feet. It seemed uncanny, standing on what seemed like thin air, with the dark waters of the lake clearly visible directly below his feet' (333). In following Vikram's cryptic emails, Vijay and Colin find *satya* (truth) in *maya* (allusion) and make it through the passageway, over the lake and into the cavern of the Nine. The cavern reveals the secret: the *vimana parva*. Vijay exclaims: 'This is the fleet of aircraft that the King of Magadha had built to defeat the Pandavas' (350). In choosing to make the *vimana parva* the 'secret', Doyle connects with the thousands of years of conjecture about the 'flying vehicles' of ancient times. Here, for those readers with little knowledge of the epics, the idea of the *vimana* is a fantastical one. For those with knowledge of the epics and with the inclination to believe these epics as *itihasa*, the idea of the *vimana* may present something of a challenge – or not. Vijay questions how such vehicles could be possible: 'Remote-controlled drones, like stealth bombers, flying over battlefields thousands of years ago? How does one explain the existence of this kind of technology in prehistoric times?' (350). As the novel closes, the cavern in which the *vimana* are found is destroyed as Farooq and his men attempt to ransack the cave in search of the blueprints for the *vimana* (and, importantly, the invisibility shield). Indian special forces storm the cavern, battle ensues and the 'unstable explosives' (367) of the *vimana* are detonated. The cavern is blown up, the hill in which the cavern was located is decimated generating a 'seismic shockwave' (367) which shatters the windows of the SUV that Vijay and the others are driving away in. No trace of the *vimana* is left in the hillside and thus the 'secret' is gone forever. In keeping with the idea of truth-telling, Vijay is not wrong in stating that 'the secret was now destroyed and beyond the reach of anyone' (382), however, back in his uncle's house, Vijay makes his way to a room containing a huge mural depicting the battlefield scene of the *Mahabharata*, wherein Sri Krishna counsels Arjun – a discourse known as *The Bhagavad Gita* – and hidden behind this mural, Vijay discovers a chamber. The space is filled with stainless steel tubes in which the 'secret' is actually stored. The secret therefore, is not actually destroyed and, in turn, it is Vijay who becomes the Nine.

Through this closing scene, Doyle foregrounds the importance of cultural and spiritual identity. Not only is the preservation of ancient Hindu knowledge kept alive, it is kept safely alive within a Hindu mind, unlike the threat of it being in the hands (and mind) of Farooq – a non-Hindu and a terrorist. In knowing the 'truth', the responsibility of carrying cultural, spiritual and scientific knowledge is significant, made more so by the fact that Vijay is young and represents, in a sense, the future generation of India. Doyle's narrative certainly speaks to ideas of the 'weird' through its engagement with the more speculative aspects of the epic stories. In bringing the reader to the edge of what may be possible, what may be believable, Doyle's novel explores an individual's relationship with *itihasa* in challenging ways, not least because the storyline focusses on matters of warfare and terrorism.

4.4 N. P. Choudhury: *Bali and the Ocean of Milk* (2011)

As the name of the novel suggests, *Bali and the Ocean of Milk* (2011) is anchored in the narrative of the Churning of the Ocean (*samudra manthan*) which features in the *Mahabharata* as well as in other Hindu texts (this epic is also discussed in Chapter 3, Section 3.2 as part of Nath's *The Guardians of the Halahala*). N. P. Choudhury's novel follows the lives of the narratives' two arch-enemies, Bali and Indrah, and how, both in need of *amrita*, the elixir of life, they work together to obtain it. The only way to release the elixir of life is to work together to churn the Ocean of Milk from where the *amrita* will be released. Bali, an *asura*, is the ruler of Tripura and Indrah is leader of the *devas*. The plot line is drawn along the lines of the epic tales of the gods (Indrah) fighting against the *asuras* (Bali), a good-versus-evil battleground in which the gods, through epic feats, sometimes resulting in epic disaster, fight for their worlds. Bali, despite being an *asura*, is regarded as a benevolent *asura* and the novel demonstrates his goodness despite his heritage.

Bali and the Ocean of Milk employs fantasy tropes, revolutionary teratology and like other Bharati Fantasy novels, plays with the idea of time, creating a sense of otherworldliness through an interweaving of ancient and contemporary sensibilities. The novel opens with a bedroom scene between the god Indrah and an apsara, Urvashi. She exclaims:

> 'Do you realize that we haven't made love one single time since that night? Do you? It's been two hundred years for heaven's sake and it's driving me up the wall. Come on, Indy darling. What's *wrong* with you?'
>
> (Choudhury, 2011: 2)

This early scene is indicative of the style in which Choudhury has written the novel. The narrative is clearly one inspired by the ancient text – the *samudra manthan* – whilst it is also littered with modern-day sensibilities, manifest in speech register, cultural references and the appearance of modern-day gadgets in the storyline.

Urvashi continues to complain about the lack of sex with Indrah, saying how she is 'a proper blue-blooded apsara, not one of those sad women from Earth who can go on for days without … TLC' (4), to which Indrah replies: 'TLC? What's that?' (4). The idea that Urvashi learns about practices on Earth of which Indrah has no idea resonates with ideas of globalisation and the Internet, both opening up vistas to seeing and living life differently. Indrah's reply is somewhat feeble, bemoaning his ageing body and mind. He is thankful when the couple are disturbed by a knock on the door. The reason for Indrah's malaise and most importantly the dissolution of his 'powers' is due to the fact that he unknowingly committed 'Brahminicide' (which according to Choudhury is when a Brahmin is killed by his own sword). With the elixir of life – the *amrita* – Indrah would be rejuvenated, his powers would be restored and, moreover, he would live eternally, that is, until the end of the Kali Yuga. On the other side of the story, the *asura* Bali, having recently survived an attempt on his life, knows only too well that other attempts will be made and so, for him, the *amrita* would mean that he would be sure to survive them.

The two enemies decide to work together to secure the *amrita* and thus plan to churn the Ocean of Milk as two distinct teams. Each team provides six members and by this, Choudhury names the project 'Oceans Twelve' after the number of those needed for the job. True to the epic story, the snake and the tortoise are used to form a churning stick to agitate the ocean. Choudhury writes:

> 'Easy, easy now ... not so hard ... owwww! That hurt real bad!' The giant snake hissed.
> 'Stop grumbling, will you?' the tortoise gurgled from below the waves. 'You volunteered for this job!'
> 'Sure, because you told me that we would be able to extract the nectar in a jiffy,' the snake replied. 'These damned guys have been pulling away at me for two bloody days now and we haven't seen the backside of a jelly fish. I'm sore and hurting all over, my bottom feels like it's been scraped with sandpaper. I am sick and tired of this tug-of-war!' (143)

The banter between the snake and the tortoise adds an element of the modern day to the story and the project's name 'Oceans Twelve' makes an obvious contemporary reference to the Hollywood film of the same name starring George Clooney and Brad Pitt. Moreover, the snake's Americanised exclamation of 'That hurt real bad!' further underscores a sense of the American and the modern.

It is during the scene of the churning of the ocean where the motifs of fantasy and the weird become more evident. The scene unfolds to reveal how the churning of the ocean results in disaster of epic proportion. As both the *devas* and the *asuras* fight to drink the *amrita*, a second jar of mixture is released from the ocean and before they can stop it, the top is released and the *halahal* powder is set free. The *halahal* powder is the opposite of the life-giving *amrita*, and consequently destroys the world, ravaging it with fire and smoke. Indrah escapes the anarchy on his chariot whilst Bali is left to survive, saving Prithvi, the earth goddess, on his way. Already this scene is replete with tropes of the fantastical, not least as Indrah leaves the scene on a chariot as the earth meets an apocalyptic end. However, the scene only increases in the fantastical as Lord Jai is summoned to save the world from complete annihilation. Lord Jai opens his mouth in an enormous yawn which draws in all the fire and smoke, saving the world from eternal catastrophe. For readers who are not familiar with the story of the churning of the ocean and the life-giving *amrita*, the plot and characters appear distinctly fantastical: the use of the tortoise and the serpent forming part of the churning stick, the idea that an ocean can be 'churned' and that such a substance as *amrita* might exist. Given that the presentation of this scene is not accompanied by a detailed construction of an alternative world (for Hindu readers this would not be necessary as the cultural fabric of this story would almost certainly be known), then the 'churning' scene might be construed as not only fantastical but also comical, given the references to American culture and use of American English.

In *Bali and the Ocean of Milk*, Choudhury includes teratology and, similar to Sanghi's use of the shape-shifter in *Chanakya's Chant*, introduces the *mayavi*. As a manifestation of revolutionary teratology, the *mayavi* appears in the novel only to inflict pain or death. The novel opens with a description of one such shape-shifter:

> It was about the size of a man's thumb but as it glided swiftly across the grounds it began to grow larger. By the time it had reached the wide stone staircase that led into the palace, it was almost half-a-hand long and thick as a fist. Black diamond-shaped scales were now visible along the length of its body. (7)

It is the *mayavi* appearing as a snake which goes on to attack King Bali, leaving him close to death. The king's personnel return to the room where he is found but no one or no thing can be found as being responsible for the attack. It is only much later in the novel that Bhrigu, the 'chief scientist of Tripura' (57) tells of the lump of mud found in the room where the king was attacked. He explains:

> All magical creatures, including Mayavis, revert to their birth form when they die – in this case a lump of clay. Traditionally, Mayavis are created from the clay of moon dust. The creator sows his own seed into the clay and gives it life. Don't ask how. It's a complicated process, but in the end, the clay can transform itself into different forms and functions, which is how a Mayavi possesses shape shifting powers. (72)

Bhrigu cannot explain how the process of creating the *mayavi* actually happens and this lack of explanation is understood as a marker of the genre of fantasy (see Roberts, 2010; Clute and Grant, 1999; Chapter 2, this volume). Indeed, Bhrigu simply describes the process of creating the *mayavi* as being 'too complicated' for explanation. Although the ability to shape-shift is a common fantasy trope, the idea of moving from one form to another has broader religious meanings here when considered with the Hindu tradition. Some Hindu gods are known in their various avatars and thus are identified through various names and forms. In this sense, these gods are also able to shape-shift, that is to appear as one and to then appear as another. Vishnu is mostly associated with various forms or avatars in Hindu scriptures, although Lord Shiva and Ganesha are also described as appearing in avatars. Although there is a link in terms of the ability to transform from one to another, the predominant difference between the two ideas, and this is explored in Choudhury's novel, is that the *mayavi*'s ability to shape-shift is primarily to attack or kill and in this sense the shape-shifting is for evil or negative ends. The avatars of Lord Vishnu, as an example, are not for such ends. On the contrary, given that Lord Vishnu is 'the Protector', Lord Shiva's forms are more eclectic in the sense that Lord Shiva appears as both creator and destroyer, foregrounding complementary forces of being, opposites in a harmonious existence.

As discussed above, for a readership with little or no knowledge of Hinduism, the idea of shape-shifting would most likely read as being of the fantasy genre and have little or no connection with Hinduism – *mayavi* or the broader notions of form-shifting and avatars. This blending of Hindu culture, practice and/or religion with 'fictional' sequences woven within is one of the most interesting developments within this body of fiction and as this chapter as well as Chapter 3 have demonstrated, is found through Bharati Fantasy texts to greater or lesser degrees. It is in Chapter 3 where the novels of Nath (Section 3.2) and Bhanver (Section 3.3) elucidate how poetic licence develops certain speculative aspects of the epic texts, wandering into the genre of fantasy per se. See in particular the author interview with Shatrujeet Nath in Section 3.6 for his responses to the use of poetic licence and the genre of fantasy.

As with other novels discussed in this chapter, *Bali and the Ocean of Milk*, despite its seemingly ancient historical context, weaves in tropes of the contemporary. Where Ashwin Sanghi's novel *Chanakya's Chant* moves between the ancient and modern through its chapter structures, Choudhury's novel brings together old and modern India within the same page. This confluence of old and new is enacted through the insertion of recognisable modern-day gadgets into the ancient context of the novel. In some instances, the gadgets are an amalgamation of the two eras, such as Indrah's 'high-pitched wailing' conch shell which he retrieves from his robes. It is vibrating, with a repeated voice in an irritating monotone saying: 'You have a message, you have a message' (Choudhury, 2011: 90). To receive his message, Indrah presses his forefinger onto the shell and a roll of parchment falls out of the conch and onto his lap. Such instances subvert a more traditional fantasy trope of an all-out 'invented' phone device; rather, here, both the ancient conch shell and the contemporary digital monotone voice (alerting the user to his message) are real world, thus resulting in a familiar yet unfamiliar phone device.

Choudhury also draws together the ancient and the modern through the figure of Privithi. As Indrah and Bali prepare to churn the ocean, Privithi, the earth goddess, has grave concerns about the damage the churning of the ocean will have on the ecosystem. Privithi is depicted as an ancient version of a modern-day 'eco-warrior' when Choudhury writes:

> She wore a plain cotton sari, the colour of young banana leaves. Her large dark eyes, usually wide open in dismay or delight, were lined thick with kohl. An oversized red bindi adorned her forehead and a

tiny silver ring flashed in her nose. She wore a tribal necklace made of wooden beads and matching earrings that rattled when she bobbed up and down during the course of her impassioned speeches. (78)

The attention to Privithi's choice of plain clothes and 'tribal' jewellery as well as her 'impassioned speeches' play to a certain stereotype of modern-day environmental activists in India as well as elsewhere, the return to 'mother-earth', which, in the case of Privithi, is embodied in herself as the 'earth goddess'. Privithi is dismayed at the thought of churning the ocean, stating her opposition strongly and reminding Bali and Indrah of how much the marine ecosystem will be destroyed by this very act. She shouts: 'Fellow gods, this is madness. Our greed is blinding us. The violence we inflict in nature will come back and destroy us' (83). Similar concerns are voiced within India today as the nation's economic boom of the noughties raises questions of 'greening' India, the installation of Liquefied Petroleum Gas (LPG) autorickshaws in the metropolises, litter campaigns and beautification programmes for urban centres. New India also looks to protect its *adivasi* or 'tribals' (a term used within India), their land and heritage. Arundhati Roy is a figurehead of the anti-globalisation/alter-globalisation movement and comparisons might be drawn between Roy's activity and the character of Privithi in Choudhury's novel, who voices the eco-concerns and consequences of the actions of the 'powerful' (in this case, the gods, Indrah and Bali) on the earth.

Protecting the earth is not the only social concern highlighted in *Bali and the Ocean of Milk*. Exploring the space between good and evil, Choudhury sets up a storyline whereby the evil Suketu, the priest leading the Brotherhood – responsible for the systematic killing of the Brahmins and who establishes the Moral Cleansing Programme within Tripura (270) – beguiles Bali, drawing him into the evil doings that the priest is involved in. Having had his life saved by Suketu, Bali is initially blind to what is happening around him. In time, however, Bali realises what is happening and unites with Indrah to put an end to the brutal programme of cultural cleansing. It is through this aspect of the novel that contemporary questions of Indianness are raised in parallel, exploring the ills of extremism within ideas of nationalism. Published in 2011, Choudhury's novel probes the idea of difference and discrimination, a timely and valid debate when we remember the Ahmedabad riots, Bombay riots, the rise of Shiv Sen and the Mumbai attacks of 26/11 in particular. Choudhury's novel foregrounds a sense of anxiety as the plot takes many twists and turns, and as the characters are loyal and disloyal at once – manifest above all through the shape-shifting – at times no one is really sure who is fighting for which side. Despite the theme of instability that the novel exudes at times, it concludes in relative harmony although this is couched in sacrifice. The novel closes as Bali and Indrah unite to kill Suketu, a battle which sees the benevolent *asura* King Bali killed by Suketu, and Suketu killed by Avani (Bali's queen) with the help of Jai. Indrah of the *devas* lives on, leaving Avani to rule over Tripura as he decides to return home to Amravati.

The novel underscores the cost of war built on difference and discrimination but, equally, it offers hope as Tripura, ruled by Queen Avani (the widow of Bali), is helped by Indrah to restore reconciliation and peace before he leaves to return to his own land.

Unlike other Bharati Fantasy novels, *Bali and the Ocean of Milk* engages in narrating the political (although Arni's *The Missing Queen* and Sangi's *Chanakya's Chant* do also explore the political in various manifestations). Anchoring the novel's politics in the ancient epic of the *samudra manthan* creates a certain distance from what appears at times to be clear lines of connection to contemporary Indian socio-political issues. The configuration of the present with the ancient past is manifest in Choudhury's novel in ways discussed earlier (gadgets, speech patterns as examples) as well as through the political echoes Choudhury creates at various points in the narrative. These types of strategies achieve what Currie (1990/2008) explains as: 'what is said in the text, together with certain background assumptions, generates a set of fictional truths: those things that are true in the fiction' (70). He goes on to say that 'anything that is true in the fiction is available for the reader to make believe' (71). Bharati Fantasy texts, as we have seen across Chapters 3 and 4, 'play' with certain truths and thus a complex, multilayered set of both truths and make-believe is constructed both within and outside of the text in terms of how the fiction is received. Currie refers to the relationship between the reader and the fictional truths (those things that are true in the fiction) as a 'game', suggesting that 'each work of fiction generates its own game, for different works of fiction differ as to what is fictionally true, and hence as to what is to be made believe' (71). *Bali and the Ocean of Milk*, alongside other Bharati Fantasy novels, invokes ancient India both in 'truth' and through make-believe and, as I have suggested in Chapter 2, it is the anchoring of the novels' narratives in *itihasa* that produce such a complex notion of truth-telling and 'truth-knowing' within the material product of a genre novel.

As we have seen in the analyses presented in Chapters 3 and 4, the creativity that, say, Choudhury or Nath (in *The Guardians of the Halahala*) or Bhanver (in *The Curse of Brahma*) bring to the reinvention of epic tales negotiates a space for a readership who has limited knowledge of the Indian epics, the line between 'truth' and 'fiction' is less connected if the reader is not aware of the 'original' (basic) premise of the storyline from the outset. We return to these thoughts as part of the concluding discussions in Chapter 5.

4.5 Interview with Author Ashwin Sanghi

Author biography: Ashwin Sanghi ranks among India's highest-selling English fiction authors. He has written several bestsellers (*The Rozabal Line, Chanakya's Chant, The Krishna Key*) and the *New York Times* best-selling crime thriller *Private India* with James Patterson. *The Sialkot Saga*

was released in the first quarter of 2016. Ashwin's first novel, *The Rozabal Line*, was self-published in 2007 under his pseudonym, Shawn Haigins. The theological thriller based upon the theory that Jesus died in Kashmir was subsequently published by Westland in 2008 in India under his own name and went on to become a national bestseller. Ashwin's second novel, *Chanakya's Chant*, a modern-day political thriller with its roots in ancient Mauryan history, shot into almost every bestseller list in India within a few weeks of launch. The novel went on to win the Crossword Popular Choice Award. The novel remained on A. C. Nielsen's India Top 10 for over two years. Ashwin's third offering, *The Krishna Key*, a fast-paced and riveting thriller that explores the ancient secrets of the Vedic age and the *Mahabharata*, was released in August 2012 and shot to number one on the A. C. Nielsen all-India fiction rankings within the first week of its release. Ashwin's fourth novel was a collaboration with James Patterson, the world's highest-selling thriller writer. The novel was an India-based crime thriller in Patterson's Private series and was released in July 2014. The book, *Private India*, hit number one on A. C. Nielsen's India Fiction list within two weeks and went on to hit the *New York Times* bestseller list.

Ashwin was included by Forbes India in its Celebrity India 100 Rankings. Educated at Cathedral & John Connon School, Mumbai and St. Xavier's College, Mumbai, Ashwin holds a master's degree in business management from Yale University. Ashwin lives in Mumbai with his wife Anushika and son Raghuvir.

E. DAWSON VARUGHESE: In your novels, you take the reader on journeys of time in the sense that your storylines play between the past and the present. Sometimes the past is the recent past whilst you also refer back to ancient times, the era of Sri Krishna, for example, in *The Krishna Key* (2012). Your work also explores science to lesser or greater degrees according to the novel at hand. Could you say a little about how, for you, the exploration of history (re earlier eras) and science in your novels elucidates some of the more pressing, contemporary themes of the post-millennial years.

ASHWIN SANGHI: As regards science, I have always maintained that God = Infinity – Human Knowledge. The ancient Egyptians saw the sun rise in the east and set in the west. They didn't know what the sun was so they made the sun into a God. They called him Ra. Ra woke in the morning and travelled across the sky in his chariot during the day until he stopped to sleep at night. Alas, in later years it was proved that the sun was a giant ball of flaming energy around which several planets rotated, thus causing the phenomenon of day and night. Once science could explain the notion of the sun, the planets and the mechanics of day and night, Ra lost his divinity. Divinity, in a sense, is that which cannot be explained. As we find rational explanations via scientific progress, we seem to leave a little less room for God in our lives.

I also believe that the ancients had far more scientific knowledge than we give them credit for. For example, the Big Bang theory tells us that the universe was created from a singularity – a thumbnail-sized point of intense energy from which the universe began expanding. Scientists tell us that our universe continues to expand. Apparently this is borne out by the fact that the distances between stars are growing. Surprisingly enough, the very notion of the Big Bang is to be found in the Sanskrit word for universe – Brahmanda. 'Brahm' means 'expanding' and 'anda' means 'egg'. Thus the word 'Brahmanda' literally means 'the expanding egg'. In effect, our ancient seers knew that the entire universe had emerged from a single point of energy. They also knew that one day the universe may collapse back into that very singularity – what physicists now call a black hole. And finally, they were aware that the process of the creation of a new universe would start from the singularity all over again. In that event, isn't it possible that mythological figures such as Brahma (creation), Vishnu (preservation) or Shiva (destruction) were simply metaphors to describe scientific phenomena?

I guess that the above pretty much explains my fascination with science as well as the ancient. For example, recent revelations from research have shown that there is no real difference between matter and energy. Of course, Albert Einstein had told us a long time ago about the interchangeability of matter and energy, but we are only now realising that the entire universe is nothing but energy. Even what we call matter is actually energy programmed to behave like matter. In effect, there is little to differentiate our human bodies from the houses we live in, the trees and shrubs around us, the air that we breathe or the fires that keep us warm. Anything and everything around us – including our own bodies – is simply energy. In that case, isn't it also possible that our thoughts are energy? That our souls are also energy?

Victor Hugo famously asked, 'Where the telescope ends, the microscope begins. Which of the two has a grander view?' The fact is that both instruments show us precisely the same thing. Looking through a microscope one sees particles in motion and looking through a telescope one sees planets in motion. We look to the skies to see the universe and forget that there is a universe within the atom. What if the outward universe that we observe is actually an atom under observation by someone else? What if the atom that we observe under the microscope is someone else's universe? The question that the physicists who gave us the Big Bang theory are unable to answer is this: what was there before the singularity? Let's assume for a moment that we accept the notion that the universe is like a balloon that periodically gets inflated and deflated via an alternating Big Bang and Big Crunch. We still cannot answer who or what created that first point of energy from which it all began. And you know what? It's fine that we can't answer it. As I see it, spirituality is not about having the answers. It's about seeking answers to the questions. In a sense, the proverb that the journey is the destination is absolutely true when one considers the spiritual journey.

EDV: Ashwin, I'd like to explore the relationship between mythology, itihasa and history with you. How do you conceive of both history and the contemporary moment as vehicles of intellectual and cultural enquiry? Moreover, as with other writers featured in this book, your novels are sometimes categorised under 'mythology'. In your mind, to what extent do the myths and the *arshamahakavya* embody *itihasa*? How does your writing engage with these ideas?

AS: Several Indian readers lump me into the 'mythological fiction' category. Mythology does not really interest me though. What possibly holds promise is the overlap between mythology and history. Ask me to retell the story of Rama or Ganesha and I'll give up within the first few pages. Ask me to write a story on whether the crossing to Lanka actually happened in history and I'll jump in with relish. My writing is an attempt to address the tantalising zone that is the overlap of history and mythology.

In 2013, I was invited to speak at a college in Kolkata. After the event, I asked the taxi driver to show me a few interesting spots in the city. He took me to the Bondel Gate area on Sridhar Roy Road. 'There's an interesting temple inside, sir,' he said, pointing to an unassuming entrance in an ordinary building. Entering, I saw a massive green throne nestling a portrait of Bollywood superstar Amitabh Bachchan (along with a pair of his shoes) inside a modest room. A Brahmin was busy performing *aarti* of the portrait while reciting verses from a little prayer book (called the Amitabh Chaleesa) that was also being sold outside. Amused by the temple, I began to wonder whether our current mythological figures – Krishna or Rama – had also started out simply as great men who began to be worshipped due to their great deeds.

It was C. S. Lewis who said that a myth is a lie that contains a truth. I like to see our mythology as precisely that but in a more literal sense. A great event like a war must have actually happened and because it was so momentous, it resulted in a work called *Jaya* that had 25,000 verses. Successive generations added to it and we had the *Bharata* of 50,000 verses. By the time we had finished the process of layering and embellishing we had the *Mahabharata* of 100,000 verses. It's a little bit like a game of 'Chinese whispers'. You sit around in a circle and one person whispers something into the ear of the person seated next to her. What goes into the circle is rarely what comes out – but is it a complete fabrication or does it also contain some of the original?

It was Edmund Burke who said, 'Those who don't know history are destined to repeat it.' I find that when I observe current events around me, I instinctively correlate these with events that happened in the past. When I read about modern-day conflicts between Islam and the Western world, I can't help thinking of the religious Crusades that were fought for most of the three hundred years following the eleventh century or the violence that was unleashed by Islamic conquests following the prophet Muhammad's death. History inevitably repeats itself, one simply needs to observe the patterns. This pattern is what interests me, not the history in itself, and this is what is central to my fiction.

EDV: *The Krishna Key* anchors itself in the life of Sri Krishna and yet, reading the novel, the rational and the logical play out alongside the ancient and the epic. In *Chanakya's Chant*, again the rational sits alongside the fantastical situated in the ancient. Could you talk a little about how and why your novels engage with ideas that seemingly present as opposites, how does the poetic licence that fiction offers help craft these ideas?

AS: But that's precisely why I love writing fiction! The Pavamana Mantra of the *Brihadaranyaka* Upanishad says: *Asato mā sad gamaya; Tamaso mā jyotir gamaya; Mṛtyor māmṛtaṃ gamaya*. Literally translated, it means 'From the unreal lead me to the real; From darkness lead me to light; From death lead me to immortality.'

For example: Hindu mythology depicts Shiva's third eye. But what if this is symbolism for something else? What if it symbolises higher consciousness and allows us to understand that we are only seeing a map; the map is a representation of an actual terrain but seeing the map is not the same as seeing the terrain. Every person possesses a third eye but it can be activated only after years of meditation. Suddenly the third eye is no longer 'fantastic' but is symbolic of something deeper. When Indian texts would talk of *Rasayana* (ancient alchemy), it seemed fantastic. Now, quantum physics is telling us about the interconnectedness of things. What we perceive to be objects are actually complex relationships—an interplay between elements. It is evidence of the fact that any element can become another. In fact, what science is telling us only now was revealed to us aeons ago by Eastern mystics. The *rishis* were entirely focussed on the awareness of the unity and mutual interrelation of all things and events. All things were seen as interdependent and inseparable parts of the cosmic whole.

EDV: I'm interested to know your thoughts on how your novels are categorised and marketed. The Westland website defines your novels as 'thrillers'. Could you say a little about how your books are categorised, about genre fiction more generally if possible and if you were give your books a genre category, what that would be and why?

AS: I pity the folks who have to categorise my books because my efforts have been entirely devoted to not getting compartmentalised. *The Rozabal Line* was a theological mystery, *Chanakya's Chant* was a political conspiracy, *The Krishna Key* was a mythological thriller ... In fact, many of my readers write to me and tell me that my books deserve a slot in the non-fiction category as well, given the extensive research that I carry out.

EDV: Could you share with me some of the key reference texts you consulted whilst writing *The Krishna Key* and any of your other novels in fact, what kind of reading has shaped your ideas about the topics explored in your novels – such as science, philosophy, belief?

AS: The list is a long one! For example, for *The Krishna Key*, some of the books that I read were: Paramahansa Yogananda (2010), *Autobiography of a Yogi*, Yogoda Satsang Society of India; A. C. Bhaktivedanta Swami Prabhupada (1986), *Bhagvad-Gita, As It Is* (Second Edition), Bhaktivedanta Book Trust; N. S. Rajaram (2006), *Search for the Historical Krishna*, Prism Publications; Michel Danino (2010), *The Lost River: On the Trail of the Sarasvati*, Penguin Books; C. Rajagopalachari (2005), *The Mahabharata Retold*, Bharatiya Vidya Bhavan.

Similarly, for *The Rozabal Line*, some of the books that I used were:

Holger Kersten (2001), *Jesus Lived in India: His Unknown Life Before and After the Crucifixion*, Penguin; Nicolas Novotitch (1990), *The Unknown Life of Jesus Christ*, Leaves of Healing Publications; Andreas Faber Kaiser (1977), *Jesus Died in Kashmir: Jesus, Moses and the Ten Lost Tribes of Israel*, Gordon & Cremonesi; Margaret Starbird (1993), *The Woman with the Alabaster Jar: Mary Magdalen and the Holy Grail*, Bear & Company.

The number of books used as reference for *Chanakya's Chant* was slightly less given that half of the story was in the present day, but the books were no less significant, here are a couple of them: *Visakhadatta's Mudrarakshasa*, translated by Prof K. H. Dhruva (1923), Oriental Book Supplying Agency; L. N. Rangarajan (1992), *Kautilya – The Arthashastra*. Penguin Books India.

Even for my latest novel, *The Sialkot Saga*, the reference list is substantial but again, here are a few of the books that have shaped my thoughts and ideas: Ramachandra Guha (2007), *India after Gandhi: The History* of the World's Largest Democracy, Harper Perennial; C. Rajagopalachari, *Ramayana*, Bharatiya Vidya Bhavan; Gary Zukav (1979), *The Dancing Wu Li Masters: An Overview of the New Physics*, Harper One; Fritjof Capra (1975), *The Tao of Physics: An Exploration of the Parallels between Modern Physics and Eastern Mysticism*, Shambhala Press; A. L. Basham (1954), *The Wonder That Was India*, Picador; S. Rizvi (2005), *The Wonder That Was India Vol. 2*. Picador.

EDV: Ashwin Sanghi, thank you.

4.6 Interview with Author Pervin Saket

Author biography: Pervin Saket was shortlisted for the Random House India Writers Bloc Award 2013 and is the author of a novel, *Urmila* (Jaico, India, 2016), and a collection of poems, *A Tinge of Turmeric* (Writers' Workshop, India, 2009). She was first published by the legendary P. Lal of the iconic Writers' Workshop, Kolkata, and much of her work is an exploration of identity, of what it means to be a woman or an Indian or a rebel or a lover negotiating a unique personal and external landscape.

Pervin's short fiction has appeared in *Journeys* (Sampad, UK, 2010), *Breaking the Bow – Speculative Fiction Inspired by the Ramayana* (Zubaan, India, 2012), *The Asian Writer Collection* (Dahlia, UK, 2010), *Aliens* (Prime Books, USA, 2013), *Earthen Lamp Journal* (2014), *Khabar* (2010), *Love Across Borders – An Anthology by Indian and Pakistani Writers* (2013), *Page Forty Seven* (2010) and others. Her short fiction stands out for its experimentation with traditional styles of structure and time. Growing up in Mumbai at the end of the 1990s, Pervin's journey is marked by an emphasis on internal landscapes and the uniquely individual perceptions of societal structures and cultural texts. The exploration moves from the political to the personal, from the activist to the artist, from the mythical to the mundane. She also uses the space afforded by fiction to explore unfamiliar voices and their silences, drawing from the anonymous characters who populate our cities.

Pervin's poetry has been featured in *Kritya*, *Platform*, *The Binnacle* (University of Maine, USA) and elsewhere. She's also shared her work with audiences at Prithvi Theatre, Mumbai, at Cappuccino Readings, Mumbai, at the Journeys Festival of the Arts, Pune, and others. Her poetry engages strongly with myth and folklore, working towards a new, edgy, raw iteration of a common tale through an uncommon hero or an unexplored perspective. Pervin is an alumnus of creative writing courses from IIT-Kanpur and from St. Xavier's College of Communication, Mumbai. She is a certified Creative Writing Trainer from the British Council and she conducts workshops at the British Council Library on reading and writing skills. Her workshops with children and adults explore, among other concerns, the role and space of mythology, the act of creating the other, the enigma of the muse and experiments with creating a unique language or register. Pervin has previously taught at St. Andrews College, Mumbai, and is a consulting editor for Ratna Sagar P Ltd, an academic publishing house.

E. DAWSON VARUGHESE: Pervin, there has been a series of retellings of the *Ramayana* from the perspective of its female protagonists, namely Sita, but Urmila too. Your novel *Urmila* (2016) draws on that recent tradition although it more reimagines than it retells. I say this because it not only moves away from the original epic through the use of the contemporary setting (of current-day India and Dubai) but also in the way that assisted fertility plays a central role in the females' lives (those of Vanita and Urmila). Could you talk about how such a reimagining of the females' experiences of marriage and fertility dovetail with the epic (in your mind) and how this strand became so central to the novel's identity?

PERVIN SAKET: The novel does reimagine the lives of its characters in a contemporary setting, and it was a conscious attempt to bring the epic within the space of modern choices and constraints. I wanted to explore a narrative that comments on and questions not the events or values of a certain (imagined or historical) era but the pervasiveness of this value system in our experiences and expectations as we live them now. This setting of course brings with it all the technological innovations that are part of our lives, medical and otherwise. Vanita and Urmila both undergo fertility treatments, one because of her miscarriages, the other because she is determined to conceive and bring up her children independently. Although lab coats and sperm straws find their way into this contemporary reimagining, they are not far removed from the possibilities explored in the epic; indeed, the underlying impetus for these threads in the novel lies in the various *Rama katha*s that form our collective cultural narratives.

Although *Urmila* presents a contemporary landscape, on closer inspection, much of this space is borrowed from the possibilities that the *Ramayana* has always held to a reader willing to go beyond the literal representation of the story. Assisted fertility, unusual conceptions and concerns over truncated bloodlines are recurrent themes and plotlines in both the *Ramayana* and the *Mahabharata*, and often define the destiny of their characters. Almost all versions of the *Ramayana* explore Dashratha's lack of a son and an heir even after three marriages, stressing on the Putrakameshtri Yagna that would grant him children. However, some regional versions also explore Dashratha's story, and describe how Dashratha married the beautiful and charming Kaushalya without knowing that they were related by blood. Their child, a girl, Shanta, is born with a physical deformity in her leg. Although the king and queen try several remedies, they are advised that Shanta's condition is the result of the mixing of genes of cousins, and can be rectified if a suitably noble and worthy couple adopt her. Subsequently, Shanta is adopted by Kaushalya's sister Queen Vershini and her husband King Lompad of Angadesh. The Adi Parva of the *Vasishtha Ramayana* further states that Dashratha married Sumitra and Keikeyi in order to beget healthy children, suggesting knowledge of the working of genetic make-up and genetic deformities. Interestingly, Shanta grows up to become a sensuous, bold woman, who undertakes the seduction of Rishyashringa, the *rishi* raised in isolation, living without even the knowledge of women. When she approaches the celibate sage, Rishyashringa is drawn to her, even as he wonders what kind of man she may be, allowing for a wide range of sexual readings of their encounter. When the heirless Dashratha later organises the Putrakameshtri Yagna for progeny, it is Rishyashringa who officiates and conducts the ceremony, eventually giving each of Dhasratha's three wives a divine potion that would help them beget sons.

As a writer I've often pondered over this narrative and the need for the wives to receive a divine potion rather than direct intervention like the kind Kunti and Madri used in the *Mahabharata*. The *Ramayana*, which is usually believed to either have been composed in or have occurred in the Treta Yuga, is a subtler and more sanitised text than the *Mahabharata* (which marks the beginning of Kali Yuga, the fourth and last thread of the circular concept of time, the age when virtue and morality have crumbled). Perhaps this accounts for veiled, indirect fertility interventions in the *Rama katha*s, where the conception of the protagonists is known only by names of ceremonies and powerful potions and all references to the women directly conceiving with the holy men are squashed (unlike the *Mahabharata* where Ved Vyasa impregnates the princesses Ambika and Ambalika in the freely accepted Niyoga tradition).

Whether suggested or stated, assisted pregnancies populate both the *Ramayana* and the *Mahabharata*, so it was an interesting prospect for me to work this into *Urmila*. While Vanita's desire for a child does stem from – and eventually leads to – strengthening familial bonds, Urmila's journey is markedly different. It was very fulfilling to see this as a movement towards Urmila becoming her own person and breaking away from the husband and the marriage that had defined her. It symbolises her rejection of his seed, of his name and eventually of his narrative.

EDV: This volume is interested in the interface of mythology, *itihasa* and history. I'm curious to know your thoughts on how you might consider both history and the contemporary moment as vehicles of intellectual and cultural enquiry?

PS: Walking down the streets of any city in India, one finds that history, legend, mythology and science are neighbours. Indeed, a structure from the 17th century may stand beside one from the 19th century, which may in turn be home to a new DNA testing laboratory, and may have a plaque announcing that this was the spot where a certain raja held his durbar or the air space through which a mythological creature once flew when on his way to meet a beloved. I've long ceased to see these as contradictions or confusions but as a unique pause where different strands of real or imagined experiences all present themselves in the now. This also allows for multipronged discussions and introspections on our priorities, our values, our heroes and perhaps our lessons as a collective cultural group. While history brings with it the lens of hindsight and patterns, mythology allows for philosophical speculations and our contemporary moment enhances the emotional and intellectual urgency of enquiry. The writing of *Urmila* in particular was a balancing act between the story as we know it (whether as history or as literature) and the exploration of why the story continues to be relevant. It is, hence, also a commentary on the previous narratives and historical values that have validated Urmila's silence as well as the current trend which explores (and often, again, justifies) Urmila's desertion. The narrative serves as a gateway to understand the culture that gave rise to Urmila's silence, the culture and the intellectual attempts that gloss over or explain away Urmila's silence and also those that are deeply uncomfortable with her lack of agency. In the Telugu ballad 'Urmila Devi Nidra' ('The Sleep of Urmila Devi'), on the first night of the exile, when Nidra the goddess of sleep approaches Laxman, he asks her to grant his share of sleep to Urmila so that he may serve Rama and Sita without fatigue. She agrees, and Urmila is depicted sleeping away the fourteen years while Laxman is awake throughout. Later, in the war against Ravana, it passes that Ravana's formidable son Meghnadh can only be destroyed by one who has not slept for fourteen years, and hence, Laxman is able to defeat him. While this is a very rich and engaging ballad, I also see it as a writer's discomfort with Urmila's pain and his/her instinct to place her in a blissfully unaware coma, and yet justifying the need for this pain in the first place by Meghnadh's condition of being invincible except to one who hasn't slept for fourteen years. Literature hence serves as a window into the possible historical and contemporary cultural questions that we continue to grapple with.

EDV: In *Urmila* it is clear from the outset that Urmila is not one to follow convention, not least when it comes to superstition, although there are points in the novel where she 'weakens', questioning if the destiny of her marriage (and life) are written in the (mis)match of her and Shree's horoscopes. How does the poetic licence that fiction offers help narrate ideas of superstition and 'truth' – specifically, in the case of *Urmila*, how does fiction allow you to move between the worlds of 'truth' (reality?) and those worlds which appear as less 'concrete' (say, where she has less control) in Urmila's life?

PS: As tempting as it to dismiss anything that is not proven in a laboratory, I always knew that I didn't want to take sides. Superstition and truth, to me, are both fluid, flexible constructs; while one might say that it is superstitious to believe Urmila's marriage was doomed because she refused to change her name, Urmila's own truth is that her name has haunted her. In fact, it's possible that the character's categorical refusal to change her name comes not from a rational, logical perspective but from an inability to fight her fate, a doom that is masked by her obstinacy; indeed, she may be the agent of her own misery. At the same time, certainly, one might argue, 'what's in a name?' Surely, she'd live the same fate even if she were a Seema or a Tanisha. And yet, we'd never know.

Fiction is the space where universal truths (if there are any, as Austen claimed) give way to personal truths. And personal truths are often messy, strange, inexplicable and routinely at odds with universal truths. *Urmila* exists at the intersection of several belief systems: the personal and the political, the mythological and the mundane, the universal and the unique – and it was very interesting for me to negotiate this space. Fiction allows not only the author to work with several (often conflicting) ideas of perception, but also enables the reader to identify, often subconsciously, the truth that works for him/her, and thereby makes his/her reading of the novel distinct from another reader's engagement with the book. It is this elasticity, this multiplicity of fiction (even with a narrative written entirely in the first person, as *Urmila* is) that is most exciting for me to explore.

EDV: I'd like to explore your position with regards to the epic narratives and the idea that these narratives are *itihasa*. As a non-Hindu, I am keen to know how you perceive the narratives of the *Ramayana* and the *Mahabharata* as a facet of an Indian 'cultural identity' given their anchorage in Hinduism. By extension, could you say how the choice of 'Urmila' came about and again, how as a non-Hindu, you engaged with her through your craft of writing, as a human being (her as a Hindu woman, caught in a loveless marriage, etc.)?

PS: My engagement with the *Ramayana* – and it is perhaps a deeper engagement than a majority of the population that gain their knowledge of the epic from television shows – is entirely as a literary and a cultural text.

I am, of course, deeply aware and respectful of the religious associations and beliefs that are linked to the epics, and also rather in awe of the fabulously intricate way in which existential issues have been explored, particularly in the *Mahabharata*. The epics are wonderfully rich in the many kinds of readings they offer, and it is entirely satisfactory, and enchanting even, to engage with them solely as literary texts. Of course, it is probably impossible to divorce literature from philosophy, however, my discussions on identity, relationships, truth, etc. with respect to the epics are comparable to how I might engage with Shakespeare or Kalidasa, i.e. as extensions of the great capacity of literature to reflect the human condition.

I do see the epics as part of the cultural pool of India, as much as texts from Buddhism or Jainism or other texts like 'Arthashastra' or 'Panchatantra' or 'Kathasaritsagara' contribute to the plural cultural heritage of India. My anxiety lies not in their religious anchorage in Hinduism or even in the claims that they are historical accounts, but rather in the tendency to impose a single *Ramayana* or a single *Rama katha*, and to reject the diversity and the hybridity of this narrative. As anyone who has worked with these texts would realise, there are episodes and characters that exist in different regional tellings of the tale, and yet each person tends to think of their own familiar version as the 'original' or the 'real' one. Further, this version is often believed to be Valmiki's *Ramayana* since Valmiki's is considered the most authoritative tale. However, many scenes that are part of our popular imagination of the *Ramayana*, such as the *Laxman rekha* scene or the episode highlighting Shabri's devotion, are not part of Valmiki's *Ramayana* at all. It is this insistence on a singular, monolithic all-encompassing text that is unnerving because it negates not just the plural voices and perspectives of the *Rama katha* but also because it fails to recognise the historical influences (the Bhakti tradition for instance) that have worked on these texts through the centuries.

As for my engagement with the *Ramayana*, A. K. Ramanujan famously said that no one ever hears the *Ramayana* for the first time; it is probably breathed in along with childhood games, stories or sweet treats. Although my childhood associations with the text are considerably loose, having been brought up in a Parsi household in Mumbai with tales of Zarathustra, Rustom and Sohrab, soon enough, the *apsaras* and *rishis* of Amar Chitra Katha comics took over my imagination. At the same time, I remember that even as I read tales of heroes and conquerors, my attention was always caught by the marginal characters who appeared for only a single scene or a single dialogue. I often wondered: how would this foot soldier tell this story or what would that handmaiden think of this decision? In fact, sometimes I was more drawn to the silent courtier or the docile sister receiving the king's instruction without any choice or opinion. Much of this is, of course, an extension of the kind of person I am – I am drawn to silence. Very often, in social gatherings, I find myself tuning out the talk and listening to the silent person in the room. And I'm quite convinced that speech, discussion, music, noise – these are actually background; the foreground, the little bursts that actually mean anything, is silence. This perspective finds its way into my reading as well, and probably explains why I find my themes and concerns reflecting in the silent or silenced stories of Urmila or Mandodari or Ahalya.

Epics from around the world have always inspired writers across religions and nations, including writers belonging to backgrounds that differ from the religious/cultural group associated with the epic. I believe much of this engagement can be attributed to the richness and depth of the epic but some of it probably lies also in the discomfort that the epic inspires. As a writer, there is an itch to set some story right, to tell it again, to tell it differently, to correct an omission or to omit an error. With a narrative like the *Ramayana* that has so much to say about good and evil, about the ideal man, the ideal woman, the ideal king, in a narrative that does not only describe the events that took place but prescribes how one must conduct their affairs, in a narrative that is so heavy with rhetoric, it is important to examine not just what it says, but also what it leaves out. And this is the space that Urmila occupies. The margins, the footnotes, the silences.

As to why I connected with Urmila from the pantheon of underrepresented women in mythology – it's something I've wondered often, considering that she's a very different person from the kind of heroine who would inspire me; if she had been a neighbour, I might have even found her too passive and conservative to relate to her. However, in the process of penning her story, I learned to let go of the 'author'ity of the writer, to refrain from imposing my feminism or my quick fixes or my rebellious dialogue on her. In fact, several scenes in earlier drafts were scrapped because they did not ring true for her, and I'm glad that I listened. I find that the sections that work best are the ones where I have just followed her, staying out of the way, giving her the time and the space she needs to find her own answers and to become her own person. I believe she taught me patience and that resolutions come from within characters, not from twists of plot or cleverness of the pen. And I believe that we are friends now.

EDV: The opening scene of *Urmila* is arresting – riotous reactions to Urmila's latest painting. In this regard, 'art' is foregrounded from the outset. Could you say how you came to portray Urmila as a successful artist and how 'art' mediates much of what takes place in the novel? I'm taken by how the idea of 'art' drives the storyline from the start, only to conclude in the realm of 'science' through the motif of the fertility clinic. What are your thoughts on how these two disciplines 'meet' in your novel (an echo of sorts on the trope of 'superstition' and 'rational thinking' that also 'meet' in your novel at certain points)?

PS: In a few regional *Rama katha*s, Urmila is depicted as an artist where she spends the fourteen years of separation painting an intricate scene of Rama and Sita's marriage – which is also the scene of her marriage to Laxman (since all four brothers married four sisters in a joint ceremony). I was taken by why a bride, particularly a woman pining away for her husband, would focus more on the depiction of another bride and another wedding instead of her own wedding. Some of the impetus behind Urmila's depiction as an artist came from this question, and some of it originates in Urmila's need to hold her husband, to etch him, to capture his gaze, even if it is only in a painting. She has always been a sensuous woman, and after the separation, becomes intensely aware of how she yearns for him visually and physically. She needs to see him but is too hurt to look at photographs; instead she draws portrait after portrait of the man, hoping to capture him and free herself of this desire, but with each painting, he eludes her. When she finally decides to address another vacuum in her life, her desire for a child, she gets busy with fertility treatments. While her twins and by extension 'science' do provide a new direction, I believe she has already found closure earlier, when Shree returns and calls her, but she refuses to go back to that house.

I see the motif of the fertility clinic, the IVF treatment, etc. as an extension of her freedom from him, perhaps even as a consequence of her freedom from him, rather than its cause. Interestingly, it is at this point that she finds she cannot paint anymore, because she has stopped seeking. So while art was her support in one stage of her life, science served the same role in another stage, both of them helping Urmila negotiate through her desires and her limitations.

EDV: I'm interested to know your thoughts on how your novel is categorised and marketed. How important a consideration is the genre classification of your writing and does this play a part in choosing a publisher for your work?

PS: The book is categorised as 'Indian fiction' and it still surprises me that in bookstores in India we need to have a shelf marked 'Indian fiction'. It probably reflects for how long and how much Indians read books in English by writers of other nationalities. In fact, the idea of foreign writers writing better is so strong that one early reader of the novel commented on *Urmila*, saying, 'it doesn't feel like this is written by an Indian writer' and meant it as a compliment! On the plus side, because we have a relatively small community of English writers, editors and publishing houses, there are fewer subdivisions of genre. Of course, writers specialise in romance or detective fiction but the genres are more fluid and easier to move across. My next books, for instance, are a collection of Mumbai-centric short stories and a historical novel set during the Indian independence movement – and this shift in theme after the mythology-inspired *Urmila* is not perceived as surprising.

At the same time, *Urmila* did receive some resistance initially because it did not fit very neatly into the genre of retold mythology. I was always very clear that I wanted a narrative which was truly inspired by the *Ramayana* and not merely derivative, but this did not work for an editor who saw an early version of the manuscript. The editor commented that the associations with the *Ramayana* were too loose and implied; the narrative wasn't ticking the boxes of the genre they had defined for it. However, not only was I happily unaware of the patterns of this new, emerging genre, I was certain that I wanted to tell a story that could be read at two levels: as a simple contemporary story of a woman looking for love and as a deeper reflection of the values we uphold as a society. I also wanted to play with time, to explore the role of art, to question Urmila's own attachments, and I decided to break the rules even as I was learning about them. Fortunately, I found first an agent and then an editor who were both very excited about the novel, in fact, who were particularly excited about the ways in which it differs from the expectations one has from this genre.

EDV: What kind of reading has shaped your ideas about the topics explored in *Urmila*? Could you cite any specific texts that have particularly shaped your thinking and writing over the years?

PS: I'm indebted of course to more writers and their works than any list can hold. However, the more direct associations with *Urmila* probably lie in Jean Rhy's *Wide Sargasso Sea*, Kiran Nagarkar's *Cuckold*, A. K. Ramanujan's essay '300 Ramayanas and Counting', Arshia Sattar's translation of the Valmiki *Ramayana*, as well as the anthology of short fiction *Breaking the Bow – Speculative Fiction Inspired by the Ramayana*, edited by Anil Menon and Vandana Singh.

Cuckold, in particular, combines history and mythology to tell the story of a Rajput prince whose wife is in love with someone else. Except his rival isn't a man but the Hindu god Krishna. It is based on the legend of Mirabai, a poet and saint of the Bhakti tradition. Nagarkar superbly weaves together an epic of love, longing and valour, through the perspective of the prince who is usually portrayed as the antagonist in Mirabai's divine love for Krishna. Although the storyline is a fictionalised introspection by the sensitive, brooding Rajput prince who focusses, to everyone's embarrassment, on the sanitation system of his kingdom, all the main characters and events are corroborated by historical accounts. At one point, the prince agonises, 'You can exorcise the devil … but how do you rid yourself of a god?' The novel is rich in historical references and political intrigue and is yet intensely personal, bringing to life the predilection of a husband who remains only an unflattering footnote in Bhakti tradition.

Another book that I've often returned to is Jean Rhys' postcolonial novel *Wide Sargasso Sea* that works as a prequel to Charlotte Brontë's *Jane Eyre* 139 years after Brontë first described the 'mad woman in the attic'.

The narrative explores the fictionalised internal truths of a white Creole heiress and her eventual descent into madness, giving not just a story but also agency to a character who was earlier little more than a speed bump in Jane and Rochester's relationship. I was particularly drawn towards the acts of naming, renaming and unnaming that weave through this narrative. A name is probably the shortest story one can tell, and *Urmila* too plays with the implications of names. Not only does the modern Urmila's life reflect that of her namesake in the *Ramayana*, but her fate seems bound to the echoes of her name. Further, her husband remains unnamed (he does have a pet name, 'Chhotu', which simply means 'small one' since he's the younger brother, and Urmila calls him 'Shree', which could be a short form of a name like Shreekant or Shreenivas, but it is mainly used since it is a generic word for Mr in Hindi), since he is the one character who cannot be grasped or contained. In some ways, it is also an act of defiance; in Laxman's story, he does not refer to Urmila, in Urmila's story, she will not name him.

EDV: Finally, I'd like to ask you about the role of 'time' in *Urmila*. The notion of 'time' plagues Urmila in a sense and I wonder how you came to integrate the 'timeless' tradition of marriage (your novel is organised by the 7 wedding vows) with 'time' as a problematic condition of human existence.

PS: *Urmila* has been structured in seven sections to reflect the *saptapadi* or the seven vows of marriage, and this not only incorporates the theme of marriage but it also allowed me to play with time. Each section unveils thematically rather than chronologically; so if the first vow is about prosperity, that section throws light on the manner in which this vow was fulfilled or not, and in Urmila's case, the expected, twisted manner in which her husband actually does inspire her commercial success as an artist. Since early in the novel, a reader would establish that the story follows the *Ramayana* trajectory, he/she brings their own information about the epic into the reading, thereby freeing me from the need to proceed in a linear, chronological manner. This allowed me to play with how and where I wanted to place events, and was very interesting for me as a writer. It enabled me to connect various incidents and emotions in a manner that heightens the theme and the emotion associated with that section. I also wanted this flexibility with time because time is experienced very differently by Urmila. While one may wonder why Urmila, particularly this modern, financially independent Urmila, waits for her husband for fourteen years, she herself doesn't register it as so long. At one point she says, 'But it couldn't have been so many years. How long is a trance, how slow an itch?' In a sense the story is also an exploration of the relative nature of time, of how one can continue to live in just a single moment, ignoring the transformations that take place externally. Urmila herself states: 'Who can calculate the length of time between my husband sprinkling sindoor into the parting of my hair and him tying the mangalsutra around my neck? It couldn't have been more than a few seconds. Yet, all these years I have lived within those moments.' So the structure of the novel stresses both, Urmila's relative time and the absolute, timeless institution of marriage that has broken down for her.

EDV: Pervin Saket, thank you.

4.7 Interview with Author Christopher C. Doyle

Author biography: Christopher C. Doyle is a bestselling author who transports the reader into a fascinating world where ancient secrets buried in legends blend with science and history to create a gripping story. His debut novel The Mahabharata Secret, released in October 2013, was an instant bestseller, featuring among the top 10 books of 2013 at Crossword, Amazon and Nielsen. It was also nominated for the Raymond Crossword Book Award 2014 as one of the top 12 books in the popular category. His second novel, The Mahabharata Quest: The Alexander Secret, was released in October 2014 and has been a bigger success than his first book, and is still among the top bestsellers in India more than a year after its release.

Brought up on a steady diet of books ranging from classical literature to science fiction and fantasy to poetry and plays, Christopher dreamed of becoming a writer from an early age. The science fiction of Jules Verne, H. G. Wells, Isaac Asimov and Robert Heinlein and the fantasies scripted by Tolkien, Robert Jordan and Terry Brooks inspired him to write from his schooldays, with the desire of seeing his name alongside his literary idols in bookshops someday. An alumnus of St Stephen's College, Delhi and IIM Calcutta, Christopher had a successful career in the corporate sector before embarking on an entrepreneurial journey. He now helps companies to achieve exponential growth and is one of India's leading CEO coaches. Over the course of his corporate career, Christopher has written articles on management and business for Indian and international publications and is also a regular invited speaker for international conventions and conferences.

Christopher lives in New Delhi with his wife, daughter and his dog and enjoys writing, reading, swimming and tennis as well as travelling and meeting people. He is also a musician and lives his passion for music through his band called Mid Life Crisis, which plays classic rock.

E. DAWSON VARUGHESE: In *The Mahabharata Secret* (2013), the narrative is set in the contemporary for the main although you begin the novel (and return briefly) to a much earlier period of time. Could you say why you chose to anchor the novel in the ancient whilst narrating a very contemporary storyline – what is the connection between the ancient and the current day for you?

CHRISTOPHER C. DOYLE: Both my books, *The Mahabharata Secret* and *The Alexander Secret* (Book 1 of 'The Mahabharata Quest' series), are anchored in the ancient, while narrating a story that takes place in our present-day world. My third book, *The Secret of the Druids* (Book 2 of 'The Mahabharata Quest' series), released in May 2016, also follows the same narrative structure, as will the rest of the books in 'The Mahabharata Quest' series. My books have three key ingredients related to the ancient past baked into the plot. The base ingredient, from which the plot springs, is a secret concealed in the myths of the *Mahabharata*. The second ingredient is an ancient, and well-known, historical figure – Asoka the Great in the case of *The Mahabharata Secret*; Alexander the Great in the case of *The Alexander Secret*; and Julius Caesar in the case of *The Secret of the Druids*. The third and, in my opinion, distinguishing ingredient is the use of established scientific fact to explain the ancient secret that is the first ingredient. The past and present are then connected through the use of fact and fiction, creating a narrative that seeks to link the *Mahabharata* (through a scientific interpretation of its stories), history and events in our present-day world. This structure is not a happy accident though the manner in which *The Mahabharata Secret* came to be written was the result of several factors coming together at the same time. Two decades ago, I read a clutch of books that raised a host of questions in my mind. I will refer to these books in more detail as part of a response to a later question in this interview but for now, I will only touch upon the thoughts that they triggered in my mind.

I guess the books that really triggered my thought process regarding mythology, history and science were *Fingerprints of the Gods* by Graham Hancock (I subsequently read *Keeper of Genesis, Underworld, Heaven's Mirror*, all by the same author, which only added to my knowledge) and *Uriel's Machine* by Christopher Knight and Robert Lomas. These authors postulated the same thing, in different ways. They spoke of a 'collective amnesia of humanity'. The essence of their writing was that there were civilisations in prehistoric times – when mankind was in the Stone Age according to traditional archaeological records – which were highly advanced in their knowledge of science and technology; and that this knowledge has been lost over the millennia and forgotten by humankind. In fact, in *Uriel's Machine*, the authors propounded a hypothesis that a key book from the Dead Sea Scrolls – 'The Book of Enoch' – was based on events that actually occurred before the Great Flood that washed over the planet Earth thousands of years ago. All these authors (including Graham Hancock, who provides further evidence of the global flood in his latest book – *Magicians of the Gods*) refer to scientific evidence to prove that the Great Flood was a real event and not just a part of over 600 myths in different cultures of the world – in itself an unbelievable coincidence. Knight and Lomas, in their book, use science to prove that 'The Book of Enoch' substantiates their hypothesis of an advanced civilisation in the British Isles, over 5000 years ago. Additional research into some of the facts mentioned in these books only served to whet my curiosity and I found myself asking some intriguing questions about Indian mythology. To my surprise, I could not find any similar work, either fictional or nonfictional, that explored the link between history, science and Indian mythology. The questions, however, remained.

First, if there is so little we know about the people who wrote the Vedas, and their history; if we have forgotten who they were and what they did, is it not possible that their know-how of science and technology may have also been forgotten as well? Second, what if the *Mahabharata* actually reveals an advanced technology and knowledge of science far beyond what we can fathom today and which, for some reason, never made it to our current recorded history? What if we have been reading it incorrectly and the traditional interpretations of the myths in that epic are concealing a deeper truth? Third, what if this knowledge of technology and science was lost as a result of the Great Flood? Or even deliberately obliterated? (I have explored this latter theme in *The Mahabharata Secret*.) These thoughts were further stoked by *The Hindu History* by Akshoy K. Majumdar, written in 1917. The author, through his extensive research into ancient Indian texts – including the *Mahabharata*, the *Ramayana*, the Puranas, the Upanishads and the Vedas – has constructed a prehistoric 'history' of ancient India, including genealogies of dynastic lines for the *Suryavansh* (Dynasty of the Sun) and *Chandravansh* (Dynasty of the Moon). This book triggered some interesting thoughts. Reading this book made me speculate if we had somehow lost a sizeable portion of our history. Is it possible, I wondered, if there was a history of India that is not popularly known, but has been captured in the ancient texts and scriptures of India in allegorical or narrative form?

At this point, I simply had to research more on the ancient science of India. It was then, during my search for material that would answer my questions, that I came across the Susruta Samhita. This is a book on surgical techniques and medicine written by a physician who lived around 3000 years ago. When I read translated versions of this ancient book, since I do not know Sanskrit, I was amazed at the surgical techniques described in this book. It established for me the fact that ancient India did, indeed, have advanced scientific and technological knowledge. I want to pause here and make it very clear that I do not subscribe to the more fantastical claims made by people who have similar views to my own. Talk of nuclear weapons in ancient India or aliens providing scientific knowledge and advanced technology is not something that I subscribe to or support. I have not found anything in the *Mahabharata*, the only ancient text that I have studied in great detail, to support either view.

At this point in time, I was sufficiently convinced that my thoughts were in the right direction. I did try to research if anyone had actually tried to interpret our epics through the lens of science but I didn't find anything. Nothing happened for several years after that. Then, in 2006, my daughter, who was seven at that time, helped trigger my journey as an author. Until then, I had been creating stories, which I would narrate to her at bedtime; stories that involved wizards, magic, high priests, mists and time travel. Pure fantasy. Influenced, no doubt, by books by Tolkien, Robert Jordan and others. But in 2006 she wanted something more cerebral. This threw up a challenge for me. I had to find material that would help me create stories that would engage her and stimulate her intellectually. Stories that moved beyond suspense and magic. Stories built on a foundation that was real while exploring themes that were new and exciting. It was easy to find the answer. My daughter was very interested in mythology and history. She knew things I didn't know about Indian mythology and the epics. It was at this time that I realised that I could fulfil my long-realised dream of interpreting Indian mythology through the lens of science. And, since I always wanted to be an author – since the age of ten, actually – this prospect excited me. And so I began researching.

I was helped, in my research, by my daughter, whose knowledge of Indian mythology was significantly superior to mine at that time. But what really intrigued me was a legend I came across on the Internet. It was a legend about Asoka the Great, one of India's greatest emperors in ancient times. The legend that captivated me was about a secret brotherhood – the most ancient secret society in the world if this legend was true – that Asoka had founded, called the brotherhood of the Nine Unknown Men. According to all the accounts I read on the Internet, the nine members of the society had published nine books on esoteric subjects like gravitation, psychological warfare, alchemy, microbiology and other such anachronistic subjects. I wasn't convinced by the legend, but it did give me some ideas for the story I wanted to write. So I decided to change the legend to suit my purpose.

As an author of fiction, what appealed to me was the fact that the *Mahabharata* had been orally transmitted for a very long time (Hundreds of years? Thousands of years? No one knows). But scholars do agree that it was committed to writing somewhere between 200 and 500 BC. Which overlapped very conveniently, from the perspective of a fictional story, with the period of Asoka's reign. Thus was born the plot of *The Mahabharata Secret*. My innate inquisitiveness and curiosity led me to ask the obvious questions: what if there was an ancient secret hidden in the *Mahabharata*? What if that secret was in a book of the *Mahabharata* that was committed to writing during Asoka's time? What if Asoka actually unearthed the secret and realised that it was a danger to the world and decided to suppress the propagation of that book of the *Mahabharata*? And, having suppressed it, then decided to hide that secret away forever by creating the Nine (the secret brotherhood) to safeguard it so that it could never harm the world? What if the legends about the Nine and their nine books were just a smokescreen to divert attention from the real secret they were guarding? What if the lost book of the Mahabharata was found later? What would happen? Between 2006 and 2008, I wrote this story for my daughter, never imagining it would turn into a bestselling book five years later. She loved it. As do legions of school-going children in India today; a substantial proportion of my readers are aged 13 to 18 years. I could have set the book in the ancient past – either in the mythological past, like some writers of mythological fiction and fantasy based on mythology; or in the ancient past, like some writers of historical fiction. But I was not inclined towards either genre. In order to create a story that would be gripping and full of suspense, it seemed logical to place the narrative in contemporary times, since I was writing for a child. And, based on my reading and research, I was able to explore the links between mythology, science, history and our present-day world. Moreover, I wanted to move beyond the conspiracy theories that swirl endlessly on the Internet, many of them touching upon themes and subjects that are similar to the theme of my books. I wanted to create my own theories, based not on pure speculation but on pure science, leveraging scientific fact rather than science fiction, exploring plausible scenarios that are logical and supported by scientific research and discoveries in our own times.

Today, science and technology are advancing at a pace never before seen in recorded history. New discoveries and new inventions are breaching barriers that, just a few decades ago, seemed to be insurmountable. As a fiction writer, I was fascinated by the opportunity to put my ideas and thoughts to work and explore the *Mahabharata*, not in a literal or philosophical manner, but using cutting-edge science and technology, based on advances made in our own times, and investigate the possibility that at least parts of that epic can be interpreted plausibly through scientific fact. For me, it was the creative challenge of credibly presenting a fresh perspective to an age, which we all associate with bows, arrows, horses, elephants and chariots, not with cutting-edge technology.

EDV: I'd like to explore the relationship between mythology, *itihasa* and history with you. How do you conceive of both history and the contemporary moment as vehicles of intellectual and cultural enquiry?

CCD: Ideally speaking, mythology and history should have a clearly demarcated boundary separating them. Let's keep *itihasa* aside for the moment. If one goes strictly by the dictionary definition of history, then the line between history and mythology blurs. If we regard history as merely the study of the past or a chronological record of past events, then where is the difference between history and mythology? Texts like the *Mahabharata*, traditionally regarded as mythology are, themselves, very well documented chronological records, as Akshoy Majumdar's research into ancient Indian texts reveals. The fact that he was able to construct a prehistoric record of people and events going back 5000 years demonstrates this. To my mind, if the two are to be clearly defined and distinguished from each other, then history should be based on evidence, preferably archaeological; evidence that is difficult to dispute. The second distinguishing factor between history and mythology should be the presence of elements influenced by the local culture that has produced the mythology. Sometimes these elements relate to the appearance of supernatural beings – gods, demons, monsters and such entities – and, at other times, they relate to abnormal events that cannot be easily explained by the laws of science or the laws of nature. Accordingly, Asoka the Great was considered a myth until 1837, when James Princep deciphered the first edicts and established Asoka as a historical figure based on the archaeological evidence of the edicts of Asoka. The problem arises when dates are ascribed to events, or historians and archaeologists create a historical record of events or establish a chronology of events without substantive evidence. A case in point is the theory of the Aryan Invasion of India. While growing up, and studying history in school, I've always had questions about the traditional theory of the Aryan Invasion of India, which essentially says that the Vedas were composed by itinerant invaders – the Aryans – from Central Asia/East Europe, who destroyed the Indus Valley Civilisation and gave India its Vedic literature. Of course, this theory, which always lacked any kind of evidence to support it, has now been effectively debunked, and many scholars now consider this theory to be a tool for Western colonial powers to deal a fatal blow to the pride and belief that Indians had in our cultural heritage, most visibly represented by the Vedas which are, arguably, the oldest verses in the world. Now that this theory has been consigned to the dustbin of fabricated historical theories, there is still a debate raging about who exactly the Vedic people were. They remain an enigma.

I believe that the pursuit of knowledge about our past based on historical discoveries can be productive only if the conclusions we reach about people, civilisations, events and locations in the past are based on facts rather than speculation or personal opinions. Unfortunately, this is not always the case, especially when it comes to ancient history. Many ancient documents have been lost over time, surviving in fragments as quotations or summaries by later writers, or as copies by scribes working to preserve the texts in medieval times. How much of the original content of those ancient texts has survived the translation and copying by hand is difficult to say. Yet, in many cases, these are the only historical records that we have of those times. In this context, I've sometimes found myself marvelling at the fact that there is no archaeological evidence to prove that Alexander the Great existed! Yes, we have accounts written by Plutarch, Arrian and Strabo, but they all wrote centuries after Alexander died and their accounts of his life are derived from the writings of others, contemporary with Alexander, whose writings are now lost. I want to stress here that I am not questioning the veracity of Alexander's existence as a real, historical figure. I am merely saying that, unlike Asoka the Great, for example, whose edicts have served to prove his existence, there is nothing similar related to Alexander that has been discovered yet. And, that brings me to *itihasa*. The *Mahabharata* repeatedly claims that it is *itihasa*, which means, approximately, 'this is how it happened' or 'this is what happened'. There is no word in the English language that can be viewed as a direct equivalent of *itihasa*. Yet, we dismiss that great epic as mythology on the basis that its transmission, first orally over hundreds if not thousands of years, and subsequently, in writing, would have distorted the original epic, so that the text that we read today is possibly quite different from the original composition. Interestingly, as I have pointed out earlier, this conclusion could just as easily be reached about ancient classical texts that we regard as historical documents. Once again, let me emphasise that I do not have a point of view either way. I am merely stating the facts as they are and not advocating any specific theory regarding the debate on dating monuments or the veracity of ancient historical records. However, as a writer of fiction, this glorious ambiguity of the ancient texts, both historical (in the widely accepted sense) and mythological, provides the opportunity for exploration of cultural and social nuances through works of fiction that attempt to fill in the missing gaps or interpret the ambiguities through speculation; it is this that creates the sense of intrigue, mystery and excitement about our past. And it is this combination of ingredients that makes for a spellbinding thriller set in modern times.

EDV: In *The Mahabharata Secret* (2013) the 'celestial weaponry' is a key aspect to the storyline and it is through these 'objects' that truth, *itihasa* and belief are all brought into question. How does the poetic licence that fiction offers help narrate these ideas and where do you stand in presenting such ideas as 'truth' or 'non-truth' – or is it not so unequivocal?

CCD: As I mention above, the ambiguity of certain portions of history offers an opportunity to interpret events, personalities and their motives in different ways, using poetic licence. And in my case, I like to combine this with my attempt to view the Mahabharata through the lens of science and technology. But before I explain further, I would like to categorically state that I write fiction. I am not rewriting or retelling the *Mahabharata* and I am definitely not writing a textbook on history. My books try and link history, mythology and science in a manner that combines fact and fiction. I do not try and present anything as a truth or non-truth. My objective is to create a story that entertains my readers, keeping them glued to the pages of my books until they reach the end, presenting them with a hypothesis that is credible and plausible. I attempt to achieve this by writing a narrative that does not allow them to distinguish easily between fact and fiction. It feels great when readers write to me and ask if the story they read is a true story. Or if they enquire which parts of the story are true facts and which parts are fiction. Thus, *The Mahabharata Secret* explores a technology that, in 2006, was at the frontiers of science, though today it is taking a form that will make it a part of our everyday lives within the next 20 years, and definitely within the lifetimes of most people alive today. The interesting part was finding a scientific explanation, which could be vetted by an expert in the field, for some of the celestial weaponry described in the *Mahabharata*. The historical angle is provided by Asoka the Great and the secret brotherhood that he is supposed to have founded, as I have explained earlier. *The Alexander Secret* studies *shlokas* (or verses) from the *Mahabharata* which, if one disregards the traditional interpretations of those *shlokas*, embody science in the Sanskrit. I have demonstrated this in the book, taking the help of PhDs in Sanskrit to ensure that I was translating the Sanskrit accurately. Once again, I took a popular myth from the epic – the *Samudramanthan* or 'Churning of the Ocean' – and created a scientific hypothesis based on real science to explain this myth and the nature of the *amrita* – the drink of immortality – that was created as a result of the process described in the myth. Again, there are mysteries about Alexander's march from Macedonia to the banks of the river Beas in modern-day Punjab that have not been satisfactorily explained. The biggest mystery was his turning back from the Beas after marching for eight years and 10,000 miles, when there was a large and rich land waiting to be conquered. Many reasons have been advanced – all speculative in my opinion – for his abrupt retreat. I find these reasons to be inadequate to explain his return from the Beas, since none of them are in keeping with the personality and character of the man whom I have researched by reading over forty books about him, from the ancient classical writers to modern researchers and historians. My own speculation, using poetic licence, was that Alexander – who portrayed himself as divine, the son of Zeus Ammon, and asked to be worshipped as a god – came to the lands of the Indus in search of the one thing that would truly make him a god – immortality. And, when he found what he sought, he decided to turn back and go home. After all, if you are immortal, where is the hurry to conquer a new land? You have eternity to do it. And Alexander had proved, in battle after battle, that he had no equal as a general. The twist in the story, of course, is the fact that Alexander died just two years after he left India. If he had, indeed, found the secret of immortality, the secret mentioned in the myth from the *Mahabharata*, then why did he die? Interestingly, the scientific explanation I have provided for the nectar of immortality also explains why Alexander died. There are no loose ends in this mystery.

The Secret of the Druids seeks to link the mysterious class of people called the Druids, about whom much has been written but little is known for certain, and the *Mahabharata*. Once again, I have used science to explain the mechanics of a well-known weapon in the *Mahabharata* and made extensive use of *shlokas* in the epic to justify my hypothesis that links the Druids with this weapon from Vedic times. In this book, the historical angle is provided by Julius Caesar who, interestingly, is one of the main sources of our knowledge today about the Druids of Gaul (modern-day France) and Britannia (Great Britain). In my view, there is a significant mystery surrounding the two invasions of Britannia mounted by Caesar from his base in Gaul. Not only were these two invasions not very successful by any measure, there was no further attention paid to Britain by the Roman empire for almost a hundred years after Caesar's second invasion of Britain. Why, then, did Caesar invade Britain not once but twice, if he was not going to return and if the Romans had no interest in colonising the island? In this case, I have speculated, through a hypothesis based on scientific fact, that the Druids possessed a secret, linked to myths in the *Mahabharata*, which Caesar learned about. Yearning to acquire this secret, which would make him the most powerful man in the world and, more importantly – for he was a general first – immune to defeat in war, he invaded Britain. Once he succeeded in his mission, he had no interest in returning.

As your question asks about *itihasa* in particular, I will only add here that, rather than engage with the historical aspect of the events and myths in the *Mahabharata*, I prefer to provide an unusual perspective – the possibility that some of the myths can be explained using real science. In this sense, I am really raising the possibility that, if the scientific hypotheses I have proposed through the fictional interpretation of the *Mahabharata*'s *shlokas* are plausible and credible, then these myths, at least, would embody *itihasa*. In effect, what I am saying through a fictionalised perspective is that the scientific explanation urges readers to believe 'this is what happened'. That is, *itihasa*.

EDV: I'm interested to know your thoughts on how your novels are categorised and marketed. You have published with both Om Books and Westland Books. How important a consideration is the genre classification of your novels and does this play a part in choosing a publisher for your work?

CCD: Let me start with the question of choosing a publisher. To start with, when I published *The Mahabharata Secret*, I really didn't have a choice. I had been rejected several times, first by 15 international literary agents (on the basis that my protagonist, being an Indian, would not be commercially accepted by a Western audience) and then by five Indian publishers. The only publisher who accepted my manuscript for publication was Om Books. Success breeds success, and when my first book became an instant bestseller, topping the Indian bestseller lists, I was approached by Westland with whom I then signed. I really had a choice only after the success of my debut novel. The genre classification really had little to do with my choice of publishers.

Coming to the question of genre, I believe there really is no established genre into which my books can be neatly slotted. There is a conceptual base of mythology, a dash of history, a dose of science and the overall format of a contemporary thriller. There is, thus, an overlap of several genres – a bit of science fiction, a thriller, a strong resemblance (in the throwback to historical references) to historical fiction, but it falls into none of these genres. On one occasion, the genre of crime fiction was used to describe my books, which isn't entirely accurate either, though there is the occasional murder, which all thrillers have. Even the genre of thrillers doesn't do justice to my books, in my opinion, because they are so richly flavoured with history, mythology and science. I have tried hard, and failed, to find any other writer in India writing similar books; I seem to be treading a lonely path. In some ways, this is positive, because there is something to appeal to lovers of all these genres, but I like to market my books for what they are: contemporary thrillers, which blend history, mythology and science.

EDV: What kind of reading has shaped your ideas about the topics explored in your novels – such as science, philosophy, belief? Could you cite any specific texts that have particularly shaped your thinking and writing over the years?

CCD: I've already briefly touched upon a few of the books that have been instrumental in shaping my ideas, philosophy and, indeed, the genre in which I write: *The Hindu History* by Akshoy K Majumdar; *Fingerprints of the Gods* by Graham Hancock; *Uriel's Machine* by Robert Lomas and Christopher Knight; the *Susruta Samhita*. I will provide some more details for each of these books since they laid the base for my writing, even though there were many more books I read that added to the flavour of the topics I explore through my writing.

Let's start with *Fingerprints of the Gods* by Graham Hancock. The book starts with the reproduction of a letter by Lt. Colonel Harold Z. Ohlmeyer of the US Air Force confirming that the Piri Reis World Map depicted a part of the coastline of Antarctica, and that the coastline would have been mapped before it was covered by the ice-cap that Antarctica now lies under. The interesting thing about this case is that this map was drawn by Admiral Piri Reis in Constantinople in 1513. As the letter from Ohlmeyer concludes: 'we have no idea how the data on this map can be reconciled with the supposed state of geographical knowledge in 1513'. According to notes made by Piri Reis on the map, he derived it from a large number of source maps, some of which dated back to the fourth century BC or earlier. Hancock concludes: '... the true enigma of this 1513 map is not so much its inclusion of a continent not discovered until 1818 but its portrayal of part of the coastline of that continent under ice-free conditions which came to an end 6000 years ago and have not since recurred.'

This sets the stage for the central theme of the book – that of an ancient civilisation, lost to human memory: '... it appears that this civilisation must have been at least in some respects as advanced as our own and that its cartographers had mapped virtually the entire globe with a uniform general level of technology, with similar methods, equal knowledge of mathematics, and probably the same sorts of instruments.'

Hancock takes the reader on a journey through the mythologies of South America, Mexico, the Indian tribes of North America and Egypt, showing similarities in their myths that support his idea of a long-lost civilisation with advanced science and technology. He shares his painstaking research, his field trips to archaeological sites, using astronomy, geology and astrophysics to substantiate his hypothesis. Throughout the book, he questions the traditional explanations of orthodox historians regarding the megalithic monuments in Egypt, Peru, Mexico and demonstrates the scientific and astronomical information encoded into prehistoric myths from these regions.

Uriel's Machine, by Christopher Knight and Robert Lomas, is intriguingly subtitled *The Ancient Origins of Science*. Its central theme is that science began in Western Europe over 5000 years ago. Using science, they demonstrate that the mythology contained in 'The Book of Enoch', an ancient Jewish text, is evidence of advanced science and technology in a civilisation that inhabited modern-day Britain and Ireland, over 5000 years ago. 'The Book of Enoch' describes events which geology has confirmed happened in 7640 BC. They provide scientific evidence for a global flood over 9000 years ago, which could have wiped out that civilisation. 'Flood legends persist worldwide, describing events which fit the geological events of that period. Enough evidence exists to show that a worldwide Flood did happen.'

They explore the mythologies of ancient Sumer, Babylon, the Australian aborigines, South America, Wales and Ireland to build their case. Their analysis of the megalithic sites in Scotland, Wales and the Orkney Islands created a long-standing ambition to visit these sites for myself, something I finally achieved in 2015 when I made two trips to Britain to research for my third book, *The Secret of the Druids*. Knight and Lomas have been able to demonstrate astronomical alignments, particularly with respect to the movement of the sun at the solstices and the planet Venus, at megalithic sites in Wales and Scotland. They describe one of these sites thus: 'Bryn Celli Ddu on Anglesey, built circa 3500 BC, is a sophisticated calendar machine which can be used to indicate the changing of the seasons. It has been so constructed that during important seasons it reflects light into different parts of its structure and produces dramatic and symbolic lighting effects ... a scientific instrument for creating and adjusting important calendar elements ... these drift out of synchronisation if not regularly corrected, so its builders used Venus to provide the means of correction.' The high point of the book is the reconstruction, by the authors, of a machine which they call 'Uriel's machine' – because the instruction to build the machine was given to Enoch by an angel whom Enoch refers to as Uriel. According to them, 'This ancient machine is nothing less than a celestial computer'.

The Hindu History, written in 1917, is a product of thirty years of research by Akshoy K. Majumdar, attempting to portray the true place of India in world history. At that time, according to Majumdar, 'in the current school history syllabuses of India, the sixth or seventh century BC is the starting point. Some even begin from 1400 BC, showing their limited faith in Hindu chronology.' His book contains some interesting references and conclusions, which not only enhanced my own knowledge but also gave birth to the thoughts I have described earlier about the ambiguity of our own conclusions about the history of India before 1400 BC. What is interesting is that, although A. K. Majumdar was a man of his times, with his book written in the context of the Aryan Invasion of India – a theory which was not just well accepted but also regarded as indisputable fact at that time – he still proposed several ideas that seem, even in today's context, far ahead of their times. One of the main themes in the early chapters of his book is the description of gods as human beings. For example, 'the moral fall of the Aryans, then living in and around the Kashmir valley was rapid ... Brahma, the greatest Aryan sage, came to know of this. To reform and regenerate the Aryans he held a council, to ask the chief sages and seers to marry ... Brahma himself married. The sages now became known as *prajapatis* i.e. progenitors ... The national character of the Aryans was soon essentially reformed by the vigorous efforts of Brahma who is further said to have drawn up a long penal code for the regulation of society. This work, condensed over the years gave rise to the *Niti-sastras* of Vrihaspati, Sukra, Kamandaka, Chanakya and others.' He based this conclusion on the *Mahabharata, Brahma Vaivarta Purana, Brahma Khanda, Srikrisha Khanda*. According to him, 'many of the prominent Devas have long passed for gods and have lost their original historical characters. Yet, doubtless they were men – excellent men – the "Shining Ones". We give below proof of the human side of the Deva Aryans, though the Sanskrit epics, the Puranas and other works have been highly saturated with their deification.' He proceeds to substantiate this with quotations from the *Mahabharata* on the subject of the mortality of the Devas, the Danavas and the Gandharvas.

He also, interestingly, speaks of 'bitter hostilities for thirty-two long years, off and on. This is known as the First Great Civil War or the Deva-Asura War ... The war began in 2850 BC or a little after and ended in 2818 BC. The Devas ... sustained great losses at first. Then, a Deva general, Purandara by name, took charge. His successes in the war led the Devas to declare him their king with the title of Indra (literally, the most exalted king). Defeat quickened the Daitya spirit and after some time they fell on the Devas with such terrible force that the Devas failed to hold their ground. The Deva cause was going to be lost when Siva, the mighty chief of the Rudras, took the field at the entreaty of the Devas and turned the tide of the battle. He inflicted a signal defeat on the Daityas ... The services of Rudra to the Deva cause have been thankfully sung by the seers ...' Once again, he provides textual references from the Vedas to substantiate his conclusions. He continues, 'Tradition bears the bright record of the deeds of one female warrior, Uma, wife of Rudra. In terrible battles, she killed the Daitya chiefs – Mahisha, Sumbha and Nishumbha (grandson of Prahlada) and their generals ... one great Daitya king, Durg by name, collected a very strong and large army ... Uma again took the field with a lion ramp ... The battle was the fiercest – Uma won the day after all ... The Devas gave Uma the title of "Durga" for having slain the most formidable foe, Durg. Her worship first began a century later, around 2700 BC. It is said that Suratha first started her puja.'

He also refers to the astronomical knowledge of the ancients, based on portions of the ancient texts that seemed to show that they knew that the earth moves around the sun; that the moon is lit by the sun; that the earth is round (hence the word *brahmanda* – mundane ball or egg); that the moon passes once in twenty-seven and one-third days through twenty-eight constellations; they knew the solar year of 364¼ days and the lunar year of 354 days; they knew the equator and the equinoxes; they could explain an eclipse, and so on. I have given but a few examples of the historical record he has tried to construct based on the ancient texts. His description of the geography of the ancient world and its link with the descriptions in the texts is fascinating, as is the list of kings from the Solar and Lunar dynasties, complete with dates of their reigns and key events that occurred in their lifetimes.

EDV: Christopher C. Doyle, thank you.

References

Banerjee, S. (2014) 'Melodrama, mimicry, and menace: reinventing Hollywood in Indian science fiction films', *South Asian Popular Culture*, vol. 12, no. 1, pp. 15–28.
Choudhury, N. P. (2011) *Bali and the Ocean of Milk*, Noida: HarperCollins India.
Clute, J. and Grant, J. (1999) *The Encyclopedia of Fantasy*, London: Orbit.
Currie, G. (1990/2008) *The Nature of Fiction*, Cambridge: Cambridge University Press.

Doyle, C. C. (2013) *The Mahabharata Secret*, Noida: Om Books International.
Roberts, A. (2010) *Science Fiction*, London: Routledge.
Saket, P. (2016) *Urmila*, Mumbai: Jaico Publishing House.
Sanghi, A. (2010) *Chanakya's Chant*, Chennai: Westland.
Sanghi, A. (2012) *The Krishna Key*, Chennai: Westland.
Vandermeer, J. (2008) 'Introduction: The New Weird 'It's Alive?'', in Vandermeer, J. and Vandermeer, A. (eds.) *The New Weird*, San Francisco: Tachyon Publications.

5 Conclusion

This volume has been interested in the interface of science, Hinduism and *itihasa*, and specifically, this interface's manifestation within mythology-inspired fiction in English from India. In turn, this trio of science, Hinduism and *itihasa* has been examined through the lens of two overarching interests: reader reception and the genre of weird fiction. Although this project has revealed significant findings with regard to these two overarching interests, it has also revealed some broader findings. These broader findings are in relation to identity and Indianness and Indian post-millennial society's interest in portraying and projecting ideas of India through its ancient cultures, epic narratives and cultural (Hindu) figures.

As Chapter 1 outlines, India has undergone immense change in terms of its economy and, for our interests here, its leisure industries and consumer spending trends. The boom of publishing post-millennial genre fiction is part of this transformation, both in terms of publishing opportunity and a strong, ready market for genre fiction. This boom continues to challenge the (erstwhile) notion of the postcolonial Indian novel given that traditionally, postcolonial literary interests have had limited engagement with popular fiction. The challenge lies not only in the popular form of this fiction but also in its appraisal, distribution and circulation patterns (see Dawson Varughese 2012; Dawson Varughese and Lau, 2015). As Gupta (2015: 47) writes, '[N]umerous academic surveys and commentaries on Indian fiction in English dwell exclusively on literary fiction and establish a canon which functions as both a repository and confirmation of literariness.'

The changes to Indian society that have taken place have happened relatively quickly and such changes are particularly visible in urban centres and as part of middle-class lifestyles. With India's predominantly young population, change is being rapidly embedded within this particular slice of the demographic through access to technology, jobs, money and loans – in short, new ways of living, making and spending money. Such accelerated alterations to lifestyle allow for greater than usual questioning of society, identity and tradition – a consequence of such a young, mobilised population with opportunity, be it through technology, enhanced personal finance or education, producing a surge of creative thinking and output. The body of mythology-inspired fiction explored here is, I suggest, part of this surge in creativity and artistic output. Moreover, this creative product of the

150 Conclusion

mythology-inspired novel engages simultaneously with questions of Indianness, identity and tradition within a domestic and global context, as Sanyal (2008) writes:

> ... as India re-emerges as a civilization in the twenty-first century, the new urban middle-class will be less apologetic about its Indianness and far more confident in its interaction with the outside world. This is an important difference with the pre-Independence middle class. Those who were entering the workforce from the nineties were more than a generation removed from British colonial rule. (181)

This concluding chapter considers both Indian and non-Indian receptions of the eight mythology-inspired novels examined in this volume. It also considers what the genre of weird fiction offers to our understanding of both the defining characteristics and the reader receptions this body of writing generates. Finally, the chapter closes in consideration of the Indianness portrayed and examined through the lens of mythology-inspired fiction and what such representations of Indianness say about the post-millennial Indian moment.

5.1 Receptions

5.1.1 A Continuum of Reception

Chapters 3 and 4 distilled what this study has postulated to be two branches of Bharati Fantasy and mythology-inspired novels: eternal *bhāva* and modern-day sensibilities. Chapter 3 discussed texts that I suggest retain a certain *bhāva* of the 'original' texts of inspiration. This is achieved through the setting of the novel in ancient (pre-)India, through the reverence of one of its characters (such as in Tripathi's *The Immortals of Meluha*, 2010) or through the text's close connection with the figures of the text of inspiration, which in the case of Arni is the *Ramayana*. On the other hand, Chapter 4 discussed texts that connect with the *Mahabharata* and the *Ramayana* through modern-day sensibilities which involve present-day or near-day (*Urmila*, 2016, is slightly speculative with regard to era) settings, real-world problems, imaginative contemporary technology or science or modern-day cultural references and speech patterns (such as in Choudhury's *Bali and the Ocean of Milk*, 2011). Although these two branches of classification are helpful in charting the trends in this relatively new body of writing, it is important to further map the 'weirdness' of each of these novels (according to the definitions of the weird set out in Chapter 2, Section 2.1) on a continuum. In mapping the eight novels across a continuum of the weird genre, we can more fully appreciate the issues of reader reception with regards to Indian and non-Indian readerships.

Out of the eight novels examined here, the two novels which demonstrate the genre of the weird the most are Nath's *The Guardians of the Halahala* (2015) and Bhanver's *The Curse of Brahma* (2015). The novels that demonstrate the genre of the weird the least are Saket's *Urmila* (2016) and Choudhury's *Bali and the Ocean of Milk* (2011). The four novels that are located in between these two ends of the continuum are Doyle's *The Mahabharata Secret* (2013), Sanghi's *The Krishna Key* (2012), Arni's *The Missing Queen* (2013) and Tripathi's *The Immortals of Meluha* (2010). It might be helpful to revisit how weird fiction is defined within this volume. Drawing on definitions of the weird from Miéville (2009) and also Vandermeer (2008), this is how the weird has been defined within this study:

- an awe at strangeness
- the numinous as a threatening force
- less narrative plot and more emphasis on 'weird presence' within the narrative
- revolutionary teratology (Miéville, 2009: 510–515)

and

- subverting traditional fantasy, largely by choosing realistic, complex, real-world models
- elements of both science fiction and fantasy (Vandermeer, 2008: xvi)

Mapping the eight novels examined in Chapters 3 and 4, the continuum of 'weirdness' reads thus:

Nath's *The Guardians of the Halahala*
Bhanver's *The Curse of Brahma*
Doyle's *The Mahabharata Secret*
Sanghi's *The Krishna Key*
Arni's *The Missing Queen*
Tripathi's *The Immortals of Meluha*
Choudhury's *Bali and the Ocean of Milk*
Saket's *Urmila*

Interestingly, there is little correspondence between the amount of 'weirdness' the novel demonstrates and the novel's classification as an 'eternal *bhāva*' (EB) text (Chapter 3) or as a 'modern-day sensibilities' (MDS) text (Chapter 4). I have marked this correspondence next to demonstrate the EB texts and the MDS texts respectively.

Nath's *The Guardians of the Halahala* – EB
Bhanver's *The Curse of Brahma* – EB
Doyle's *The Mahabharata Secret* – MDS
Sanghi's *The Krishna Key* – MDS
Arni's *The Missing Queen* – EB
Tripathi's *The Immortals of Meluha* – EB
Choudhury's *Bali and the Ocean of Milk* – MDS
Saket's *Urmila* – MDS

What this mapping exercise concludes is that mythology-inspired or Bharati Fantasy novels can be weird whether they are set in ancient or contemporary periods. What the examination of the eight novels here reveals though is that the most 'weird' narratives are set in ancient times and the defining characteristics of their weirdness are namely teratology, emphasis on weird presence, the numinous as a threatening force and an awe at strangeness. Bharati Fantasy texts that exude modern-day sensibilities are more likely to demonstrate defining characteristics of weirdness such as elements of science and fantasy, the numinous as a threatening force mediated through (dark) science and technology and awe at highly developed scientific and technological advances. Where texts display less weirdness, it is the trope of time or era that is evident, subverting traditional fantasy by using real-world contexts that don't seem to quite 'fit'; they are otherworldly and disturbing in a near-now sense of setting, for example, Arni's *The Missing Queen* and Saket's *Urmila*.

5.1.2 Indian Receptions

Chapter 2 looked in some detail at the issues around *itihasa* and the *itihasa* texts of the *Mahabharata* and the *Ramayana*. The chapter acknowledged that in terms of reception, the body of mythology-inspired fiction engages with a reader's own perception and understanding of the very term *itihasa*. So even before issues of reader reception outside of India are to be considered, it is important to note that within India, or within 'Indian readerships' (I speak of the Indian diaspora as a readership in Chapter 2), the issue of reception with specific regard to the anchoring of these novels in *itihasa* texts is a significant one. Juluri (2014) writes on the personal engagement with the Hindu epics when he talks about the sensitive matter of representing and storying Hindu gods. He says:

> No matter how much secular writers and historians insist that the *Ramayana* or *Mahabharata* are merely stories and the heroes in one version can be villains in another, the fact is that these are not perceived as merely works of fiction by most Hindus, but as stories of the gods. That, more than anything else, is the question that the commentators on the Hindu culture wars of the past few decades have failed to address.
>
> (Juluri, 2014: online)

The presence of the *itihasa* text as a cultural (and for some, religious) anchor to the fiction's plotline, characterisation and style is an important factor for both reader and author. Within an Indian readership, the engagement with the *itihasa* inspiration is various and the novels themselves offer various degrees of connectivity to the epic text. Arni's *The Missing Queen*, Saket's *Urmila*, Choudhury's *Bali and the Ocean of Milk* and Sanghi's *The Krishna*

Key all make very clear connections with the *Ramayana*, the *Mahabharata* or in the case of Choudhury's novel, the *samudra manthan*. Tripathi's novel *The Immortals of Meluha*, although based on the early life of Lord Shiva as he discovers his divine status, does not follow an established text in the same way as the aforementioned novels, rather, the life of Lord Shiva, as it has been documented variously, is synthesised (and retold) through Tripathi's work. In Nath's novel *The Guardians of the Halahala* and in Bhanver's novel *The Curse of Brahma* the narratives are momentarily connected to Hindu epics and sacred texts, in Nath's case through the reference to the *halahala* (we join the story as the *halahala* has been released, thus Nath does not narrate the story of the Churning) and in the case of Bhanver, although some readers may recognise the story of the time preceding the birth of Sri Krishna, it is the focus on the Dark Lord, Lord Brahma's once star pupil, that sets up and drives the storyline. Doyle's contemporary tale of *The Mahabharata Secret* connects to the epic text through the novel's title. The novel makes reference to various elements of the epics and to Hindu sacred texts, thus, overall, the novel is not supremely anchored in any one narrative. Rather, the 'secret' of the *Mahabharata* is discovered through a series of clues which themselves are embedded within the sacred and epic texts.

It is important to recognise these different approaches to *itihasa* and how these approaches are manifest in the eight novels explored here, because although a common thread of Hindu epic narrative may connect them (and they are all variously referred to as mythology-inspired novels regardless of how the author classifies her/his work), the novels engage with the *itihasa* texts and inspirations in very different ways and for different ends.

The author interviews at the end Chapters 3 and 4 explore the craft of building on the inspiration of the *itihasa* text. Amish Tripathi highlights how the English word 'mythology' is often conflated with the Hindi word *mithya* which translates as 'untruth' and that, although for him, he writes about 'his gods' and that for him 'they exist' (see interview in Chapter 3, Section 3.5), when he addresses what he calls a 'Western or Westernised audience' he uses the word 'mythology' to convey what he is talking about. Given that the *itihasa* texts have long inspired other Indian language fiction, the issue of genre labelling and the translatability of *itihasa* prove problematic for Indian writing in English, its receptions and the language used to talk about and critique this body of fiction. Indeed, the genre terms 'mythology-inspired' or even 'Bharati Fantasy' signal to non-Indian readerships that the fiction these terms represent is 'untrue' or 'fantastical'. Shatrujeet Nath, in his interview, says how he mindfully set out to write a series of novels which are 'not bound by the pressure of history' (see interview in Chapter 3, Section 3.6). In taking such a decision, Nath set out to write a fantasy series, but given that the series is anchored in the character of the legendary King Vikramaditya and that the narrative is linked to the Churning of the Ocean and the *halahala*, Nath was obliged to make his narrative 'fit' a certain historical context for it to 'make sense' to an Indian readership. His portrayal of ancient Indian society, politics and whether the novel should be set in an era before or after the *Mahabharata* war were all considerations that had to be taken in order for the fiction to be convincing for certain Indian readerships. For non-Indian readerships, these details would not have greatly mattered given that the introduction into the world of King Vikramaditya is fantastical from the outset. Doyle, in his interview (Chapter 4, Section 4.7), also comments on how elements of history can come together in a way that encourages poetic licence. For Doyle, the fact that the *Mahabharata* had been orally transmitted for so long and that dating the *Mahabharata* is so heavily contested, a certain space for creativity opened up, knowing that he is free to connect up aspects of ancient history whilst weaving in a storyline of his own. In *The Mahabharata Secret*, Doyle brings together the idea that the *Mahabharata* holds a secret and that Asoka, during his reign, fathomed out this secret. In knowing how powerful the secret of the *Mahabharata* really is, Asoka decides to hide it away from the world, burying it within the Nine (a secret brotherhood of nine men). For an Indian readership, both elements of Doyle's story are part of India's cultural fabric and are thus easily connected with, even when the 'original' is significantly driven in new fictitious directions.

For Samhita Arni, the combination of *itihasa* and the speculative as a genre allowed her to narrate a story that mapped the past onto the future. Speaking in her interview here (Chapter 3, Section 3.7), Arni highlights how India's past has often been glorified, revealing a golden age and an ideal era of living. Unlike Western notions of linear time and development, whereby development only ever lies before us, in the future, Arni reminds us that the past (and within this, *itihasa* texts) can provide answers and solutions to contemporary problems and that a more (Indian) cyclical view of time disturbs the idea that development only lies in the future, meaning that the past has little to offer, given that it has now been surpassed by the present. In *The Missing Queen*, Arni harnesses the power of the speculative to narrate the 'now' (see her comments on Ursula Le Guin in the interview). In a break from popular practice, Arni maps the (Hindu) past not onto the present but rather onto the future, using the epics 'not to imagine a utopia, as most do today, but to suggest the frightening possibility that by invoking the epics as we do in mainstream discourse and creating a Hindu Nationalist identity we will actually create a dystopia'.

5.1.3 Non-Indian Receptions

As we have seen in the analyses of the novels in Chapters 3 and 4, the creativity that, say, Bhanver (in *The Curse of Brahma*) or Nath (in *The Guardians of the Halahala*) bring to the re-invention of epic tales negotiates a space for a readership which has limited knowledge of the Indian epics. The line between 'original' and 'fiction' is irrelevant if the reader is not aware of the 'original' (or at the very least, the basic) storyline in the first place. As the continuum of reception demonstrates (see Section 5.1.1), the non-Indian reader (or the reader with little or no knowledge of the *itihasa* texts and Hinduism) is able to engage more easily with the novels that find themselves at the (opposing) ends of the continuum. Novels which exude the most weird or fantastical tropes, such as Nath's *The Guardians of the Halahala* (2015), present less issues of cultural untranslatability given that the worlds created in the novels are more fantastical than they are *itihasa*. Such a novel as Nath's does not require the reader to know the epics, to know the story of the Churning or to understand the true relevance (and religious significance) of Lord Shiva. Rather, the reader engages with all aspects of the text within the genre of the weird or fantasy. This reader experience is vastly different from engaging with novels which occupy the midway position on the continuum. Novels such as Sanghi's *The Krishna Key* require the reader to engage with the cultural and religious contexts in order to connect all aspects of the narrative together. This is especially the case with regard to *The Krishna Key*, where each chapter is prefaced by text narrating Sri Krishna's life. This demonstrative connection between *itihasa* text and fictional (thriller) text cannot be *fully* appreciated without some cultural (and religious) understanding on the part of the reader. Interestingly, at the other the end of the continuum, where novels demonstrate the least 'weirdness', the specific cultural and religious contextual knowledge that the Sanghi novels might require is not necessary for the reading of these texts, rather, it is possible to read Arni's *The Missing Queen* or Saket's *Urmila* without making the connections to the text of inspiration, namely the *Ramayana*. That said, such readings would be different, if not lacking somewhat, given the connections these novels make to the *Ramayana*. For Arni's novel, the movement from Ayodhya, through the forest, to Lanka and the return to Ayodhya has obvious connection to Valmiki's *Ramayana*, whilst Saket's exploration of 'Urmila' as the wife of Laxman in the *Ramayana* has more impact on the reading of a situation when the reader knows the text from which the story is inspired, but, importantly, for our interests here, a non-Indian readership is not precluded from reading and understanding Arni's and Saket's novels as the cultural specificity of the works is not so great as to impede engagement with the text.

    The ability to connect with the text within a non-Indian cultural context is important given the discussion in Chapter 1 of this volume. As distribution channels open up and Indian fiction in English becomes more available to a global readership, questions of genre classification, marketing and reception become ever more pertinent. In his interview (Chapter 3, Section 3.6), Shatrujeet Nath comments on his desire to create an 'Indian version of the Arthurian legend' and how, for him, the emphasis on genre in terms of publisher choice was negligible, rather, the publisher of his Vikramaditya series, Jaico, offered a good publishing deal and the CEO was excited by his idea for the series. As the body of mythology-inspired fiction continues to grow, it proves interesting to chart how these novels travel outside of India and to gauge how they are received. To date, the novels of Sanghi and Tripathi have been made fairly visible through e-retailer Amazon.com (as I discuss in Chapters 1 and 2) and as Tripathi's novels are distributed through the UK-based Jo Fletcher Books, there is a commitment to regional distribution outside of India. Although some of the other novels discussed in Chapters 3 and 4 are equally available through Amazon.com (such as *The Missing Queen*), it is the body of work of Sanghi and of Tripathi, as well as the genre labels of 'mythology- inspired', 'fantasy' and 'thriller', which mark out a place for these novels in the Western e-markets. If the flows of distribution continue to be enhanced through both electronic sales and regional distribution agreements, then the role of reader reception discussed in this volume will clearly evolve and move in new directions. It is to this idea of increased global readership flows and the internationalisation of fiction that the next chapter section moves.

5.2 Genre – The Weird

This volume has been somewhat restricted in its scope, only being able to discuss the reception of Bharati Fantasy novels in terms of an Indian and a Western divide (or rather an 'Indian readership' and 'non-Indian readership' divide). I readily acknowledge that this binary is problematic given that the fertile ground for research lies in the space to be found in between these binary positions. Nonetheless, what this volume has attempted to establish is a debate around how genre fiction of this kind – 'mythology-inspired', 'Bharati Fantasy' or 'weird' – can be variously received across geographies, cultures and belief systems. This ability to be received variously extends to how the books are received as 'popular' or 'commercial' fiction and Chapter 1 defines these ideas in an attempt to think *across* the terms in order to understand this body of writing through its supposed 'non-literariness' (Gupta, 2012), its sales performances (Joshi, 2015) and through its engagement with the 'now' (McCracken, 1998).

Although the study has mindfully looked to map the novels onto definitions of weird fiction, it remains useful to think of this body of fiction through all three terms ('mythology-inspired', 'Bharati Fantasy' and 'weird). The term 'mythology-inspired' has been used because of its established presence in the domestic Indian fiction market. This term acknowledges the inspiration or anchoring of the narrative in an Indian epic (or sacred) story whilst simultaneously conveying this cultural connection to an English-speaking readership. The term 'mythology-inspired' is not without its issues as it conveys a sense of the mytho-historic, but in doing so glosses over the role and place of *itihasa* in these fictions by the fact that it uses the English word 'myth'. As Chapter 2 details at some length, the idea of 'mythology' in the English language at least is one of untruth and legend. In employing the term 'mythology-inspired' fiction, the notion of *itihasa* is lost to the idea that Malhotra describes as 'imaginary, fantastical, fictional, or even superstitious, primitive or false' (2013: 63), expressed, that is, through the word 'mythology'.

The second term, 'Bharati Fantasy', has been presented in Chapter 2 as a potential theoretical framework for the genre classification of this body of fiction articulating how this body of new writing is not simply 'commercial Indian fantasy'. This term is particularly useful in acknowledging the role of reader reception with regard to cultural (un)translatability issues surrounding this body of writing. Moreover, the term is particularly valuable when categorising the novels of Nath and Bhanver, located as they are at the 'most weird' end of the reception continuum (see Section 5.1.1). Indeed, Nath concedes in his interview (Chapter 3, Section 3.6) that the Vikramaditya series is a fantasy series per se, not as the domestic Indian market might describe it, a 'mythology-inspired' series. Although the framework of Bharati Fantasy does not offer a hard and fast definition of this body of writing, it does offer various modes of reading for a body of fiction which itself manifests as a continuum. Bharati Fantasy suggests modes of reading such as historical fiction, fantasy fiction, historical fantasy (Schanoes, 2014) and fantasies of history and religion (Sleight, 2014), and although there are distinct differences between the writing Sleight interrogates and our interests here with Bharati Fantasy, what Sleight suggests does resonate with the examination of the texts in Chapters 3 and 4: '[I]n the case of the fantasy of history, it may be that the writer feels certain ideas about our past and culture can only be made apparent by going beyond the facts and physics of the world we know' (2014: 256). In coining the genre term Bharati Fantasy, the anchoring in ancient (pre-)India with its practices, customs and epic tales is recognised, whilst the established (Western) genre term of fantasy recognises how reception of this body of writing is akin to the reception of fantasy novels of the West.

It is the third term, 'weird fiction', however, that this volume has been particularly keen to explore, mainly because the two preceding terms are established and settled (in that Bharati Fantasy is anchored in the established fantasy traditions of the West). The New or Recent Weird, on the other hand, is a developing genre given that its defining characteristics continue to be charted and established through the work of Vandermeer, Miéville and various contributors to sites and blogs such as the Weird Review (www.weirdreview.com). Moreover, what the weird offers as a genre term through its Lovecraftian genealogy is its connection with the numinous, and for the mythology-inspired novels this connection is paramount. All eight novels examined in Chapters 3 and 4 of this volume connect in some sense with the numinous. In the weird sense, this numinosity presents as a threatening force, and this is the case in *The Guardians of the Halahala* through the character of the Healer, in Bhanver's *The Curse of Brahma* through the Dark Lord and the inhabitants of *Paatal Lok*, in *The Mahabharata Secret* it is Farooq, in *The Krishna Key* it is Taarak Vakil and the mysterious Mataji and in Arni's *The Missing Queen* it is the spectral character of the Washerman. In the other novels, namely Tripathi's *The Immortals of Meluha*, Choudhury's *Bali and the Ocean of Milk* and Saket's *Urmila*, the numinous is more manifest through the novel's connection with the epic or in the case of Tripathi's novel, the life of Lord Shiva specifically. Within these three novels, there is a strong mystical sense to the narrative although no threatening numinous presence is as apparent as it is within the other novels.

Another way in which mythology-inspired fiction from post-millennial India connects with characteristics of the Lovecraftian weird is through the idea of the cosmos and of human existence released from the limitations of (earthly) time and space. Through the medium of the epics as inspiration (to whatever degree this may be), mythology-inspired novels connect with notions of fate, destiny, of powers and 'shapers' beyond the earthly realm and thus connect not only with the Lovecraftian pursuit of imagining beyond the limitations of natural law but also connect with the linguistic etymology of the word 'weird', namely that of the 'wyrd' (see Chapter 2, this volume, for this discussion in full).

Thinking of Indian mythology-inspired fiction in this manner opens up avenues of discussion on how such fiction forms part of a more global body of writing that interrogates the human condition in relation to the cosmos and the shattering of natural law. The inclusion of not only Indian but other cultural, speculative aesthetics in this emerging global canon of contemporary writing allows for a wider representation of what speculative fiction can mean. Not unlike Bharati Fantasy, Afrofuturism combines elements of science fiction, historical fiction and fantasy alongside inspiration from non-Western cosmologies. Womack (2013) says of Afrofuturist works that they: 'analyse dynamics of race and culture specific to the experiences of black people through sci-fi and fantasy works. They use it as a platform to assess humanity issues – including war, apartheid, and genocide – while also exploring class issues, spirituality, philosophy, and history' (23). The use of the speculative in order to interrogate the Indian now or near now has already been raised in Arni's interview (Chapter 3, Section 3.7, this volume), but just as Womack suggests, the speculative can act as a vehicle to reassess culture and race dynamics, although Menon (2016) suggests that the speculative can achieve something more ambitious – it can open up the opportunity to reassess the idea of storytelling per se. He says:

> Speculative Fiction at its best undermines linear narratives – even the idea of story-telling itself because it can question the reasons stories offer. I'm not calling for abandoning stories. Far from it. But I reject the utilitarian explanations often given for why stories are needed. I do not believe we need stories to make us more human, teach us empathy, reveal the eternal verities, help us make sense of the world, or give meaning to our lives. I write because I cannot control the reader's response.
> (Menon, 2016: 27)

As this volume has foregrounded, reader response is various and layered when it concerns the reception of mythology-inspired or Bharati Fantasy novels, and this is further advanced when such fiction travels within generous global distribution circuits. Furthermore, other aspects of globalised living where people, language, ideas and artistic expressions intermingle, travel and settle, future configurations of both the hybridised *production* of science fiction and fantasy narratives and the *receptions* of such fiction are myriad. Csicseroy-Ronay (2012) writes:

> With the availability of sf by more non-European – and especially second-generation, émigré, and multilingual – writers on the rise, we can expect to see the interflow of fantastic elements – oneiric, visionary, hallucinatory, folkloric, mythological, supernatural, surrealistic – to increase, not just as entertainment augmentors or artistic experiments, but as naturalized alternative rationalities, aspects of a larger commitment to breaking down technoscientism and its plausibility norms from within the myth itself, simultaneously reflecting the blending of alternative ontologies and prefiguring the inevitable spectralization of material science as it encounters spookier and spookier phenomena in the folds of matter. (481)

What Csicseroy-Ronay puts forward here is an exciting proposition, albeit surrounded by potential 'reception' difficulties. As of yet, globalisation has been articulated in fairly straightforward ways in terms of the flow, exchange and mixing of people, languages and cultures. As the distribution of fiction becomes a truly global endeavour, whereby 'domestic' narratives are made available to global audiences, meaning that cultural specificity and particular traditions, practices and expressions travel freely within these narratives, then it is possible that globalisation will take on new meanings and directions. A step further, as Csicseroy-Ronay suggests, would mean that ideas of science, technology and belief would appear through speculative fiction, drawing on all kinds of cultural and social traditions, lessening the cultural anchor of the West (and thus hegemonic ideas of scientific tradition, technology and creationism, as examples) in the craft of such genre fiction. Such a move would offer new ways to read the world and the human condition, advancing a globalisation of a more nuanced and comprehensive kind. This type of move within the humanities was called for by Brennan in the early 2000s when he wrote of an 'ethical program' involving the reorientating of the field of humanities, saying:

> [I]t seeks to reorient cultural values attendant upon learning to understand and appreciate aesthetically the cultural achievements of those outside the European sphere. It seeks to show how earlier scholars in the West have been narrowly obsessed, culturally limited, and tendentiously ignorant of many of the world's most consequential artistic and intellectual creations. (2004: 132)

What the 21st-century world *might* offer is an opportunity to better know and understand aesthetic and cultural achievements outside of one's cultural sphere. What it *certainly* offers is an opportunity to explore the lives of other people, removed not only in geography but also in cultural and material ways, and nowhere is this more evident than through the violent upheaval of people from their homelands, especially through the major waves of migration we are currently witnessing from the Middle East towards and into Europe. Chapter 2 has already cited some disasters – natural and otherwise – of the post-millennial years to date. The increasing sense of fear propounded by terrorist cells, in particular the so-called Islamic State, the overwhelming sense of connectivity to all things digital and the (unwanted) consequences of this, the spread of the Ebola or Zika viruses, barely containable despite our 21st-century technology, the continued abhorrent sexual violence towards women hallmarked through the Delhi gang-rape case of 2012 (also known as the Nirbhaya case) and the crisis over food security all dominate lives in the 21st century, piercing the day-to-day humdrum as high-pitched outbursts only to settle down as a constant, threatening background noise. Of this 21st-century condition, Csicseroy-Ronay (2012: 479) writes: '… the current culture of hybridism is produced by the violent deterritorializing of peoples and the ever-accelerating entrainment of populations in technological systems with ever more sophisticated ways of manipulating desires and fears.'

The genre of the speculative has been popularly conceived as one that 'imagines the future', whether that be a near future or one that lies in the next century or even beyond. As Arni states in her interview (Chapter 3, Section 3.7, this volume), invoking the sentiments of Ursula Le Guin, the employment of the speculative as a genre is more descriptive than it is predictive. Today's speculative fiction says more about the now than it might about the future, but in any case, what it does say about the now cleverly describes the future we will most likely come to know. The novels examined in Chapters 3 and 4 echo Le Guin's idea through the themes, story arcs and plot lines that the authors have crafted. Doyle's *The Mahabharata Secret* opens with the destruction of the Bamiyan Buddhas in 2001, the storyline charts a terrorist's desire to get hold of the 'celestial weaponry' mentioned in the *Mahabharata* in order to attack the G20 summit in Washington and wreak havoc around the world. Doyle, in his interview (Chapter 4, Section 4.7, this volume), states that he attempts to write a narrative that does not allow the reader to distinguish between fact and fiction. He goes on to say that the technology that his novel explores was at the time of writing (2006) at the frontiers of science, whereas now he says 'it is taking a form that will make it part of our everyday lives within the next 20 years, and definitely within the lifetimes of most people alive today'. For Doyle, his fiction foregrounds the scientific as part of the contemporary Indian experience. This connection between science and Indian identity is taken up by Harder (2001), who, writing about science fiction works in Marathi (published around the 1970s), explores Narlikar's work called *Yakśophār*. He says:

> … it is exactly through scientific achievements that Indians prove their international worth. Science is the adequate mode of living for the age

and goes perfectly well with a religious tradition that even approves of it (*Vijñān-yug mem Nāradjī*). It helps save human civilisation (*Himpralay*), and the knowledge of cosmic events inspires an awe of truly religious dimensions (*Visphoṭ*).

(Harder, 2001: 118)

Indeed, Doyle's novel makes contentious links with what Harder writes of, demonstrating that 'science', even the science of the Vedas (or the science of the epics), can be harnessed for wicked purposes if such knowledge falls into the wrong hands. This idea of spiritual and cultural 'gate-keeping' that is set up here – manifestly through the idea of the Nine – is challenging for New India as its achievements in technology, science and space exploration are a national endeavour, supposedly a point of pride for *all* Indians, irrespective of spiritual or religious belief.

In Sanghi's *The Krishna Key*, the motif of the manner in which Sri Krishna is killed is traced through the novel, manifest at each murder scene. The killer, Taarak, executes his victims by thrusting a scalpel into their left foot; this scene re-enacts the death of Sri Krishna, who is inadvertently shot in the left foot by a hunter's arrow whilst meditating in the forest. The echo of the past in the contemporary is central to Sanghi's approach to writing fiction. His interview (Chapter 4, Section 4.5, this volume) reveals how he instinctively links current-day events with similar events of the past. Sanghi is fascinated by how history repeats itself and his observance of these patterns shapes how he approaches the writing of his novels.

In Saket's *Urmila*, the reader is challenged by the near-now setting of the novel. Looking for references that firmly place the narrative in the contemporary moment is challenging as very few clues are given and the story reads familiar yet estranged all at the same time. Despite the challenge of situating this novel in an era, it is clear to readers who know (of) the *Ramayana* that the protagonist Urmila is narratively linked to the Urmila of the epic. Saket's novel connects with the older narrative in what appear to be the most unorthodox ways, namely through the fertility treatment that both Urmila and her sister-in-law Vanita (the wife of Urmila's brother-in-law) undergo. This contemporary re-visioning of the women and reproductive medicine may seem at odds with the older narrative, creating a disjuncture that shatters any sense of continuum (if indeed, such is needed), but as we are reminded by Saket in her interview (see Chapter 4, Section 4.6, this volume), this aspect of the women's lives is not so displaced: '[A]ssisted fertility, unusual conceptions and concerns over truncated bloodlines are recurrent themes and plotlines in both the *Ramayana* and the *Mahabharata*, and often define the destiny of their characters.'

What we might say about the eight novels examined in Chapters 3 and 4 of this volume is that they explore the human condition, philosophies of life and of belief and that this is the reading experience for Indian and non-Indian readers alike. In invoking the Indian epics in various ways and to varying degrees, the novels engage readers with ideas of science, technology, history and *itihasa* but they also, through the very fact of being a material 'Indian' product, explore post-millennial dynamics of Indianness. Moreover, the narratives of these novels further examine what it is to be Indian and what it means to engage with those strands of the (national) cultural weave that are the *Ramayana* and the *Mahabharata* and that this engagement is offered whether one is Hindu or otherwise and to whatever extent one believes in these texts as *itihasa*.

5.3 Post-Millennial Indianness

At the time of India's independence, what it meant to be Indian was, unsurprisingly, a matter of great debate. Gandhi recognised that Hinduism was part of what it meant to be Indian, however, it was a broad and inclusive sense of Hinduism that shaped his particular idea of India and one consistent with his non-aggressive philosophy. In early 2016, the matter of Indianness was once again revived as students at the Jawaharlal Nehru University campus protested over the hanging of Afzal Guru on terrorism charges. News channels were flooded with debate about not only what it meant to be Indian but also what it meant to live in a society of free speech. Indeed, it was Jawaharlal Nehru who, at the point of independence, looked to create an India which was secular, and through his vision of a nation as a hegemonic entity, Nehru pursued a model which was 'committed to protecting cultural and religious difference rather than imposing a uniform "Indianness"' (Khilnani, 1999: 167). Given that identity is closely bound to language, Nehru's idea of what it meant to be Indian was reflected in his views on India's languages; English was recognised as the language of state, Hindi as an 'official' but not 'national' language – other regional languages were also recognised as 'official' – and of this debate Khilnani (1999) writes:

> This technique of compromise refused to anchor an Indian identity to a single trait – an option which, had it been chosen, would have suborned regional cultures to majoritarian definitions of a national one. [...] Indianness was defined not as a singular or exhaustive identity, but as one which explicitly recognized at least two other aspects. Indian citizens were also members of linguistic and cultural communities: Oriyas or Tamils, Kashmiri or Marathi. (175)

Following Nehru's death in 1964, and then later on during the 1970s, Indian politics began moving in very different directions and various social groups and movements took precedence over the more hegemonic sense of Nehru's original view of Indianness. By the 1980s, demands for regional autonomy grew – such as the cases in Punjab and Kashmir – each looking for more independence and self-rule. This desire for autonomy ostracised the various peoples seeking regional independence as their demands were interpreted as being 'anti-national'. General elections in 1991 and again in 1996 produced hung parliaments and coalition governments, and it was in this political vacuum of sorts that the Bharatiya Janata Party was born out of a Hindu nationalist party – the Bharatiya Jan Sangh. Known as the BJP, the Bharatiya Janata Party's sense of 'Indianness' stood in opposition to Nehru's ideas of what being Indian entailed. Although the BJP claimed that all Indians need not be Hindu to be Indian, it claimed that India needed to be recognised as Hindu. Events such as the Jawaharlal Nehru University (JNU) campus debacle in early 2016 reignited the fires of identity politics, ideas of what it is to be Indian and what it is to be Indian when you are not Hindu. Such questions and concerns can be found in what Mondal (2005) speaks of when he reminds us that despite leaders who have pioneered secular notions of Indianness since independence, the result has often proved to encode a Hindu majoritarian point of view 'even in the most secular-seeming and tolerant formulations' (22). Furthermore, Bery (2005) goes on to suggest that such a (Hindu) nationalism is able to develop because 'although this nationalism, like the modernizing one, is primarily a product of the nineteenth century, it projects itself backward into ancient India as its source' (118).

New India and its economic prosperity have certainly impacted many aspects of post-millennial society and Khilnani goes so far as to suggest that the more radical ideas of Hinduism evident in previous years have been tempered by a 'rebranding' of India's Hinduism. He says:

> For many in India modernity has been adopted through conservative filters of religious piety, moralism and domestic virtue. This has spawned a novel Hinduism, where holographic gods dangle on well-used keychains and cassettes of devotional *ragas* are played in traffic jams: instances of a religious sentiment freed from its original defining contexts, from the subtle iconography of materials and the punctual divisions of the day into sacred and mundane time.
> (Khilnani, 1999: 187, original emphasis)

In an echo of some sort, the mythology-inspired novels examined in this volume might also be considered part of what Khilnani describes here as 'instances of a religious sentiment freed from its original defining context[s]'. Yet, what we might glean from this rise in the domestic popularity of mythology-inspired or Bharati Fantasy novels currently remains unclear. Tripathi, author of the 'Shiva Trilogy' and the 'Ram Chandra Series', has been criticised for 'supposedly' peddling a Hindutva agenda through his novels. Tripathi dismisses the claims and states in the interview here (Chapter 3, Section 3.5, this volume): 'I am a believer, so I write about my Gods with respect. And yes, I believe they exist. But I am not forcing that point of view on anyone else. If someone does not want to believe, it's their choice. Everyone has a right to believe what gives them peace.'

There is a risk that the unanticipated popularity of mythology-inspired fiction when seen in conjunction with the landslide victory of the BJP and

Narendra Modi's 2014 inauguration as prime minister might be considered as feeding into a Hindu-orientated discourse of 'Indianness' and the promotion of India as a Hindu nation. However, I suggest that the consumption of this body of fiction needs to be seen as part of a larger project.

Post millennium, the production of fiction in English *generally* in India, as discussed in Chapter 1, has risen to an all-time high, and we should remember that this wave of genre fiction consumption also includes significant sales in other genres such as chick lit, what I call Crick Lit (see Dawson Varughese, 2016), murder mystery and 'young India' narratives, and it is therefore unwise to speculate about correlations between the popularity of mythology-inspired fiction in relation to 'Hindu' Indianness post millennium. This is not to say that there is no anxiety around contemporary ideas of Indianness in relation to Hinduism – such a concern is voiced in several of the author interviews in this volume. Samhita Arni talks about how *The Missing Queen* invokes the epic of the *Ramayana* not to imagine a utopia but a dystopia which she says manifests in the creation of a Hindu Nationalist identity, something she asserts as being her 'great fear' (see interview, Chapter 3, Section 3.7, this volume). In the interview with Shatrujeet Nath, I ask about the revival of telling tales of ancient India through genre fiction that has come to be called mythology-inspired fiction and Nath concedes that there is 'a general revival of interest in ancient India – or Hindu India' and that this revival of interest is 'quite in keeping with the Hindu assertiveness that is prevalent in India these days' (see Chapter 3, Section 3.6, this volume for the broader context of the discussion). What Nath's interview does also remind us of is the necessity to call into question the role of the English-speaking/writing author and the inspiration of the English language novel in their craft. Rather than seeing the rise of mythology-inspired fiction as being related to the renewed 'Hindu assertiveness' that Nath speaks of in his interview, we might instead recognise that many of the English language authors publishing in India have grown up reading Western authors through formal education (or through pleasure) and that these inspirations have acted as a 'template' or 'springboard', as Nath describes them, for the author's own works. Indeed, in the author interviews with Arni, Nath, Saket and Doyle in particular, English language (Western) novelists are cited as inspiration for the author's ideas of characterisation, plot line or story arc. Where Arni cites Asimov, Nath talks of the Arthurian legend, Saket mentions Rhys' *Wide Sargasso Sea*, and Doyle cites Tolkien.

Professor of Indian politics and intellectual history Sudipta Kaviraj writes that:

> Questions – about the rationalization of society; the altercations in fundamental religious beliefs; the decline of traditional authority of the king in the political world, of Brahmins in social life, and of the father inside the family; the immense changes in habits of intimacy between the sexes – asked and answered by social theory in the West, are all analysed and answered through literary writing. (2015: 25)

It could be argued that mythology-inspired fiction continues the tradition Kaviraj speaks of here as it explores the changing face of Indian society, the connection with the past, with *itihasa* and with the philosophical and moral directives that the epics and other sacred texts communicate. As Morey (2000: 10) writes, '… reading, like writing, responds to history as well as helping to shape it', and in this sense the circulation of such popular genre fiction novels, where questions of identity and Indianness can be found amongst the tropes of the fantastic and the weird, is an important vehicle in examining what it is to be Indian (in India) today. If nothing else, the proliferation of mythology-inspired fiction does attend to the following (somewhat disturbing) sentence '[A] couple of hundred years ago it was stated that Indian civilization was unique in that it lacked historical writing and, implicitly therefore, a sense of history' (Thapar, 2014: 3). The body of fiction examined in this volume, through the resplendent tradition of the 'many *Ramayanas*', venerates the unique nature of Indian thought and civilisation whilst simultaneously celebrating its sense of history, heritage and its various identities.

References

Bery, A. (2005) '"Reflexive Worlds": the Indias of A.K. Ramanujan', in Morey, P. and Tickell, A. (eds.) *Alternative Indias Writing, Nation and Communalism*, Amsterdam: Rodopi.

Brennan, T. (2004) 'From development to globalization: postcolonial studies and globalization theory', in Lazurus, N. (ed.) *The Cambridge Companion to Postcolonial Literary Studies*, Cambridge: Cambridge University Press, pp. 120–138.

Csicsery-Ronay Jr., I. (2012) 'What do we mean when we say "Global Science Fiction"? Reflections on a new nexus', *Science Fiction Studies*, vol. 39, no. 3, pp. 478–493.

Dawson Varughese, E. (2012) *Beyond the Postcolonial: World Englishes Literature*, Basingstoke: Palgrave.

Dawson Varughese, E. (2016) 'Genre fiction of New India: post-millennial configurations of Crick Lit, Chick Lit and crime writing', in Tickell, A. (ed.) *South Asian Fiction in English: Contemporary Transformations*, Basingstoke: Palgrave.

Dawson Varughese, E. and Lau, L. (2015) *Indian Writing in English and Issues of Visual Representation: Judging More Than a Book by Its Cover*, Basingstoke: Palgrave Macmillan.

Gupta, S. (2012) "Indian 'commercial' fiction in English, the publishing industry, and youth culture." *Economic and Political Weekly*, vol. 46, no. 5, pp. 46–53.

Gupta, S. (2015) *Consumable Texts in Contemporary India: Uncultured Books and Bibliographical Sociology*, Basingstoke: Palgrave Macmillan.

Harder, H. (2001) 'Indian and international: some examples of Marathi science fiction writing', *South Asia Research*, SAGE, vol. 21, no. 105, pp. 105–119.

Joshi, P. (2015) 'Chetan Bhagat: remaking the novel in India', in Anjaria, U. (ed.) *A History of the Indian Novel in English*, New York: Cambridge University Press.

Juluri, V. (2014) 'Hinduism and its culture wars', http://www.theindiasite.com/hinduism-and-its-culture-wars/ [accessed January 2016].

Kaviraj, S. (2015) *The Invention of Private Life*, New York: Columbia University Press.

Khilnani, S. (1999) *The Idea of India* New Delhi: Penguin Books India.

Malhotra, R. (2013) *Being Different: An Indian Challenge to Western Universalism*, Noida: HarperCollins Publishers India.

McCracken, S. (1998) *Pulp: Reading Popular Fiction*, Manchester: Manchester University Press.

Menon, A. (2016) 'The future arrives earlier in Palo Alto (but when it's high noon there, it's already tomorrow in Asia): a conversation about writing science fiction and reimagining histories and technology', in Phalkey, J. and Lam, T. (eds.) *British Journal of the History Science*, Special Issue on the History of Science in India & China Vol – TBC.

Miéville, C. (2009) 'Weird fiction', in Bould, M., Butler, A. M., Roberts, A. and Vint, S. (eds.) *The Routledge Companion to Science Fiction*, New York: Routledge.

Mondal, A. (2005) 'The limits of secularism and the construction of composite national identity in India', in Morey, P. and Tickell, A. (eds.) *Alternative Indias Writing, Nation and Communalism*, Amsterdam: Rodopi.

Morey, P. (2000) *Fictions of India: Narrative and Power*, Edinburgh: Edinburgh University Press.

Sanyal, S. (2008) *The Indian Renaissance: India's Rise after a Thousand Years of Decline*, Gurgaon: Penguin Books.

Schanoes, V. (2014) 'Historical fantasy', in James, E. and Mendlesohn, F. (eds.) *The Cambridge Companion to Fantasy Literature*, Cambridge: Cambridge University Press.

Sleight, G. (2014) 'Fantasies of history and religion', in James, E. and Mendlesohn, F. (eds.) *The Cambridge Companion to Fantasy Literature*, Cambridge: Cambridge University Press.

Thapar, R. (2014) *The Past Before Us: Historical Traditions of Early North India*, Ranikhet: Permanent Black.

Vandermeer, J. (2008) 'Introduction: The New Weird 'It's Alive?"', in Vandermeer, J. and Vandermeer, A. (eds.) *The New Weird*, San Francisco: Tachyon Publications.

Womack, Y. (2013) *Afrofuturism: The World of Black Sci-Fi and Fantasy Culture*, Chicago: Lawrence Hill Books.

Index

21st century crisis 26

advaita Vedanta 29, 48, 49
Afrofuturism 45, 158
ancient civilisation 99, 145
Arthurian 85, 89, 155, 164
Arundhati Roy 8, 9, 37, 38, 118
awe at strangeness 17, 25, 26, 29, 63, 96, 106, 151, 152

Bharati Fantasy **28–30, 32–45**
BJP 163
Brouillette, S. 8

Capra, F. 46–48
changes to Indian society 1, 149
Chaudhuri, A. 7, 8, 35
Churning of the Ocean 35, 54, 60–62, 88, 113, 115–118, 142, 153
cloning 71, 100
Clute, J. and Grant, J. 38, 59, 116
commercial fiction **9–13**, 35–37, 40, 156
creationism 21, 22, 29, 48, 159
Crick Lit fn19, 12, 164
cyclical narrative 74

dharma 29–31, 34, 38, 56, 67, 80
distributor 37

fantasy **40–41**
fertility 103, 105, 107, 126, 127, 131, 132, 161

Gandhi 162
genre classification 38, 40, 42, 89, 132, 143, 155, 157
genre marketing 36
globalisation 12, 114, 118, 159
Gupta, S. 9–12, 37, 40, 150, 156

Hanuman 72, 73, 77, 78
Healer 65, 157

Hellfires 62, 64
Hindutva 39, 163
historical fiction 29, 34, 35, 39, 40, **41–43**, 139, 144, 157, 158
History (as a subject) 17, **30, 34, 35,** 38, 41, 44, 47, 48, 55, 61, 74, **83–86,** 92, **93,** 102, 104, 109, 110, **122, 123, 128, 137, 140,** 141, 144, 146, 153, 154, 157, 161, **165**
Huggan, G. 8

India and modernity 4, 12, 80, 85, 93, 163
India and science 17, 29, 33, 42, **43–50,** 59, 63, 81, 82, 97, 99, 100, 102, **121,** 123, **128,** 132, 137, 139, 141, **142,** 143–145, 152, **160–161**
India's outer space activity 44, 45
Indian postcolonial literature 1, 7, 9, 13, 14, 17, 18, 35, 49, 149
Indian thought 39, 165
Indianness (identity) 8, 9, 12, 18, 39, 40, 43, 44, 101, 102, 118, 149, 150, **162–165**
invisibility 112, 113
Islamic State 26, 160
Itihasa **29–35,** 38, 39, 42, 48, 49, 61, 73, 76, 80, 81, 85, 86, 92, 102, 109, 112, 113, 119, 122, 128, 129, 139, 141, 143, **152–156,** 165

Jaipur Literature Festival (JLF) 3, fn18
Joshi, S.T. 21, 22

Lashkar-e-Taiba 110
legend 54, 55, 57, 84–90, 104, 110, 128, 133, 139, 145, 153, 155, 156, 164
literary prizes 3, 9
Lovecraft **21, 22,** 24, 25, **26, 27,** 157, 158

Index

Mangalyaan (India's Mars Orbiter) 45
McCracken, S. 11, 12, 16, 36, 156
Mendlesohn, F. 38, 40, 42, 63
Miéville, C. 21, 22, 24, 25–28, 54, 60, 106, 151, 157
mythology **22, 23**, 30, b31b, 66, **80**, 85, 86, 87, **89**, 90, 92, 93, 104, 122, 123, 128, 131, 138, 139, 140, 144, 153, 156

Narendra Modi **2**, fn18, 164
narrative interviews 18
natural law 22, 25, 29, 30, 158
near-future 54, 73, 74, 78, 91
Nehru 44, 162, 163
numinous 17, 21, 22, 24, 25, 26, 29, 49, 60, 62, 67–70, 96–98, 151, 152, 157, 158

oracle 64, 65

paraliterature 9
Poetic Edda 23, 24, 46
poetic licence 64, 86, 87, 117, 124, 129, 141, 142, 154
popular fiction 11, **12**, 16, 35, 36, 149
predestiny 96, 101
proto-scientific 23
publishing within India **4–7**

reader reception theory **14–18**, 149, 150, 152, 156
real-world 28, 64, 67, 102, 111, 150, 151, 152
reversed time 103
Roberts, A. 38, 40, 116

Schanoes, V. (historical fantasy) 41, 157
science fiction 25, 27, 28, 29, 37, 40, 45, fn50, 69, 92, 94, 135, 140, 144, 151, 158–160
shape-shift 42, 43, 116, 117

Shiva Trilogy 3, 6, 10, 11, 16, 32, 34, 36, 37, 54, **55**, 79, 163
Sleight, G. (fantasies of history and religion) 41, 157
slipstream 27
somras (magical drink) 58, 59
speculative fiction 13, 27, 90, 94, 158, 159, 160
Squires, C. 8, 9
steampunk 63
suspended animation 99

teratology 25, 26, 42, 60, 62, 67, 86, 96, 100, 106, 114, 116, 151, 152
terrorism 113, 162
Thapar, R. 30, 31, 165
The Nine 108, **109–113**, 138, 139, 154, 161
the Weird; New Weird **27–29** 64, 96; Recent Weird **24–27**, 157
thriller (genre) 11–13, 42, 120, 124, 141, 144, 155, 156
Tolkien 56, 135, 138, 164
truth-telling 73, 78, 93, 109, 111, 113, 119

universalism in story **17**
utopia 12, 56, 72, 92, 111, 154

values (in society) 47, 126, 129, 133, 159
Vandermeer 21, **28**, 54, 60, 96, 106, 151, 157

weaponry 48, 86, 111, 112, 141, 142
weird presence **25**, 64, 67, 74, 78, 106, 151, 152
Western academy 1, 6, 7, 13, 14, 17, 18, 22, 28, 40, 42
wyrd **22–25**, 29, 158

For Product Safety Concerns and Information please contact our EU representative GPSR@taylorandfrancis.com
Taylor & Francis Verlag GmbH, Kaufingerstraße 24, 80331 München, Germany